Bill Colegrave has collected and been inspired by travel books for more than four decades. He also published them as owner of Cadogan Guides. His own book *Halfway House to Heaven* (2011) tells the story of his journey up the Wakhan Corridor in Afghanistan to find the source of the Oxus River in the High Pamirs. He has visited more than 110 countries. He has represented Great Britain (seniors) at real tennis and also in the World Pétanque Championships. He lives in London.

SCRAPS OF WOOL

A Journey Through the Golden Ages of Travel Writing

Bill Colegrave

Unbound

This edition first published in 2017

Unbound
6th Floor Mutual House, 70 Conduit Street, London W1S 2GF
www.unbound.com
All rights reserved

For legal purposes the copyright acknowledgements on p. 367
constitute an extension of this copyright page. While every reasonable
effort has been made to trace the owners of copyright material reproduced
herein, the publisher would like to apologise for any omissions and will be
pleased to incorporate missing acknowledgements in any further editions.

Text Design by Ellipsis, Glasgow

A CIP record for this book is available from the British Library

ISBN 978-1-78352-423-5 (trade hbk)
ISBN 978-1-78352-424-2 (ebook)
ISBN 978-1-78352-425-9 (limited edition)

Printed in Great Britain by Clays Ltd, St Ives Plc
1 3 5 7 9 8 6 4 2

Arne Naess 1937–2004

'Arne was a superb leader, choosing the right people to work with and consult, then making firm clear decisions. He was always a delight to be with, on a mountain or ski slope, in a restaurant or pub; that wicked smile, boundless enthusiasm and warmth of spirit that led to so many great adventures.'

Sir Chris Bonington, who joined Arne and his Norwegian team on the successful 1985 Everest expedition

'A buccaneer adventurer, he always wanted to defy the odds and the conventions. His great gift was to enthuse others in these endeavours; it was my privilege to be one of them.'

Bill Colegrave

A dedication to our father who left us too young from his kids, Chris, Katinka, Leona, Ross, Evan, Nicklas, Louis

Special thanks to Camilla Astrup and Ross Arne Naess for sponsoring this page.

'. . . these bits and pieces of the random world are little more than scraps of wool on a barbed wire fence; they're there to be collected, spun and woven into the fiction of the book . . .'

Jonathan Raban, *For Love and Money: A Writing Life,* 1989

Dear Reader,

The book you are holding came about in a rather different way to most others. It was funded directly by readers through a new website: Unbound. Unbound is the creation of three writers. We started the company because we believed there had to be a better deal for both writers and readers. On the Unbound website, authors share the ideas for the books they want to write directly with readers. If enough of you support the book by pledging for it in advance, we produce a beautifully bound special subscribers' edition and distribute a regular edition and e-book wherever books are sold, in shops and online.

This new way of publishing is actually a very old idea (Samuel Johnson funded his dictionary this way). We're just using the internet to build each writer a network of patrons. At the back of this book, you'll find the names of all the people who made it happen.

Publishing in this way means readers are no longer just passive consumers of the books they buy, and authors are free to write the books they really want. They get a much fairer return too – half the profits their books generate, rather than a tiny percentage of the cover price.

If you're not yet a subscriber, we hope that you'll want to join our publishing revolution and have your name listed in one of our books in the future. To get you started, here is a £5 discount on your first pledge. Just visit unbound.com, make your pledge and type **wool5** in the promo code box when you check out.

Thank you for your support,

Dan, Justin and John
Founders, Unbound

Contents

———————

1   INTRODUCTION: A Scrap of Wool   1

2   THE SKIN OF A BRONTOSAURUS   4
    Dervla Murphy, *Full Tilt*
    Judith Schalansky, *Atlas of Remote Islands*
    Joseph Conrad, *Heart of Darkness*
    Bruce Chatwin, *In Patagonia*

3   'OUR FEEBLE HEARTS COULD NOT STAND MORE'   20
    Nicolas Bouvier, *The Way of the World*
    John Steinbeck, *Travels with Charley*
    Henry Miller, *The Colossus of Maroussi*
    Raja Shehadeh, *Palestinian Walks*
    Paul Bowles, *Without Stopping*
    John Masters, *Bugles and a Tiger*
    Ana Briongos, *Black on Black*

4   ALONE   37
    Paul Heiney, *One Wild Song*
    Isabella Bird, *A Lady's Life in the Rocky Mountains*
    Mary Kingsley, *Travels in West Africa*
    Ejnar Mikkelsen, *Lost in the Arctic*

Joshua Slocum, *Sailing Alone Around the World*
Sylvain Tesson, *Consolations of the Forest*

5   'BECAUSE IT'S THERE'   54
Maurice Herzog, *Annapurna*
Heinrich Harrer, *The White Spider*
Wade Davis, *Into the Silence*
John Hunt, *The Ascent of Everest*
W. E. Bowman, *The Ascent of Rum Doodle*

6   *NE VAUT PAS LE VOYAGE*   73
Redmond O'Hanlon, *In Trouble Again*
Rudyard Kipling, *American Notes*
Mark Twain, *The Innocents Abroad*
John Gimlette, *At the Tomb of the Inflatable Pig*
John Betjeman, *Shell Guide to Cornwall*

7   '. . . LET THE BOY FLAUNT HIS GENIUS SOMEWHERE'   92
Bruce Chatwin, *What Am I Doing Here?*
Patrick Leigh Fermor, *Mani*
Peter Matthiessen, *The Snow Leopard*
Wilfred Thesiger, *The Marsh Arabs*
Freya Stark, *Ionia: A Quest*
Isabelle Eberhardt, *The Oblivion Seekers*
Barry Lopez, *Arctic Dreams*
Patrick Leigh Fermor, *The Broken Road*
Ryszard Kapuściński, *The Shadow of the Sun*

8   UNEXPECTED ENCOUNTERS   128
Alexander Kinglake, *Eothen*

Joseph Thomson, *Through Masai Land*
Jonathan Raban, *Driving Home*
Ryszard Kapuściński, *Travels with Herodotus*
Redmond O'Hanlon, *Congo Journey*

9   AMERICANS LEAVING HOME   149
Bill Bryson, *The Lost Continent*
Mark Twain, *Life on the Mississippi*
Jack Kerouac, *On the Road*
William Least Heat-Moon, *Blue Highways*

10   THE ROMANCE OF ARABIA   164
Charles Doughty, *Travels in Arabia Deserta*
T. E. Lawrence, *Seven Pillars of Wisdom*
Wilfred Thesiger, *Arabian Sands*

11   'A BOOK ABOUT HIMSELF (HERSELF). . .'   178
V. S. Naipaul, *An Area of Darkness*
Robert Louis Stevenson, *Travels with a Donkey in the Cévennes*
Richard Holmes, *Footsteps*
Pico Iyer, *The Lady and the Monk*
Jenny Balfour Paul, *Deeper Than Indigo*
Cheryl Strayed, *Wild*

12   THE CITIES OF ITALY   197
Italo Calvino, *Invisible Cities*
Jan Morris, *Venice*
Johann Wolfgang von Goethe, *Italian Journey*
Norman Lewis, *Naples '44*
Dana Facaros and Michael Pauls, *Cadogan Guide to Rome*

13   Destinations Achieved   213

George Nathaniel Curzon, *The Pamirs and the Source of the Oxus*

Alexandra David-Néel, *My Journey to Lhasa*

Colin Thubron, *To a Mountain in Tibet*

Alexander Frater, *Chasing the Monsoon*

14   '. . . so long all you want is a penguin's egg.'   230

Mungo Park, *Travels in the Interior Districts of Africa in the Years 1795, 1796 and 1797*

Francis Younghusband, *The Heart of a Continent*

Apsley Cherry-Garrard, *The Worst Journey in the World*

Sir Ernest Shackleton, *South*

15   'I never knew of a morning in Africa when I woke that I was not happy'   251

Ernest Hemingway, *True at First Light*

Isak Dinesen, *Out of Africa*

Elspeth Huxley, *The Flame Trees of Thika*

Paul Theroux, *Dark Star Safari*

Alexandra Fuller, *Scribbling the Cat*

16   The Journey is the Destination   263

Patrick Leigh Fermor, *A Time of Gifts*

Colin Thubron, *Behind the Wall*

Paul Theroux, *The Great Railway Bazaar*

Robert Macfarlane, *The Old Ways*

17   Opium and Kif Dens   280

Isabelle Eberhardt, *The Oblivion Seekers*

Jon Swain, *River of Time*

18 A Supper in Capri   289
    Sybille Bedford, *Pleasures and Landscapes*
    Norman Douglas, *Siren Land*
    Martha Gellhorn, *Travels with Myself and Another*
    Sybille Bedford, *A Visit to Don Otavio*

19 The Thirties and Their Heritage   305
    Peter Fleming, *News from Tartary*
    Graham Greene, *Journey Without Maps*
    Sir Fitzroy Maclean, *Eastern Approaches*

20 The Lure of Afghanistan   318
    Freya Stark, *The Minaret of Djam*
    Eric Newby, *A Short Walk in the Hindu Kush*
    Jason Elliot, *An Unexpected Light*
    Rory Stewart, *The Places in Between*

21 Seeking Coloured Architecture   335
    Gertrude Bell, *Persian Pictures*
    Vita Sackville-West, *Twelve Days in Persia*
    Robert Byron, *The Road to Oxiana*

22 Herodotus   352
    Herodotus, *The Histories*

23. Who Made Scraps?   354

Copyright Acknowledgements   367
Index   371
Supporters   379

ONE

———

Introduction

A Scrap of Wool

We used to play a game over dinner using *The Times Complete Atlas*, which has 220,000 place names. We were blindfolded and had to select places from the index until we had one in each of Asia, the Americas, Europe and Africa. The idea was that we all had to leave the next day and go to each of our places in turn. The first time we tried my pin landed on: Butuceni, a village in Moldova near the Dniester River, in what was once called Bessarabia; the city of Guwahati in Assam on the Brahmaputra, whose waters have flowed as the Tsangpo across much of Southern Tibet; a place called Tumatumari Landing, near the confluence of the Potaro and Essequibo Rivers in Guyana and home to the Arawak and Akawaio tribes; and then a wadi in Niger, which I realised I had crossed ten years before, when travelling the Sahara north to south.

The piquancy was in the anticipation of the unknown, the excitement of getting to somewhere that hitherto has been only a name on a map, a heady temptation for wanderlust.

Scraps of Wool is the story of travel writers titillating that wanderlust. It is told through the advocacy of many correspondents, all of them sharing a love of the adventure, and some, the writers themselves, having the enviable talent to communicate it. In no way is this collection a critique of travel writing or an accolade for individual titles. It is

1

simply a celebration of writers who have inspired and amused. These are writers who understand that a simple narrative of a journey tends towards the dull. Their responsibility is to fashion a flowing story from their collection of incident and experience. As one of them, Jonathan Raban, wrote: '. . . these bits and pieces of the random world are little more than scraps of wool on a barbed wire fence; they're there to be collected, spun and woven into the fiction of the book . . .' The noun is fiction, not fabric. There are over one hundred different writers from eighteen countries of origin, that have followed these principles. Even the books that appear to be in diary form, such as Byron's *Road to Oxiana* and Kinglake's *Eothen*, have been carefully crafted, written and rewritten many times, so as to create a work that demands and deserves the readers' attention.

For more than forty years I have collected and read travel books. The process was more dilettante than disciplined. But I had marked passages that enthused me and so had gathered a library that was annotated by triangular corner-folds and barely decipherable jottings. This was my own inadvertent wool gathering. As I have expanded the process to build this book, I have learned and been stimulated by how little I really know, and how much more there is to discover. It has been a pleasure to which I could turn at any moment; the library is a big barrel of refrigerated chocolate truffles, from which I have been allowed to choose more than a hundred, without any fear of getting fatter. The only pain has been a hankering after those left uneaten.

Scraps of Wool can be no more than an interim report on a burgeoning library; the classics of future years are now being written by writers ever more perceptive, as they must be in a world already so intimately explored.

I have had a treasure chest of recommendations from others and continue to receive them, the most valuable of which have been those accompanied by some personal anecdote or comment. Some of these are reproduced in the final chapter. The result is this collection of passages, sometimes no more than a sentence, that have inspired us to go or at least to dream of going.

My own first taste came one evening lying in a bunk in a yacht club in Cowes, Isle of Wight, with wind-blown rain on the porthole windows. I chanced upon a copy of Wilfred Thesiger's *The Marsh Arabs*. There is only one paragraph in the book that is not about the Iraqi Marshes and the waterborne life of the Madan Arabs. It is hidden in chapter sixteen. It refers to what he had done between visits to the Madan, in a completely different part of the world. This is the paragraph that would inspire in me a lifetime's interest in Central Asia.

> I had left in the last week of July 1952 and it was now an early afternoon in February. Seven months later; it seemed longer. In that time I had crossed high passes through the snows of the Hindu Kush to the cold blue lake of Korombar where the Chitral river rises; I had looked out over Wakand from the Borogil Pass and seen in the distance a glint that was the Oxus; I had slept on the glaciers at the foot of Tirich Mir, and in dark, verminous houses among mulberry orchards, where the last of the Black Kafirs lived on the borders of Nuristan.

I had no idea where the Chitral River or Tirich Mir were to be found or what the Wakand was, although the latter was to play a part in my life much later. But I knew I had to go to find them.

This book is for those who understand that feeling. It is for those who have what John Steinbeck and Ryszard Kapuściński both call the disease of travel, a disease that is 'essentially incurable'.

TWO

The Skin of a Brontosaurus

Some writers only discovered the thrill of the journey after they had already embarked. It hit them like a new love, a revelation, and they have remembered and recorded that moment. Others knew they were travellers from long before they even left for abroad. Here are four such writers, connected by their pre-adolescent urge to travel.

There is Dervla Murphy's realised ambition to cycle to India, and there is the young Judith Schalansky, entirely ignorant of the outside world whilst growing up in an East Germany that hardly admitted its existence. There follow two of the most celebrated openings to books: Joseph Conrad explaining how he came to want to go to Africa, the experience which he fictionalised in *Heart of Darkness*. Then the opening pages of Bruce Chatwin's *In Patagonia*, which has been the first and best-remembered travel book for many. Chatwin got the 'skin of the brontosaurus' opening so right that it has been a bane of comparison for writers that have followed. Many have been asked by their editor: 'Can't you find an opening like . . .?' The editor is always thinking of Chatwin. Nearly every writer of his generation and the next has wanted, at some point, to be Bruce Chatwin; wanted, like him, to talk of Fez, Firdausi, Nigeria and Nuristan with equal apparent authority.

'I was quite confident that one day I would cycle to India'

DERVLA MURPHY

Full Tilt: Ireland to India with a Bicycle (1965)

Dervla Murphy (b. 1931), an intrepid Irish woman of the old school, is a doyenne of living travel writers, with more than twenty books to her name. Dervla is the opposite of the many British travel writers of the previous generation. They set out to enhance literary reputations by writing about the world; Dervla left school at fourteen to look after her mother in Lismore, County Waterford, and was rarely able to travel until she was thirty-two. Then she set out on her bicycle Roz to achieve the ambition that she had nurtured for twenty-two years. Full Tilt, *her first book, tells the story of that journey. In later books she is often accompanied by Rachel, her daughter, who first travelled with her aged five. Dervla is not one of those seeking to impress with her hardiness or exclusive access; she is not one who wants to impress with accomplished philology and erudition. She just wants to take us on a holiday to unlikely places in the company of her bicycle or daughter.*

On my tenth birthday a bicycle and an atlas coincided as presents and a few days later I decided to cycle to India. I've never forgotten the exact spot on a hill near my home at Lismore, County Waterford, where the decision was made and it seemed to me then, as it still seems to me now, a logical decision, based on the discoveries that cycling was a most satisfactory method of transport and that (excluding the U.S.S.R. for political reasons) the way to India offered fewer watery obstacles than any other destination at a similar distance.

However, I was a cunning child so I kept my ambition to myself, thus avoiding the tolerant amusement it would have provoked among my elders. I did not want to be soothingly assured that this was a passing whim because I was quite confident that one day I would cycle to India.

That was at the beginning of December 1941, and on 14 January 1963, I started to cycle from Dunkirk towards Delhi.

The preparations had been simple; one of the advantages of cycling is that it automatically prevents a journey from becoming an Expedition. I already possessed an admirable Armstrong Cadet man's bicycle named Rozinante, but always known as 'Roz'. By a coincidence I had bought her on 14 January 1961, so our journey started on her second birthday. This was ideal; we were by then a happy team, having already covered thousands of miles together, yet she was young enough to be dependable.

Six months later Dervla is at the Babusar Pass at the end of the Kaghan Valley going north towards Gilgit and Baltistan in North Pakistan.

For a combination of beauty, danger, excitement and hardship (of the enjoyable variety) today wins at a canter.

As I was resolutely chewing my breakfast of beans and one chapatti (made from about two ounces of maize flour and given me in honour of the occasion) an incoherent but kindly old man came along and told me that a pony-caravan had left the hamlet about three hours ago in a desperate attempt to cross the pass on the Mahomet-Mountain principle; they hope to collect essential stores from the camel-caravan which has now been held up at Butikundi for ten days. At the time I didn't quite grasp why the old man was telling me this – but before long I got the message!

Roz and I started out at 7 a.m. (it was rather a holiday feeling not having to be up at 4 a.m. to beat the sun) and it took me nearly two and a half hours to walk slowly up the six miles I came down yesterday in less than one and a half hours. On this stretch I passed several groups of nomads, the smoke from their little camp-fires sending an incongruously cosy smell across the bleak landscape. Equally incongruous seemed the persistent call of a cuckoo. Apart from this, the only sounds to break the distinctive silence of high places were the whistles of nomads directing their flocks and the careless melody of sheep and goat bells.

I reached the first glacier in good shape, but the sun was now high and I noted with some alarm that this great bank of melting snow had moved a few yards since yesterday. However, the pony-trail was encouragingly clear and we were soon safely over; it was at this point that the penny dropped and I saw the import of the old man's information. I stopped here to eat some of the glacier, remembering my last meal of snow in the mountains between Yugoslavia and Bulgaria. Already I was almost painfully hungry and apart from quenching my thirst the feel of the solid snow in my mouth was absurdly welcome.

For another mile the track remained clear, though so torn by the thaw that it resembled a river-bed. At this height no trees grow and the rock-strewn pastures, which in a few weeks will be a rich green, were wearily yellow after the long winter. Ahead I could now see a gigantic glacier, more than two miles wide, extending to the Top. The track disappeared beneath this about a mile to the west of where it crossed the Top and hoof-prints in the thaw-soft earth showed me that the ponies had branched off to take a direct route up, cutting all the hairpin bends which obviously lay beneath the glacier.

At this point I stopped to consider what I should do. To follow the track approximately would be much less exhausting than to take the short-cut, but it might be much more dangerous for someone ignorant of the idiosyncrasies of glaciers. So I decided to drag Roz up the direct route, not suspecting that what looked like a twenty-minute climb would take almost two hours.

By now clouds were dark and close, and a sharp wind sent gusts of little snow-flakes whirling around me at intervals. I revelled in this and went bare-headed, enjoying the keenness of the air. High peaks surrounded me, cutting off the valley below, and it was a rare joy to move alone among them with the chaotic symphony of re-echoing thunder as background music.

I was now higher than I had ever been before and when I stopped at six-minute intervals to regain breath my heartbeats sounded as loud as the thunder. This suffocating sensation frightened me until I realised that the illusory feeling of repeatedly coming to the point of death was simply the mountains' way of teasing novices. By the time I was halfway up the ponies' wisdom seemed open to doubt – their trail crossed many outcrops of rock and every time I lifted Roz over one of these barriers I collapsed with exhaustion. In places the snow was so soft that I sank into it up to the knees. Elsewhere it was so hard that even the ponies' hoofs had made little impression and I kept upright only by driving my specially nailed boots into it at each step – a process which still further exhausted me. After about an hour and a half of this struggle I was at that peculiar stage when one doesn't really believe that one's objective will ever be reached, and when one's only mental awareness concerns the joy (to some incomprehensible, if not downright unnatural) of driving one's body far beyond the limits of its natural endurance. Then, having dragged Roz up another savage gradient, and over yet another litter of boulders, we suddenly found ourselves on a level plateau, about a quarter of a mile square. Sitting where I had subsided beyond the rocks, and still clutching Roz, I slowly assimilated the unlikely fact that we were on Babusar Top.

I was understandably anxious to photograph Roz at this historic point where, because of her owner's mental unsoundness, she had become the first bicycle to cross the Babusar Pass; but though I took

8

three shots I doubt if the light was strong enough for a cheap camera. Yet, between the intermittent snowfalls, I had a clear view to east and south, where the sun was bright on a sparkle of angular peaks and on the flawless, smooth curves of the glaciers that united them.

By now the thunder had ceased and when the wind dropped the overwhelming silence of the mountains reminded me of the hush felt in a great empty Gothic Cathedral at dusk – a silence which is beautiful in itself. However, I could afford no more than half an hour on the Top, for I was still fifteen miles from the head of the Kagan Valley. In my enthusiasm to get up, the process of getting down again had not been very seriously considered; possibly I was suffering from lack of vitamins to the brain, because I'd assumed that once on the south side all hazards would be left behind. This delusion was fostered during the first stage of the descent.

From the plateau, I could see, about 1,000 feet below me, a vividly green valley some eight miles long and two miles wide, with a foam-white nullah flashing down its centre, and a reasonably-surfaced earth track descending at a comfortable gradient along the flank of the mountain, where snow had lain too recently for any growth to have covered the brown scree. On reaching the valley floor the track crossed the nullah and was visible running level along the base of the opposite mountains before curving away out of sight halfway down the valley. As we began to free-wheel I reflected that this was a delightful road to follow, with all the characteristics which thrill a wanderer's heart.

Half-an-hour later I was rapidly revising my opinion. The track's first imperfection was revealed when we arrived at the nullah, to find that where a bridge should be stood two supports, stoutly upholding nothing. I looked up- and downstream with wild surmise. The ponies had not returned, therefore the ponies had forded the nullah at some point. But at what point? Unfortunately the ground here was so firm, and the bank

9

so stony, that my diligent search for prints yielded no clues. Then, as I stood looking pathetically around me, in the faint hope of seeing some nomads, a solitary black cow (for all the world like a good little Kerry) appeared some twenty yards upstream, walking purposefully across the meadow towards the torrent. There was no other sign of life in the valley, either human or animal, and in retrospect I tend to believe that she was my guardian angel, discreetly disguised. But when I first noticed her I did not pause to speculate on her nature or origin. She was obviously going to ford the nullah for some good reason of her own, and we were going with her. I pedalled rapidly and bumpily over the grass to the point for which she was heading. There I hastily unstrapped the saddle-bag, tied it to my head with a length of rope mentally and appropriately labelled 'FOR EMERGENCIES', and was ready to enter the water.

The cow, when she joined us on the bank, showed no surprise at our presence, nor did she register any alarm or despondency as I put my right arm round her neck, gripped Roz's cross-bar firmly with my left hand, and accompanied her into the turmoil of icy water. It had occurred to me that if I found myself out of my depth this could become an Awkward Situation, but actually the water was never more than four feet deep, though its tremendous force would have unbalanced me had I been alone. My friend, however, was clearly used to this role and we crossed without difficulty, unless the agony of being two-thirds submerged in newly melted snow counts as a difficulty. I felt that there was a certain lack of civility about our abrupt parting on the opposite bank, after such a meaningful though brief association, but our ways lay in different directions and I could do nothing to express my gratitude. So I can only record here my thanks for the fairy-tale appearance of this little black cow.

'I probably loved atlases so much because . . .'

JUDITH SCHALANSKY

Atlas of Remote Islands (2009)

Judith Schalansky (b. 1980), who lives in Berlin, was brought up in the German Democratic Republic in the 1980s. Her illustrated account of 'visiting' fifty of the world's most distant islands, first published in 2009, was also voted the most beautiful German book of that year.

I grew up with an atlas. And as a child of the atlas, I had never travelled. The fact that a girl in my class had actually been born in Helsinki felt unimaginable. But there it was in her passport: H-e-l-s-i-n-k-i. Those eight letters became a key into another world. To this day I am baffled by Germans born, for example, in Nairobi or Los Angeles. They might as well claim to come from Atlantis, Thule or El Dorado. Of course I know that Nairobi and Los Angeles exist – they are on the maps. But that someone has actually *been there or even been born there* still feels incredible to me.

I probably loved atlases so much because the lines, the colours and the names replaced the real places that I could not visit. When I was eight, I saw a documentary about the Galapagos Islands. I stared, fascinated by the enormous iguanas with their tiny heads and jagged combs. I still remember the breathless commentary: *Day after day these animals bask motionless on the rocks. This is how the earth must have looked millions of years ago.* My reaction was immediate: I was going to be a naturalist and travel to these islands. I dragged our atlas down from the shelf and, as the researchers on the television inched their way towards some nesting birds, I heaved open our map of the world. I quickly found the Galapagos. They were a cluster of dots in the light blue ocean. *I want to go there now,* I announced. *Maybe one day,* said my mother, sadly.

But I wasn't to be deflected, and I pushed my index finger across the Atlantic to the tip of South America, turning before the southern polar circle and taking a new direction north at Tierra del Fuego. *Take the Panama Canal, that's shorter,* she recommended, tapping on the line that separated North from South America. And thus I undertook my first voyage round the world.

This map had several colours. The Soviet Union was a bibulous pink. The USA was a reserved blue, nearly as bright as the sea. Then I looked for my country: the German Democratic Republic. East Germans could not travel, only the Olympic team were allowed beyond our borders. It took a frighteningly long time to find. It was as pink and tiny as my smallest fingernail. This was hard to equate: at the Seoul Olympics we had been a force to reckon with, we had won more medals than the United States: how could we suddenly be so infinitesimal?

My love for atlases endured when a year later everything else changed: when it suddenly became possible to travel the world, and the country I was born in disappeared from the map. But by then I had already grown used to travelling through the atlas by finger, whispering foreign names to myself as I conquered distant worlds in my parents' sitting room.

The first atlas in my life was called *Atlas für jedermann (Everyman's Atlas)*. I didn't realise then that my atlas – like every other – was committed to an ideology. Its ideology was clear from its map of the world, carefully positioned on a double-page spread so that the Federal Republic of Germany and the German Democratic Republic fell on two separate pages. On this map there was no wall dividing the two German countries, no Iron Curtain; instead, there was the blinding white, impassable edge of the page. That, in turn, the provisional nature of the

GDR was depicted by the mysterious letters SBZ (*Sowjetische Mesatzungs-zone*, 'Soviet-occupied territory') in the atlases used in West German schools was something that I only found out later, when I had to memorise the rivers and mountains of a home country that had more than doubled in size.

The rest of the book is a little treasure house, a guide to tiny islands and enclaves that neither we nor Schalansky are likely to visit. Or maybe we will. They are attainable and provide a store of possibilities for those who love the adventure of being somewhere that they have only ever known from a map, which can create an anticipation that a photograph may only blunt.

This is Brava, one of the Islands Under the Wind (Cape Verde Islands):

This clenched heart lies untamable, protected from the wind by the great volcano of the neighbouring island. Here, at the outermost edge of the archipelago, the clouds hang low and it rains more than on the other islands, which are continually battered by desert winds. Dew forms on the leaves of the almond trees and the date and coconut palms, on the petals of the fringing lobelia, oleander, hibiscus, jasmine and bougain-villea. This island has veins of rivers and strong muscles in its mountain range. The faint beat of the melancholy *morna* sounds, and the old song pulses relentlessly in a minor key, a lament about the inescapability of fate. It is the longing for an unnameable moment in the past, for a distant land, for a long-lost home. A feeling, scattered like these islands, the yearning for a place that is at once everywhere and nowhere. This is the song of a land without original inhabitants. Everyone who lives here is descended from the planters who stayed behind and from their slaves, from those who chose to move here and those who were forced to, a people with blue eyes and black skin. // The melody starts hesitantly, following the wide arc of a legato. The guitar adds a bass line in four-four time, accompanied by the plucking syncopations of the cavaquinho, sometimes backed up by a violin. These songs live in the bars and dance halls of the harbour: Who goes with you / on this long journey? / Who goes with you / on this long journey? // This journey / to São Tomé // Homesick, homesick / homesick/ For my country São Nicolau // When you write to me / I will write to you / When you forget me / I will forget you // Homesick, homesick / homesick / For my country São Nicolau // Until the day / that you return. // Two-thirds of Cape Verdeans do not live on the islands any more.

'The snake had charmed me'

JOSEPH CONRAD

Heart of Darkness (1899)

Heart of Darkness *is a novel, but is included because the opening passages are autobiographical with Joseph Conrad putting his own story into the mouth of Marlow, the narrator of the novel. Conrad (1857–1924) was Polish, but was born in what is now the Ukraine. Although one of the most admired of all English language writers, he did not even speak it until his mid twenties. He began a nineteen-year career in the merchant marine on French ships. He joined the British merchant fleet in the late 1880s. Much of his writing drew closely from his experience in the merchant marine in in India, Borneo, Australia and South Africa. It was a three-year employ-ment as a captain of a steamer on the Congo River that enabled him to write his most celebrated work,* Heart of Darkness.

'Now when I was a little chap I had a passion for maps. I would look for hours at South America, or Africa, or Australia, and lose myself in all the glories of exploration. At that time there were many blank spaces on the earth, and when I saw one that looked particularly inviting on a map (but they all look that) I would put my finger on it and say, "When I grow up I will go there." The North Pole was one of these places, I remember. Well, I haven't been there yet, and shall not try now. The glamour's off. Other places were scattered about the Equator, and in every sort of latitude all over the two hemispheres. I have been in some of them, and ... well, we won't talk about that. But there was one yet – the biggest, the most blank, so to speak – that I had a hankering after.

'True, by this time it was not a blank space any more. It had got filled since my boyhood with rivers and lakes and names. It had ceased to be a blank space of delightful mystery – a white patch for a boy to dream gloriously over. It had become a place of darkness. But there was in it one river especially, a mighty big river, that you could see on the map, resembling an immense snake uncoiled, with its head in the sea, its body at rest curving afar over a vast country, and its tail lost in the depths of the land. And as I looked at the map of it in a shop-window, it fascinated me as a snake would a bird – a silly little bird. Then I remembered there was a big concern, a Company for trade on that river. Dash it all! I thought to myself, they can't trade without using some kind of craft on that lot of fresh water – steamboats! Why shouldn't I try to get charge of one? I went on along Fleet Street, but could not shake off the idea. The snake had charmed me.

'Please can I have the piece of brontosaurus'

BRUCE CHATWIN

In Patagonia (1977)

In 1972, Bruce Chatwin (1940–89) was working for the Sunday Times. *He interviewed the ninety-three-year-old architect and designer Eileen Gray in her Paris salon, where he noticed a map she had painted of the region of South America called Patagonia. 'I've always wanted to go there,' Chatwin told her. 'So have I,' she replied. 'Go there for me.' He went.*

In my grandmother's dining-room there was a glass-fronted cabinet and in the cabinet a piece of skin. It was a small piece only, but thick and leathery, with strands of coarse, reddish hair. It was stuck to a card with a rusty pin. On the card was some writing in faded black ink, but I was too young then to read.

'What's that?'

'A piece of brontosaurus.'

My mother knew the names of two prehistoric animals, the brontosaurus and the mammoth. She knew it was not a mammoth. Mammoths came from Siberia.

The brontosaurus, I learned, was an animal that had drowned in the Flood, being too big for Noah to ship aboard the Ark. I pictured a shaggy lumbering creature with claws and fangs and a malicious green light in its eyes. Sometimes the brontosaurus would crash through the bedroom wall and wake me from my sleep.

This particular brontosaurus had lived in Patagonia, a country in South America, at the far end of the world. Thousands of years before, it had fallen into a glacier, travelled down a mountain in a prison of blue ice, and arrived in perfect condition at the bottom. Here my grand-mother's cousin, Charley Milward the Sailor, found it.

Charley Milward was captain of a merchant ship that sank at the entrance to the Strait of Magellan. He survived the wreck and settled nearby, at Punta Arenas, where he ran a ship-repairing yard. The Char-ley Milward of my imagination was a god among men – tall, silent and strong, with black mutton-chop whiskers and fierce blue eyes. He wore his sailor's cap at an angle and the tops of his sea-boots turned down.

Directly he saw the brontosaurus poking out of the ice, he knew what to do. He had it jointed, salted, packed in barrels, and shipped to the Natural History Museum in South Kensington. I pictured blood and ice, flesh and salt, gangs of Indian workmen and lines of barrels along a shore – a work of giants and all to no purpose; the brontosaurus went rotten on its voyage through the tropics and arrived in London a putre-fied mess; which was why you saw brontosaurus bones in the museum, but no skin.

Fortunately cousin Charley had posted a scrap to my grandmother. My grandmother lived in a red-brick house set behind a screen of yellow-spattered laurels. It had tall chimneys, pointed gables and a garden of blood-coloured roses. Inside it smelled of church.

I do not remember much about my grandmother except her size. I would clamber over her wide bosom or watch, slyly, to see if she'd be able to rise from the chair. Above her hung paintings of Dutch burghers, their fat buttery faces nesting in white ruffs. On the mantelpiece were two Japanese homunculi with red and white ivory eyes that popped out on stalks. I would play with these, or with a German articulated monkey, but always I pestered her: 'Please can I have the piece of brontosaurus.'

Never in my life have I wanted anything as I wanted that piece of skin. My grandmother said I should have it one day, perhaps. And when she died I said: 'Now I *can* have the piece of brontosaurus,' but my mother said: 'Oh, that thing! I'm afraid we threw it away.'

At school they laughed at the story of the brontosaurus. The science master said I'd mixed it up with the Siberian mammoth. He told the class how Russian scientists had dined off deep-frozen mammoth and told me not to tell lies. Besides, he said, brontosauruses were reptiles. They had no hair, but scaly armoured hide. And he showed us an artist's impression of the beast – so different from that of my imagination – grey-green, with a tiny head and a gigantic switchback of vertebrae, placidly eating weed in a lake. I was ashamed of my hairy brontosaurus, but I knew it was not a mammoth.

It took some years to sort the story out. Charley Milward's animal was not a brontosaurus, but the mylodon or Giant Sloth. He never found a whole specimen, or even a whole skeleton, but some skin and bones, preserved by the cold, dryness and salt, in a cave on Last Hope Sound in Chilean Patagonia. He sent the collection to England and sold it to the British Museum. This version was less romantic but had the merit of being true.

My interest in Patagonia survived the loss of the skin; for the Cold War woke in me a passion for geography. In the late 1940s the Cannibal of the Kremlin shadowed our lives; you could mistake his moustaches for teeth. We listened to lectures about the war he was planning. We watched the civil defence lecturer ring the cities of Europe to show the zones of total and partial destruction. We saw the zones bump one against the other leaving no space in between. The instructor wore khaki shorts. His knees were white and knobbly, and we saw it was hopeless. The war was coming and there was nothing we could do.

Next, we read about the cobalt bomb, which was worse than the hydrogen bomb and could smother the planet in an endless chain reaction.

I knew the colour cobalt from my great-aunt's paintbox. She had lived on Capri at the time of Maxim Gorky and painted Capriot boys naked. Later her art became almost entirely religious. She did lots of St Sebastians, always against a cobalt-blue background, always the same beautiful young man, stuck through and through with arrows and still on his feet.

So I pictured the cobalt bomb as a dense blue cloudbank, spitting tongues of flame at the edges. And I saw myself, out alone on a green headland, scanning the horizon for the advance of the cloud.

And yet we hoped to survive the blast. We started an Emigration Committee and made plans to settle in some far corner of the earth. We pored over atlases. We learned the direction of prevailing winds and the likely patterns of fall-out. The war would come in the Northern Hemisphere, so we looked to the Southern. We ruled out Pacific Islands for islands are traps. We ruled out Australia and New Zealand, and we fixed on Patagonia as the safest place on earth.

I pictured a low timber house with a shingled roof, caulked against storms, with blazing log fires inside and the walls lined with the best books, somewhere to live when the rest of the world blew up.

Then Stalin died and we sang hymns of praise in chapel, but I continued to hold Patagonia in reserve.

THREE

'Our Feeble Hearts Could Not Stand More'

I was eight when I first crossed the Channel. We flew from Lydd Airport in Kent in a short fat aircraft; we drove our car onto it. It flew us and three other cars to Le Touquet. Then we were on to the French roads. We stopped at a café. We had no cafés in late 1950s Britain, at least where I lived. I remember the wide green ribbed coffee cup, the smell of the coffee and fresh croissants. This was the smell of abroad.

A few years later my father took me on a boat from London's Tilbury Docks. It was Union Castles' *Braemar Castle*. I shared a cabin with my twin sister. We went to Gibraltar, Genoa ('avoid the beaches at Rapallo; there may be topless girls'; there were), past Stromboli, erupting gently at night, then silently eased through the Strait of Messina, seeming to push the shore lights apart for a channel, and across to Alexandria. I did not sleep that night, just knelt at a hotel window and watched. Nightlife was new to me – men in white dresses, talking, bargaining, scurrying, just *doing*, all night – and by early morning a bustling, spicy market, urgent with opportunity for an innocent boy from Sussex.

We docked at Aden, where they walked around with guns on the street and even at midnight it was hotter than the best English August. Across the equator with all the ceremonies, accompanied by dolphins and phosphorescent flying fish, and then we nosed our prow through green tropical channels up into Mombasa. Real Africa.

I had fallen in love with abroad. I still am.

In this chapter others describe how they fell in love with abroad, or bits of abroad. The first is Nicolas Bouvier, whose tribute to the excitement of new feelings of liberation gives the title to the chapter. I have felt the same; until I read Bouvier I would call these pinnacle moments 'feeling in the chest events,' after a line that I so clearly recall from Gavin Young's *Return to the Marshes* but now cannot trace. They happen for me without warning: in a fly-swarmed meat market on a Kabul hill; whilst wandering among sheep on a stony dune south of Laghouat in the Algerian Sahara; the first glimpse of the Oxus after a fifteen-hour journey through a Tajikistan night in the back of a hijacked military truck; the first view of the Potala Palace. It is the drug that finds you, not the other way around.

Some, such as Bouvier, Jack Kerouac and John Masters, are young and on their first adventure. Or they may be on their first journeys to a particular destination, like Henry Miller in Greece and Paul Bowles in North Africa. Some, such as John Steinbeck, have many years of adventure behind them but are still thrilled at the new and searching for the meaning of their yen for travel.

'Our feeble hearts could not stand more'

NICOLAS BOUVIER

The Way of the World (1963, 2007)

It's a gap year 1953-style. Bouvier (1929–1998) is a twenty-four-year-old Swiss, travelling and exploring for the first time. In this passage he finds himself in eastern Turkey. First published in 1963, L'Usage du Monde *appeared in English translation in 2007 as* The Way of the World. *The first extract comes from his preface and the second is the last three paragraphs of the chapter 'The Road to Anatolia' and ends with the glorious words that give this chapter their title and represent the spirit of all of* Scraps of Wool *as a collection.*

From ten to thirteen I had stretched out on the rug, silently contemplating the atlas, and that makes one want to travel. I had dreamed of regions such as the Banat, the Caspian, Kashmir, of their music, of the glances one might meet there, of the ideas that lay in waiting... When desire resists commonsense's first objections, we look for reasons – and find that they're no use. We really don't know what to call this inner compulsion. Something grows, and loses its moorings, so that the day comes when, none too sure of ourselves, we nevertheless leave for good.

Travelling outgrows its motives. It soon proves sufficient in itself. You think you are making a trip, but soon it is making you – or unmaking you.

. . .

East of Erzurum the road is very lonely. Vast distances separate the villages. For one reason or another we occasionally stopped the car, and spent the rest of the night outdoors. Warm in big felt jackets and fur hats with ear-flaps, we listened to the water as it boiled on a primus in the lee of a wheel. Leaning against a mound, we gazed at the stars, the ground undulating towards the Caucasus, the phosphorescent eyes of foxes.

Time passed in brewing tea, the odd remark, cigarettes, then dawn came up. The widening light caught the plumage of quails and partridges . . . and quickly I dropped this wonderful moment to the bottom of my memory, like a sheet-anchor that one day I could draw up again. You stretch, pace to and fro feeling weightless, and the word 'happiness' seems too thin and limited to describe what has happened.

In the end, the bedrock of existence is not made up of the family, or work, or what others say or think of you, but of moments like this when you are exalted by a transcendent power that is more serene than love. Life dispenses them parsimoniously; our feeble hearts could not stand more.

'I fear the disease is incurable.'

JOHN STEINBECK

Travels with Charley (1962)

In 1960, at the age of fifty-eight and possibly already aware of his failing health, John Steinbeck (1902–1968), author of Grapes of Wrath, East of Eden *and* Of Mice and Men, *set out with his French poodle Charley and his camper pick-up truck on a journey across his native America. Two years later Steinbeck would become one of the more controversial Nobel laureates in literature.*

When I was very young and the urge to be someplace was on me, I was assured by mature people that maturity would cure this itch. When years described me as mature, the remedy prescribed was middle age. In middle age I was assured that greater age would calm my fever and now that I am 58 perhaps senility will do the job. Nothing has worked. Four hoarse blasts of a ship's whistle still raise the hair on my neck and set my feet to tapping. The sound of a jet, an engine warming up, even the clopping of shod hooves on pavement brings on the ancient shudder, the dry mouth and vacant eye, the hot palms and the churn of stomach high up under the rib cage. In other words, I don't improve; in further words, once a bum, always a bum. I fear the disease is incurable. I set this matter down not to instruct others but to inform myself.

When the virus of restlessness begins to take possession of a wayward man, and the road away from Here seems broad and straight and sweet, the victim must have, in himself a good and sufficient reason for going. This to the practical bum is not difficult. He has a built-in garden of reasons to choose from. Next he must plan his trip in time and space, choose a direction and a destination. And last he must implement the journey. How to go, what to take, where to stay. This part of the process is invariable and immortal. I set it down only so that newcomers to bumdom, like teenagers in new-hatched sin, will not think they invented it.

Once a journey is designed, equipped and put in process, a new factor enters and takes over. A trip, a safari, an exploration is an entity different from all other journeys. It has temperament, individuality, uniqueness. A journey is a person in itself; no two are alike. And all plans, safe-guards, policing, and coercion are fruitless. We find after years of struggle that we do not take a trip; a trip takes us. Tour masters, sched-ules, reservations, brass-bound and inevitable, dash themselves to wreckage on the personality of the trip. Only when this is recognised can the blown-in-the-glass bum relax and go along with it. Only then do the frustrations fall away. In this a journey is like marriage. The certain way to be wrong is to think you control it. I feel better now, having said this, although only those who have experienced it will understand it.

—•━•—

'Christ, I was happy'

HENRY MILLER

The Colossus of Maroussi (1941)

The American Henry Miller (1891–1980) is best known for his novels Tropic of Cancer *and* Tropic of Capricorn, *but he was also a travel writer of note. He lived in Paris in the 1930s, where he met Anaïs Nin, who became his lover and financed the first printing of* Tropic of Cancer. *He was invited to Greece by Lawrence Durrell (*Bitter Lemons, *The Alexandria Quartet) in 1939. The title of the book refers to the dominant character, the Greek writer and raconteur George Katsimbalis, whom Miller admired and may have viewed as a Greek version of himself.*

I would never have gone to Greece had it not been for a girl named Betty Ryan who lived in the same house with me in Paris. One evening, over a glass of white wine, she began to talk of her experiences in roaming about the world. I always listened to her with great attention, not only because her experiences were strange but because when she talked about her wanderings she seemed to paint them: everything she described remained in my head like finished canvases by a master. It was a peculiar conversation that evening: we began by talking about China and the Chinese language which she had begun to study. Soon we were in North Africa, in the desert, among peoples I had never heard of before. And then suddenly she was all alone, walking beside a river, and the light was intense and I was following her as best I could in the blinding sun, but she got lost and I found myself wandering about in a strange land listening to a language I had never heard before. She is not exactly a storyteller, this girl, but she is an artist of some sort, because nobody has ever given me the ambience of a place so thoroughly as she did that of Greece. Long afterwards I discovered that it was near Olympia that she had gone astray and I with her, but at the time it was just Greece to me, a world of light such as I had never dreamed of and never hoped to see.

For months prior to this conversation I had been receiving letters from Greece from my friend Lawrence Durrell, who had practically made Corfu his home. His letters were marvellous too, and yet a bit unreal to me. Durrell is a poet and his letters were poetic: they caused a certain confusion in me, owing to the fact that the dream and the reality, the historical and the mythological, were so artfully blended. Later I was to discover for myself that this confusion is real and not due entirely to the poetic faculty. But at the time I thought he was laying it on, that it was his way of coaxing me to accept his repeated invitations to come and stay with him.

. . .

We didn't go through the Corinth canal because there had been a landslide: we practically circumnavigated the Peloponnesus. The second night out we pulled into Patras opposite Missolonghi. I have come into this port several times since, always about the same hour, and always I experienced the same fascination. You ride straight into a big headland, like an arrow burying itself in the side of a mountain. The electric lights strung along the waterfront create a Japanese effect; there is something impromptu about the lighting in all Greek ports, something which gives the impression of an impending festival. As you pull into port the little boats come out to meet you: they are filled with passengers and luggage and livestock and bedding and furniture. The men row standing up, pushing instead of pulling. They seem absolutely tireless, moving their heavy burdens about at will with deft and almost imperceptible move-ments of the wrist. As they draw alongside a pandemonium sets in. Everybody goes the wrong way, everything is confused, chaotic, disorderly. But nobody is ever lost or hurt, nothing is stolen, no blows are exchanged. It is a kind of ferment which is created by reason of the fact that for a Greek every event, no matter how stale, is always unique. He is always doing the same thing for the first time: he is curious, avidly curious, and experimental. He experiments for the sake of experimenting, not to establish a better or more efficient way of doing things. He likes to do things with his hands, with his whole body, with his soul, I might as well say. Thus Homer lives on. Though I've never read a line of Homer I believe the Greek of today is essentially unchanged. If anything he is more Greek than he ever was. And here I must make a parenthesis to say a word about my friend Mayo, the painter, whom I knew in Paris. Malliarakis was his real name and I think he came originally from Crete. Anyway, pulling into Patras I got to thinking about him violently. I remembered asking him in Paris to tell me something about Greece and suddenly, as we were coming into the port of Patras, I understood everything he had been trying to tell me that night and I felt bad that he was not alongside me to share my enjoyment. I remembered how he had said with quiet, steady conviction, after describing the country for me as best he could – 'Miller, you will like Greece, I am sure of it.' Somehow those words impressed me more than anything he had said about Greece. You will like it . . . that stuck in my crop. 'By God, yes, I like it,' I was saying to myself over and over as I stood at the rail taking in the movement and the hubbub. I leaned back and looked up at the sky. I had never seen a sky like this before. It was magnificent. I felt completely detached from Europe, I had entered a new realm as a free man – everything had conjoined to make the experience unique and fructifying. Christ, I was happy. But for the first time in my life I was happy with the full consciousness of being happy. It's good to be just plain happy; it's a little better to know that you're happy; but to understand that you're happy and to know why and how, in what way, because of what concatenation of events or circumstances, and still be happy, be happy in the being and the knowing, well, that is beyond happiness, that is bliss, and if you have any sense you ought to kill yourself on the spot and be done with it. And that's how I was – except that I didn't have the power or the courage to kill myself then and there. It was good, too, that I didn't do myself in because there were even greater moments to come, something beyond bliss even, something which if anyone had tried to describe to me I would probably not have believed. I didn't know then that I would one day stand at Mycenae, or at Phaestos, or that I would wake up one morning and looking through a port hole see with my own eyes the place I had written about in a book, but which I never knew existed nor bore the same name as the one I had given it in my imagination. Marvellous things happen to one in Greece – marvellous good things which can happen to one nowhere else on earth. Somehow, almost as if He were nodding, Greece still remains under the protection of the Creator. Men may go about their puny, ineffectual bedevilment, even in Greece, but God's magic is still at work and, no matter what the race of man may do or try to do, Greece is still a sacred precinct – and my belief is it will remain so until the end of time.

'It is a drug-free high, Palestinian-style'

RAJA SHEHADEH

Palestinian Walks: Notes on a Vanishing Landscape (2007)

Raja Shehadeh was born in 1951 in Jaffa in Israel and now lives in Ramallah on the West Bank. He had grown intimate with the West Bank landscape, walking with his grandfather, when he was young. In Palestin-ian Walks *he returns to the same paths and celebrates the memories of his early discoveries, whilst lamenting the transformation caused by the encroachment of new town settlements from across the border.*

In the uneasy first years of the new millennium I felt that my days in Palestine were numbered. But whether Palestine or myself would slip away first was an open question. Cities were being erected in its midst, as were industrial and theme parks, and wide, many-laned highways more suited to the plains of the Mid-West of America than the undulat-ing hills of Palestine. In two and a half decades one of the world's treasures, this biblical landscape that would have seemed familiar to a contemporary of Christ, was being changed, in some parts beyond rec-ognition.

The biography of these hills is in many ways my own, the victories and failures of the struggle to save this land also mine. But the persistent pain at the failure of that struggle would in time be shared by Arabs, Jews and lovers of nature anywhere in the world. All would grieve, as I have, at the continuing destruction of an exquisitely beautiful place.

As a child I used to hear how my grandfather, Judge Saleem, liked nothing more than coming to Ramallah in the hot summer and going on a *sarha* with his cousin, Abu Ameen, leaving behind the humid coastal city of Jaffa and the stultifying colonial administration which he served and whose politics he detested. It was mainly young men who went on these expeditions. They would take a few provisions and go to the open hills, disappear for the whole day, sometimes for weeks and months. They often didn't have a particular destination. To go on a *sarha* was to roam freely, at will, without restraint. The verb form of the word means to let the cattle out to pasture early in the morning, leaving them to wander and graze at liberty. The commonly used noun *sarha* is a colloquial corruption of the classical word. A man going on *sarha* wanders aimlessly, not restricted by time and place, going where his spirit takes him to nourish his soul and rejuvenate himself. But not any excursion would qualify as a *sarha*. Going on a *sarha* implies letting go. It is a drug-free high, Palestinian-style.

. . .

It had been a long winter, continuing to rain throughout April and during the first few days of May, which is most unusual for this part of the world. I set out on my *sarha* just two days after the rain had stopped. The sun had emerged and the earth was not too muddy. The sky was blue with low scattered clouds that sometimes blocked the sun, making it very pleasant to walk.

My starting point on that day was behind the Anglican School in a north-western neighbourhood of Ramallah. I walked down the newly paved road, which continued northward towards the unfinished hous- ing development, at that time the farthest incursion of the town into the hills. I found the path almost immediately; once on it, a certain peace and tranquility descended upon me. Now I could go on with no need to worry, just walk and enjoy the beauty of the nature around me.

I ambled alongside the western side of the valley across from the hill referred to as El Batah (the duck), so called because of the way it sits on the valley. Along the path the wild flowers were in abundance. Most were in miniature, blue iris only a few centimetres high, pink flax also very close to the ground and the slightly taller Maltese Cross and pyra- mid orchids, a colourful but thin carpet covering the vibrant land. I had assumed a pace that was neither hurried nor dawdling. I was heading towards the appropriately named Wadi El Wrda (the flower) across the shoulder of the hill, a gentle descent that took me over one fold, down a small incline and up another in a diagonal trajectory towards the valley.

I could see that the wadi had longer grass and plants because it was fed by the sweet water of A'yn El Lwza (the almond). I crossed over and listened to the faint sound of the dripping of the water down to a pool. Then I bent and looked into the hollow in the rocks from which the water oozed. I stretched out my hand and let the cold water run over it. There were plenty of stones and weeds. The spring was in bad need of cleaning – otherwise the water would be gushing out. I sat nearby smelling the moist soil and looking at the impressive mossy brown cliff across the wadi. It was studded with cyclamens that grew out of every nook and cranny. They always seemed to grow in rocks that shielded them from the glare of the midday sun, squeezing themselves between cracks to protect their bulbs from drying up. And despite their precarious position their delicate flowers grew straight up and were hooked at the top like a shepherd's staff. Their large variegated leaves, similar to those of the grapevines but thicker and a deeper green, seemed suspended from nowhere, miraculously hanging on the high steep rock. Above the cliff the hill was steep and from this vantage point seemed high and formidable.

Nearby I found a well-preserved *qasr*. The word, which literally means a 'castle', refers to the mainly round stone structures dotting the land where farmers kept their produce and slept on the open roof. It was in one of these structures that my grandfather Saleem and my uncle Abu Ameen camped out when they went on their *sarha* together. It must have taken a good degree of skill to build one on this slope, where it has lasted for more than a hundred years. Before visiting the qasr, I took a moment to look around. It was as though the earth was exploding with beauty and colour and had thrown from its bosom wonderful gifts without any human intervention. I wanted to cry out in celebration of this splendour. As I shouted 'S-A-R-H-A!' I felt I was breaking the silence of the past, a silence that had enveloped this place for a long time. My cry of greeting echoed against one hill then another and another, returning to me fainter and fainter until I felt I had somehow touched the entire landscape.

⸻⸰⸱⸰⸱⸰⸱⸰⸻

'Like any Romantic, I had always been vaguely certain that sometime during my life I should come into a magic place'

PAUL BOWLES

Without Stopping (1972)

Paul Bowles, born in Queens, New York in 1910, had prodigious literary and musical talent from a very young age and was befriended by the avant-garde of the day in both fields. He dropped out of university to travel to Paris with Aaron Copland, who had been his music teacher in New York. In Paris he was assimilated into the literary and artistic circle of Gertrude Stein. In 1931 he and Copland travelled to Morocco, arriving by boat at Tangier. The moment described here is his first sight of Africa from that boat. Tangier would later be his home for much of the rest of his life, where he was to become the pivotal intellectual figure of the large expatriate community in the city. But first he returned to New York and established a reputation as a composer before leaving again for Morocco after the end of the Second World War. By then he was in a marriage of social rather than sexual convenience with the author Jane Auer. His travels in North Africa inspired his novel The Sheltering Sky *(1949), the work for which he remains best known. His autobiography* Without Stopping *was not published until 1972.*

⸻⸰⸱⸰⸱⸰⸱⸰⸻

Straightway I felt a great excitement; much excited; it was as if some interior mechanism had been set in motion by the sight of the approaching land. Always without formulating the concept, I had based my sense of being in the world partly on an unreasoned conviction that certain areas of the earth's surface contained more magic than others . . . Like any Romantic, I had always been vaguely certain that sometime during my life I should come into a magic place which in disclosing its secrets would give me wisdom and ecstasy – perhaps even death. And now, as I stood in the wind looking at the mountains ahead, I felt the stirring of the engine within, and it was as if I were drawing close to the solution of an as-yet-unposed problem. I was incredibly happy as I watched the wall of mountains slowly take on substance, but I let the happiness wash over me and asked no questions.

'I knew then I had caught . . . a passionate love of mountains'

JOHN MASTERS

Bugles and a Tiger (1937)

John Masters (1941–83), later much better known as a novelist, was a subaltern serving with the 4th Gurkha Rifles based in Bakloh, a hills garrison up in Himachal Pradesh, northern India. His regiment was deployed to the Northwest Frontier and the twenty-two-year-old Masters remained behind – the only British officer in the depot, tasked with training recruits. He took them on a trek across the mountains into Chamba, which the following piece describes.

The recruits sang with joy to be back in the mountains. By day we curved round the forested shoulders of great hills and climbed over bare spurs and toiled up steep valleys. At night we camped in clearings among the pines, beside running streams full of fish. At Jhot the little rivulet would not do for their fishing, and they insisted on taking me down to the Ravi, four thousand feet almost vertically below. In the morning we had marched twelve miles; all afternoon we ran up and down in the burning valley with our nets; by evening the recruits had to help me back up that gigantic slope from the river to the camp. They seemed surprised at my flabbiness – but they had to discover sometime that British officers were not demigods, and now they enjoyed their opportunity to be solicitous. When I reached my tent and flopped down I found a half-dead crab in the pocket of my shorts. Recruit Manparsad had put it there during the fishing.

In Chamba, the tiny capital of a small hill state, the Ravi was one hundred and fifty feet wide and a hundred feet deep and ran at ten or twelve knots, grey with melted snow. An icy breath blew on us out of its gorge as we walked with broken step across the jouncing suspension bridge into the town. The rajah was a slight, dark boy of fifteen, not yet invested with ruling powers. He gave us permission to camp on the miniature parade ground below his palace and then invited me to dine with himself and his English tutor. After an unostentatious meal in a mid-Victorian room, they came out to our campfire. The young rajah laughed with pleasure and clapped his hands while the recruits danced the *jaunris* and sang the hill songs of Nepal.

When he had gone back to the palace with his tutor, and the recruits were asleep in the low bivouacs, I walked alone by the bank of the Ravi in the moonlight. Here and now a breath of relaxation and pure happiness came to me for perhaps the first time in my life – certainly it was the most strongly felt. Inside me my spirit sang: this is our life, you and

I, the body and the spirit, the lonely mountains, running water, and friends. The Himalaya had breathed its breath into my nostrils while I lay asleep on the trail. The night was beautiful down by the river; the land was beautiful; but nothing was as beautiful as the feeling inside me. I wanted to share it and open my heart and love to a woman who would know without words what was in me, in whose nostrils too there was this mingled majesty and peace and excitement. But there was no such woman, not then, not there.

The next day, as we went back over a high pass into India, the strange feeling of utter content, yet with striving, came on me again, for now the main chain of the Himalaya stood up blindingly blue and white to the north beyond the Chamba valley, and we climbed in slow sweat through meadows blinking with the flowers of early summer.

After our return to Bakloh I knew I had caught two germs – in the low country, a second dose of malaria, and in the Himalaya, a passionate love of mountains.

'It's important to travel when you're young: you travel light and cheap, and your heart is like a sponge'

ANA BRIONGOS

Black on Black: Iran Revisited
(2000; first published in Spanish as *Negro Sobre Negro*)

Ana Briongos (b. 1946) studied and worked in Iran in the 1960s and then returned there to see what had changed in the 1990s, working for a while in a carpet store in Isfahan.

The second time, some months later, I arrived on a coach again, but this time I had crossed Turkey: Istanbul, Trabzon, Erzurum, Tabriz, Tehran. A day in the city to get the Afghan visa, then a coach to Mashhad, on the north-eastern border of Iran. I was twenty, travelling on my own, and I never had any problems. I had deferred my course at the Faculty of Physics in Barcelona, with its classes and exams, to immerse myself in the permanent university of travelling through other countries and getting to know their people. It isn't just the forests, the seas, the rivers, the deserts, the paths and the daybreaks that teach you things; it isn't just the monuments and the museums: it's also the men, the women and the children who live by those paths and in those deserts. It's important to travel when you're young: you travel light and cheap, and your heart is like a sponge. The paths across the world make up a school which tempers the character and reinforces tolerance and solidarity. You learn to give and take, to keep the doors open in the house of the spirit, and above all to share. You learn to enjoy small things, to value what you have, to be happy in times of scarcity and to celebrate abundance. You learn to listen, to watch, and to love.

FOUR

Alone

While many travel writers travelled alone all or some of the time, there is a group for whom their aloneness and isolation was the essence of the adventure. These include the two nineteenth-century women travellers, Mary Kingsley and Isabella Bird, the round-the-world sailor Joshua Slocum, and the ever-optimistic Dane Ejnar Mikkelsen, marooned with a colleague in the Arctic just before the First World War. The two more contemporary writers included here are Sylvain Tesson, who deliberately marooned himself on the shores of Lake Baikal for a winter, and Paul Heiney, who also deliberately isolated himself, but on a boat and for very different reasons.

'the other one I would have given anything to avoid'

PAUL HEINEY

One Wild Song (2015)

An important aspect of the voyage for all these writers is what is left behind, as well as what is sought. None had a fiercer and less tractable catalyst for departure than Paul Heiney, as he explains here in his

37

introduction. He left the English coast in Cornwall to sail alone in his small boat around Cape Horn, the southernmost tip of the Americas and possibly the most forbidding destination in any marine atlas.

Land slips from sight very slowly, often more slowly than you would wish. But eventually it goes and in that moment, when the coast finally disappears and you, your little ship and your crew are alone on the sea, lies the torment; for a bit of you wants rid of the sight of land and the real journey to begin, but if you are honest you secretly crave its comforting presence. This is the voyaging paradox and has been for all sailors who take to deep waters. On that fine July afternoon, as the green and secure Cornish landscape dwindled behind me and the blank, grey ocean lay ahead, I was torn over where my true ambition lay; wouldn't life be simpler and safer at home, on land? Yet isn't an ocean voyage the greatest of achievements, if an often dangerous and uncertain business? Which way do you turn your head? Forwards to the unknown or backwards to the safe? The only answer has to be ever forwards, towards the bow. Backward glances are not the ingredients of true adventures.

The start of a new voyage is a time of confused emotions, a tumult of thoughts and feelings every bit as wild as the tumbling of the waves around you. This must be accepted and relished, for if depth of feeling is lacking then there can be no sense of adventure. On the one hand it is also a time of urgency in which you are drawn with all haste to the horizon like a gull to a scrap of fish: you want to be on your way, devouring the journey, making progress, putting miles beneath the keel getting there. But a little bit of you wishes the land would stay with you, for it spells comfort and refuge while, increasingly, all around you is becoming less certain and you more isolated. On land you can walk with others, at sea you always stand alone.

It doesn't do to look over your shoulder too often, watching for the once distinct outline of land to fade to a blur and then be lost in the haze: this leads to an unnerving feeling that a door has finally closed on the world behind you. This thought will make you swallow hard. Yet once it is admitted, that things have changed and that which was is now gone, and only what lies ahead matters, then you are relieved and rise to the challenge. This transition does not always come easily, but it is at the heart of the satisfaction of voyaging. People talk of 'voyages of discovery' and imagine only of arrivals in new, romantic worlds; but the beginnings and the ends in themselves are the least part of it, for true voyages are an unfolding process of self-discovery and the true drama lies not in the starting or the finishing, but is made along the way.

I have made two of my life's toughest voyages in the past few years; one I had always wanted to make, and the other I would have given anything to avoid. Both involved letting go of one world, and finding the courage to live in the next. One is the long trek, under sail, to one of the most profoundly remote parts of the world; to an often bleak land of rock, ice and near overwhelming storms – these are the waters of the infamous Cape Horn. The other is the long, hard journey through the death of my son, Nicholas, who took his own life at the age of twenty-three; to travel this road is to suffer desolation that no earthly place can inflict upon you. The two journeys are not unconnected; they are both tales of high adventure and discovery through some of life's most difficult landscapes, and both begin, as all voyages must, with finding the courage to face the future, reserving the past as a fond memory and not something you should cling to like a drowning soul. Your strength must come from what lies ahead. That is true voyaging.

'A more successful ascent of the Peak was never made'

ISABELLA BIRD

A Lady's Life in the Rocky Mountains (1873)

Isabella Bird is one of the most admired of all the travel writers of any age. She freed herself from a male dominated society, overcame her own perennial ill health and ventured forth to Japan, Tibet, China, the Americas, Persia, Kurdistan and Korea. Dervla Murphy wrote to me of Isabella: 'I think of long dead authors as my friends. Among the dearest is Isabella Bird, a clergyman's daughter, born exactly a century before me in 1831. For decades, while travelling in far-flungery, she wrote to her sister in Edinburgh, who represented all the mid-Victorian virtues from which Isabella needed to escape.' She visited the Sandwich Islands (now called Hawaii) in 1873, and on the way back led anything but a lady's life in the Rocky Mountains of the USA, riding a horse more than 800 miles in three months over unpredictable terrain. Here she is at Estes Peak in Colorado.

Long's Peak, the 'American Matterhorn' as some call it, was ascended five years ago for the first time. I thought I should like to attempt it, but up to Monday, when Evans (a hunter) left for Denver, cold water was thrown upon the project. It was too late in the season, the winds were likely to be strong, etc; but just before leaving, Evans said that the weather was looking more settled, and if I did not get farther than the timber line it would be worth going. Soon after he left, 'Mountain Jim' came in, and he would go up as a guide, and the two youths who rode here with me from Longmount and I caught at the proposal. Mrs Edwards at once baked bread for three days, steaks were cut from the steer which hangs up conveniently, and tea, sugar, and butter were benevolently added. Our picnic was not to be a luxurious or 'well-found' one, for, in order to avoid the expense of a pack mule, we limited our luggage to what our saddle horses could carry. Behind my saddle I carried three pairs of camping blankets and a quilt, which reached to my shoulders. My own boots were so worn that it was painful to walk, even around the park, in them, so Evans had lent me a pair of his hunting boots, which hung to the horn of my saddle. The horses of the two young men were equally loaded, for we had to prepare for many degrees of frost. 'Jim' was a shocking figure; he had an old pair of high boots, with a baggy pair of old trousers made of deer hide, held on by an old scarf tucked into them; a leather shirt, with three or four ragged unbuttoned waistcoats over it; an old smashed wide awake, from under which his tawny, neglected ringlets hung; and with his one eye, his one long spur, his knife in his belt, his revolver in his waistcoat pocket, his saddle covered with an old beaver skin, from which the paws hung down; his camping blankets behind him, his rifle laid across the saddle in front of him, and his axe, canteen, and other gear hanging to the horn, he was as awful-looking a ruffian as one could see. By way of contrast he rode a small Arab mare, of exquisite beauty, skittish, high spirited, gentle, but altogether too light for him, and he fretted her incessantly to make her display herself.

Heavily loaded as all our horses were, 'Jim' started over the half mile of level grass at a hard gallop, and then throwing his mare on her haunches, pulled up alongside of me, and with a grace of manner which soon made me forget his appearance, entered into a conversation which lasted for more than three hours, in spite of the manifold checks of fording streams, single file, abrupt ascents and descents, and other incidents of mountain travel. The ride was one series of glories and surprises, of 'park' and glade, of lake and stream, of mountains on mountains, culminating in the rent pinnacles of Long's Peak, which looked yet grander and ghastlier as we crossed an attendant mountain 11,000 feet high. The slanting sun added fresh beauty every hour. There were dark pines against a lemon sky, grey peaks reddening, and etherealising, gorges of deep and infinite blue, floods of golden glory pouring through canyons of enormous depth, an atmosphere of absolute purity, an occasional foreground of cottonwood and aspen flaunting in red and gold to inten-sify the blue gloom of the pines, the trickle and murmur of streams fringed with icicles, the strange sough of gusts moving among the pine tops – sights and sounds not of the lower earth, but of the solitary, beast-haunted, frozen upper altitudes. From the dry, buff grass of Estes Park we turned off up a trail on the side of a pine-hung gorge, up a steep pine-clothed hill, down to a small valley, rich in fine, sun-cured hay about eighteen inches high, and enclosed by high mountains whose deepest hollow contains a lily-covered lake, fitly named 'The Lake of the Lilies.' Ah, how magical its beauty was, as it slept in silence, while there the dark pines were mirrored motionless in its pale gold, and here the great white lily cups and dark green leaves rested on amethyst-colored water!

. . .

Unsaddling and picketing the horses securely, making the beds of pine shoots, and dragging up logs for fuel, warmed us all. 'Jim' built up a great fire, and before long we were all sitting around it at supper. It didn't matter much that we had to drink our tea out of the battered meat tins in which it was boiled, and eat strips of beef reeking with pine smoke without plates or forks.

'Treat Jim as a gentleman and you'll find him one,' I had been told; and though his manner was certainly bolder and freer than that of gentlemen generally, no imaginary fault could be found. He was very agreeable as a man of culture as well as a child of nature; the desperado was altogether out of sight. He was very courteous and even kind to me, which was fortunate, as the young men had little idea of showing even ordinary civilities. That night I made the acquaintance of his dog, 'Ring,'

42

said to be the best hunting dog in Colorado, with the body and legs of a collie, but a head approaching that of a mastiff, a noble face with a wistful human expression, and the most truthful eyes I ever saw in an animal. His master loves him if he loves anything, but in his savage moods ill-treats him. 'Ring's' devotion never swerves, and his truthful eyes are rarely taken off his master's face. He is almost human in his intelligence, and, unless he is told to do so, he never takes notice of anyone but 'Jim.' In a tone as if speaking to a human being, his master, pointing to me, said, 'Ring, go to that lady, and don't leave her again tonight.' 'Ring' at once came to me, looked into my face, laid his head on my shoulder, and then lay down beside me with his head on my lap, but never taking his eyes from 'Jim's' face.

. . .

We reached Estes Park at noon of the following day. A more successful ascent of the Peak was never made, and I would not now exchange my memories of its perfect beauty and extraordinary sublimity for any other experience of mountaineering in any part of the world. Yesterday snow fell on the summit, and it will be inaccessible for eight months to come.

'Fortunately my terror is a special variety'

MARY KINGSLEY

Travels in West Africa (1897)

*Mary Kingsley (1862–1900) came from a family with a literary and naturalist bent; she was the niece of Charles Kingsley (*The Water Babies*) and* *admired Charles Darwin, T. H. Huxley and, most of all, Isabella Bird. She arrived in Sierra Leone in 1893 and initially followed a similar route to that taken by Mungo Park, a hundred years earlier, and Graham Greene forty years later.* Travels in West Africa *covers an eleven-month journey among the 'inland tribes'. Kingsley roamed from Sierra Leone as far as Angola, explored almost unknown parts of Gabon and even pioneered a new route up the 14,000-foot Great Peak of the Cameroons. She is another of Dervla Murphy's heroes: 'Of my chosen octet, Mary Kingsley is the best writer and wittiest commentator.' Kingsley was to die at only thirty-seven, having volunteered as a nurse during the Second Boer War. She developed typhoid in Cape Town and asked to die alone and be taken out to sea for burial.*

I must say the African leopard is an audacious animal, although it is ungrateful of me to say a word against him, after the way he has let me off personally, and I will speak of his extreme beauty as compensation for my ingratitude. I really think, taken as a whole, he is the most lovely animal I have ever seen; only seeing him, in the one way you can gain a full idea of his beauty, namely in his native forest, is not an unmixed joy to a person, like myself, of a nervous disposition. I may remark that my nervousness regarding the big game of Africa is of a rather peculiar kind. I can confidently say I am not afraid of any wild animal – until I see it – and then – well I will yield to nobody in terror; fortunately as I say my terror is a special variety; fortunately because no one can manage their own terror. You can suppress alarm, excitement, fear, fright, and all those small-fry emotions, but the real terror is as dependent on the inner make of you as the colour of your eyes, or the shape of your nose; and when terror ascends its throne in my mind I become preternaturally artful, and intelligent to an extent utterly foreign to my true nature, and save, in the case of close quarters with bad big animals, a feeling of rage against some unknown person that such things as leopards, elephants, crocodiles, &c., should be allowed out loose in that disgracefully dangerous way, I do not think much about it at the time. Whenever I have come across an awful being in the forest and I know it has seen me I take Jerome's advice, and instead of relying on the power of the human eye rely upon that of the human leg, and effect a masterly retreat in the face of the enemy. If I know it has not seen me I sink in my tracks and keep an eye on it, hoping that it will go away soon. Thus I once came upon a leopard. I had got caught in a tornado in a dense forest. The massive, mighty trees were waving like a wheat-field in an autumn gale in England, and I dare say a field mouse in a wheat-field in a gale would have heard much the same uproar. The tornado shrieked like ten thousand vengeful demons. The great trees creaked and groaned and strained against it and their bush-rope cables groaned and smacked like whips, and ever and anon a thundering crash with snaps like pistol shots told that they and their mighty tree had strained and struggled in vain. The fierce rain came in a roar, tearing to shreds the leaves and blossoms and deluging everything. I was making bad weather of it, and climbing up over a lot of rocks out of a gully bottom where I had been half drowned in a stream, and on getting my head to the level of a block of rock I observed right in front of my eyes, broadside on, maybe a yard off, certainly not more, a big leopard. He was crouching on the ground, with his magnificent head thrown back and his eyes shut. His fore-paws were spread out in front of him and he lashed the ground with his tail, and I grieve to say, in face of that awful danger – I don't mean me, but the tornado – that depraved creature swore, softly, but repeatedly and profoundly. I did not get all these facts up in one glance, for no sooner did I see him than I ducked under the rocks, and remembered thankfully that leopards are said to have no power of smell. But I heard his observation on the weather, and the flip-flap of his tail on the ground. Every now and then I cautiously took a look at him with one eye round a rock-edge, and he remained in the same position. My feelings tell me he remained there twelve months, but my calmer judgment puts the time down at twenty minutes; and at last, on taking another cautious peep, I saw he was gone. At the time I wished I knew exactly where, but I do not care about that detail now, for I saw no more of him. He had moved off in one of those weird lulls which you get in a tornado, when for a few seconds the wild herd of hurrying winds seem to have lost themselves, and wander round crying and wailing like lost souls, until their common rage seizes them again and they rush back to their work of destruction. It was an immense pleasure to have seen the great creature like that. He was so evidently enraged and baffled by the uproar and dazzled by the floods of lightning that swept down into the deepest recesses of the forest, showing at one second every detail of twig, leaf, branch, and stone round you, and then leaving you in a sort of swirling dark until the next flash came; this, and the great conglomerate roar of the wind, rain and thunder, was enough to bewilder any living thing.

'I'm glad we didn't shoot those guillemots yesterday'

EJNAR MIKKELSEN

Lost in the Arctic: Being the Story of the Alabama *Expedition, 1909–1912* (1913)

Ejnar Mikkelsen (1880–1971) was a Danish explorer who led an expedition to Greenland. Their wooden vessel, the Alabama, *was trapped in the ice off Shannon Island. Mikkelsen and his engineer, Ivesen, were separated from the rest of the crew, who were rescued by a whaler. The two remained marooned on Shannon Island for 865 days . . . no one knew where they were. As compensation for his adventure he has had a mountain range in Greenland named for him.*

And the days go on, one just like another, all wearily long, and always the same striving to occupy our thoughts with the present or the past, anything but the painful doubt of the future. The possibilities are too awful. And yet we cannot help following in our minds the ships that now may be on their way towards us – we see them entering the ice, striving to get through to land – they should soon be able to reach us now, if it is no worse out there than what we can see here close in to land. Or we follow the movements of a single ship – today it has reached the ice, and each day it comes nearer – we let it lie up when fogs or storm hinder its passage, until at last the day comes when it should have been here, if it had entered the ice on the day we fancied it there. A mad existence – another year of this would be too much for us.

Now all the snow has gone and the running water stopped. It is impossible to leave Bass Rock now, for the ice is full of cracks and pools of water. We are prisoners upon this little patch of rock, but still we climb up as before, spending the most of our time gazing out over the sea, and waiting. The land ice goes – breaking up and drifting away to southward, floe after floe goes floating away, and we wish for our boat, that we might follow – anything rather than this ceaseless waiting.

We sit out on the farthest point of rock, looking at the water lapping against its foot. It is a fine day, warm and bright, without a cloud in the sky, and all about looks fair and kindly. But the flowers are gone, the sun is declining and soon the autumn will be here with its boisterous gales. It is a lovely scene, but it is rarely that we care to talk now of the beauty of the scenery; we sit in silence, looking out over the sea.

A whirr of wings in the air wakes us from our dreams: it is a flock of guillemots that have their home on the cliffs, and are now making for the water. So happily they splash about down there – and how we envy them! The gun lies ready between us, the birds are good eating, and it is always something to do. Moreover, we need meat. The guillemots shall die. Cautiously we creep along the shore to get within range, but the little black birds disarm us after all, we cannot find it in our hearts to shoot them. It is cheering to have some few living things about us, we sit on a stone and look at them; their young ones are waiting for them up on the cliff, they will die of hunger if their parents do not return – and we know what hunger is; no, let them live! Besides, there may come a ship – and then it would be a pity. We can wait until tomorrow, all sorts of things may have happened by then.

We are well paid for having spared them by the feeling of quiet content which takes possession of us as we sit there watching the happy little creatures. At last they fly off, and we feel quite sorry they are gone. Well, it is getting near our bedtime too; we may as well go back to the house and turn in.

Half-an-hour later we are lying in our sleeping bags, and have said good-night to each other, repeating once more the old refrain, 'Who knows – there may be a ship tomorrow!' And as I lie there, my eyes wander over the wall of the cabin – there is the picture of the four generations, there the street scenes from Copenhagen, and then a little empty space, always the first and last I see. There was a picture there once, a little card with the woods of Frederiksdal, so green and splendid – but I had to take it down, it was too painful. I burnt the card, but I could not burn the place where it had hung, and the empty space grins at me now, as if to say, 'Do you remember?' And I remember all too well, it was a foolish thing to burn the card, for the empty place is worse.

'Coward,' it seems to say, 'you dare not think of the future, you dare not hope ever to reach home again!'

Soon all is still in the house, and we sleep. Suddenly I am wakened by the noise of a case upset outside, and as I open my eyes, there is Iversen dashing across the room, bare-legged, with nothing on but a striped jersey, and with a wild look in his eyes. A bear! is my first thought, and in a moment I am out of my bunk, seize my gun, and am about to follow, but before I have got halfway, I stop, petrified with astonishment – Iversen has got the door open, and is crying 'Morning – good-morning!'

God – a ship at last! In a moment I am standing beside my faithful comrade, staring at a host of men – an endless army of men – the whole shore is full of men.

What happened next I do not know. We put some clothes on, I suppose, but there is a blank spot in my memory, and the next thing I remember is that Iversen has disappeared, and going out to look for him, I find him standing on a rock, waving his cap and shouting, 'A ship! a ship! a ship!'

With a bound I am at his side. True enough, out there where we have never seen anything but water and ice, a little steamer is lying. We look at each other with bright eyes, and do not know what to say. It is eight-and-twenty months since we last saw a human face. Then we go up behind the house, where nobody can see us, and shake hands – hard. We have been through a rough time together, and now it is over. A moment we stand holding each other's hands, then Iversen bursts out suddenly – 'I say – I'm glad we didn't shoot those guillemots yesterday – jolly little things!'

'Many a long talk since then have I had with the man in the moon'

JOSHUA SLOCUM

Sailing Alone Around the World (1899)

Joshua Slocum (1844–1901) became for a while the world's most celebrated traveller, and his 36-foot gaff rigged sloop Spray *the most famous boat, after his achievement of being the first man to sail alone around the world. He and* Spray, *which was no more than a converted oyster boat, left Boston in April 1895 and arrived back in Newport, Rhode Island in July 1898 after a 46,000-mile journey. He fended off pirates by spreading tin tacks about the deck at night; the squeals of the first barefooted boarders were enough to discourage any more. After this record-breaking voyage he continued to sail alone, usually to winter away from New England. On 14 November 1909 he set off on one of these voyages, having indicated an interest in exploring the Orinoco, Rio Negro and Amazon Rivers. He was never heard from again.*

On the evening of July 5 the *Spray*, after having steered all day over a lumpy sea, took it into her head to go without the helmsman's aid. I had been steering southeast by south, but the wind hauling forward a bit, she dropped into a smooth lane, heading southeast, and making about eight knots, her very best work. I crowded on sail to cross the track of the liners without loss of time, and to reach as soon as possible the friendly Gulf Stream. The fog lifting before night, I was afforded a look at the sun. Just as it was touching the sea, I watched it go down and out of sight. Then I turned my face eastward, and there, apparently at the very end of the bowsprit, was the smiling full moon rising out of the sea. Neptune himself coming over the bows could not have startled me more. 'Good evening, Sir,' I cried, 'I am glad to see you.' Many a long talk since then have I had with the man in the moon; he had confidence in my voyage.

About midnight the fog shut down again denser than ever before. One could almost 'stand on it.' It continued so for a number of days, the wind increasing to a gale. The waves rose high, but I had a good ship. Still, in the dismal fog I felt myself drifting into loneliness, an insect on a straw in the midst of the elements. I lashed the helm, and my vessel held her course, and while she sailed I slept.

During these days a feeling of awe crept over me. My memory worked with startling power. The ominous, the insignificant, the great, the small, the wonderful, the commonplace – all appeared before my mental vision in magical succession. Pages of my history were recalled which had been so long forgotten that they seemed to belong to a previous existence, I heard all the voices of the past laughing, crying, telling what I had heard them tell in many corners of the earth.

The loneliness of my state wore off when the gale was high and I found much work to do. When fine weather returned, then came the sense of solitude, which I could not shake off. I used my voice often, at first giving some order about the affairs of a ship, for I had been told that from disuse I should lose my speech. At the meridian altitude of the sun I called out aloud, 'Eight bells,' after the custom of a ship at sea. Again from my cabin I cried to an imaginary man at the helm, 'How does she head, there?' and again, 'Is she on her course?' But getting no reply, I was reminded the more palpably of my condition. My voice sounded hollow on the empty air, and I dropped the practice.

'Something fairly close to the sheer happiness of being alive'

SYLVAIN TESSON

The Consolations of the Forest (Une Vie à Coucher Dehors) (2013, 2011)

Baikal is a rift created lake in the mountainous region of Siberia, north of the Mongolian border. It is more than 600 kilometres long and ten kilometres deep in places and contains over 20 per cent of all the fresh water in the world. It is surrounded by mountains and taiga forests. It is very cold in winter. Sylvain Tesson (b. 1972) spent six winter months in a cabin beside the lake. His enforced loneliness was mitigated by dogs, the occasional visits of fishermen and a supply of cigars and vodka, with which, as a sensible Frenchman, he had equipped himself.

26 July

'I'm leaving now, but have barely passed the first of the elms that line the road . . .' André Chenier, guillotined on 25 July 1794.

Sergei will come to get me the day after tomorrow. We'll drop the dogs off at Elohin, where they'll stay until they find a master in a different cabin in the reserve.

I came here without knowing whether I'd find the strength to stay; I leave knowing that I will return. I've discovered that living within silence is rejuvenating. I've learned two or three things that many people know without having to hole up somewhere. The virginity of time is a treasure. The parade of hours is busier than the ploughing-through of miles. The eye never tires of splendour. The more one knows things, the more beautiful they become. I met two dogs, I fed them and, one day, they saved me. I spoke to the cedars, begged forgiveness from the char, and thought about my dear ones. I was free because without *the other*, freedom knows no bounds. I contemplated the poem of the mountains and drank tea while the lake turned pink. I killed the longing for the future. I breathed the breath of the forest and followed the arc of the moon. I struggled through the snow and forgot the struggle on the mountaintops. I admired the great age of trees, tamed titmice, and perceived the vanity of all that is not reverence for beauty. I took a look at the other shore. I knew weeks of silent snow. I loved to be warm in my hut while the tempest raged. I greeted the return of the sun and the wild ducks. I tore into the flesh of smoked fish and felt the fat of char eggs refresh my throat. A woman bade me farewell but butterflies alighted on me. I lived the most beautiful hours of my life until I received a message and the saddest hours afterwards. I watered the earth with tears. I wondered if one could become a Russian not through blood but through tears. I blew my nose on mosses. I drank litres of poison at 104° F, and I enjoyed pissing with a wide-screen view of Buryatia. I learned to sit at a window. I melted into my realm, smelled the scent of lichen, ate wild garlic and shared trails with bears. I grew a beard, and time unfurled it. I left the cave of cities and lived for six months in the church of the taigas. Six months: a life.

It's good to know that out there, in a forest in the world, there is a cabin where something is possible, something fairly close to the sheer happiness of being alive.

FIVE

Because it's There

Mountaineers did not set out to write books, but did so in response to achievements or to record disaster. Here are the stories of the men who are drawn to the mountains and feel, as Robert Macfarlane (*Mountains of the Mind*) put it, 'something between lust and fear' that draws them. George Mallory, writing to his wife Ruth in 1921, said: 'Everest has the most steep ridges and appalling precipices I have ever seen. My darling, it possesses me.' Look at Kilimanjaro from Amboseli, at Aconcagua from the 5,000m Base Camp, at Rakaposhi from the mellow Hunza Valley or, most tellingly, at the Eiger from Kleine Scheidegg and you will know the lust and the fear if you are susceptible.

Maurice Herzog went to the Himalayas as a highly respected mountaineer from Chamonix with no literary training, but wrote one of the classics of the genre. Heinrich Harrer was a dare-devil young Austrian alpinist when he attempted one of the two pinnacle challenges of his generation, the North Face of the Eiger.

The other challenge was Everest. Here Wade Davis records the 1924 Mallory led Everest expedition; it could be a long time before another so compelling and meticulously researched account of any expedition is written.

The first confirmed ascent of Everest is recorded in expedition leader Sir John Hunt's book in the words of Sir Edmund Hillary, who made that first ascent with his climbing partner Tensing Norgay.

The W. E. Bowman piece is in an entirely different category.

———•❖•———

'Victory is ours if we all make up our minds not to lose a single day, not even a single hour!'

MAURICE HERZOG

Annapurna (1951)

Maurice Herzog (1919–2012) represented the finest tradition of French Alpinism. His objective for a 1950 expedition to Nepal was the first ever ascent of an 8,000-metre mountain, Annapurna. It took more than twenty days to get near the mountain from the last road and when they reached the area, no one knew how to find the mountain as they had no accurate maps and the name Annapurna meant nothing to the local Nepalis. After some failed sorties, they succeeded, as he describes here.

They had no idea how to attempt the mountain or even where to start. Their efforts all but failed, but eventually he and Louis Lachenal spider-crawled up the last rock and ice band to the summit. In a state of numbed serenity they had long since lost understanding of the damage being done to their bodies. 'All sense of exertion was gone, as though there was no longer any gravity. This diaphanous landscape, this quintessence of purity. These were not the mountains I knew; they were the mountains of my dreams.'

The terrible toll that the mountain took on Herzog all but killed him; indeed many times he asked for death instead of the pain when most of his fingers and toes had to be amputated on the way down. But he had possessed and been possessed by Annapurna and that was enough.

———•❖•———

An astonishing sight greeted me next morning. Lachenal and Rébuffat were sitting outside on a dry rock, with their eyes riveted on Annapurna. A sudden exclamation brought me out of my tent: 'I've found the route!' shouted Lachenal. I went up to them, blinking in the glare. For the first time Annapurna was revealing its secrets. The huge north face with all its rivers of ice shone and sparkled in the light. Never had I seen a mountain so impressive in all its proportions. It was a world both dazzling and menacing, and the eye was lost in its immensities. But for once we were not being confronted with vertical walls, jagged ridges and hanging glaciers which put an end to all thoughts of climbing.

'You see,' explained Lachenal, 'the problem . . . is to get to that sickle-shaped glacier high up on the mountain. To reach the foot of it without danger of avalanches, we'll have to go up well over on the left.'

'But how the hell would you get to the foot of your route?' interrupted Rébuffat. 'On the other side of the plateau that we're on there's a glacier which is a mass of crevasses and quite impossible to cross.'

'Look.'

We looked hard. But I am bound to admit I felt almost incapable of following Lachenal's explanations. I was carried away on a wave of enthusiasm, for at last our mountain was there before our eyes.

This May the twenty-third was surely the Expedition's greatest day so far!

'But look,' insisted Lachenal, his knitted cap all askew, 'we can avoid the crevassed section by skirting round to the left. After that we'll only have to climb the icefalls opposite, and then make gradually over to the right towards the Sickle.'

The sound of an ice-axe distracted our attention for a moment; it was Ajeeba breaking up ice to melt into water.

'Your route isn't direct enough, Biscante,' I told him. 'We'd be certain to sink up to our waists in the snow: the route must be the shortest possible, direct to the summit.'

'And what about avalanches?' asked Rébuffat.

'You run a risk from them on the right as well as on the left. So you may as well choose the shortest way.'

'And there's the couloir too,' retorted Lachenal.

'If we cross it high enough up, the danger won't be very great. Anyway, look at the avalanche tracks over on the left on your route.'

'There's something in that,' admitted Lachenal.

'So why not go straight up in line with the summit, skirt round the seracs and crevasses, slant over to the left to reach the Sickle, and from there go straight up to the top?'

Rébuffat struck me as being not very optimistic. Standing there, in the old close-fitting jersey that he always wore on his Alpine climbs, he seemed more than ever to deserve the name the Sherpas had given him of Lamba Sahib, or 'long man'.

'But,' went on Lachenal, 'we could go straight up under the ice cliff and then traverse left and reach the same spot . . .'

'By cutting across to the left it's certainly more direct.'

'That should be quite feasible,' agreed Lachenal, letting himself be won over.

Rébuffat's resistance yielded bit by bit.

'Lionel! Come and have a look . . .'

Terray was bending over a container and sorting out provisions in his usual serious manner. He raised his head: it was adorned with a red skiing bonnet, and he sported a flowing beard. I asked him point-blank what his route was. He had already examined the mountain and come to his own conclusion:

'My dear Maurice,' he said, pursing up his lips in the special way that marked a great occasion, 'it's perfectly clear to me. Above the avalanche

cone of the great couloir, just in line with the summit . . .' and he went on
to describe the route we had worked out.

So we were all in complete agreement.

'We must get cracking,' Terray kept saying in great excitement.
Lachenal, no less excited, came and yelled in my ear:

'A hundred to nothing! That's the odds on our success!'

And even the more cautious Rébuffat admitted that 'It's the least difficult proposition and the most reasonable.'

The weather was magnificent; never had the mountains looked more
beautiful. Our optimism was tremendous, perhaps excessive, for the
gigantic scale of the face set us problems such as we had never had to
cope with in the Alps. And above all, time was short. If we were to succeed not a moment must be lost. The arrival of the monsoon was
forecast for about June 5th; so that we had just twelve days left. We would
have to go fast, very fast indeed. I was haunted by this idea. To do so we
should have to lengthen out the intervals between the successive camps,
organise a shuttle service to bring up the maximum number of loads in
the minimum time, acclimatise ourselves and, finally, maintain communications with the rear. This last point worried me. Our party was
organised on the scale of a reconnaissance and the total supply at our
disposal was only five days' food and a limited amount of equipment.

How was I possibly to keep track of the thousand and one questions
that buzzed round in my head? The rest of the party were all highly
excited and talked away noisily while the Sherpas moved about the tents
as usual. Only a couple of them were here, and there could be no question of beginning operations with just these two. So the Sahibs would set
off alone and carry their own loads: in this way we should be able to get
Camp II pitched the next day. When I asked the others what they
thought they enthusiastically agreed to make this great effort, which
would save us at least two days. Ajeeba would go back to the Base Camp

and show the people there the way up to Camp I, which would have to be entirely re-equipped since we were going to take everything up with us for Camp II. For Sarki there was an all-important job: he would have to carry the order of attack to all the members of the Expedition.

I took a large sheet of paper and wrote out:

Special message by Sarki, from Camp I to Tukucha. Urgent.

23.5.50
Camp I: Annapurna glacier.
Have decided to attack Annapurna.
Victory is ours if we all make up our minds not to lose a single day, not even a single hour!

'And there the "Spider" waits'

HEINRICH HARRER

The White Spider (1958)

I, an acrophobe who loves mountains, have many times sat underneath the compellingly forbidding sheer North Face of the Eiger (Eigerwand in German), forcing myself to imagine the horror of being up there, exposed and helpless for escape.

Harrer's book is the history of attempts on the North Face of the Eiger. The denouement of The White Spider *is Harrer's own successful first ascent of the North Face on 21–24 July 1938 with his Austrian and German co-climbers Anderl Heckmair, Ludwig Vörg and Fritz Kasparek. In the following passage he describes the eponymous feature that looms large in the apprehension of Eiger climbers.*

On the 'Spider' in the Eiger's North Face I experienced such borderline situations, while the avalanches were roaring down over us, endlessly. This sector of the Eiger's upper wall has won its name from its external likeness to a gigantic spider. Seldom has an exterior attracted a name which at the same time suits the inner nature of the object named so completely. The 'Spider' on the Eiger's Face is white. Its body consists of ice and eternal snow. Its legs and its predatory arms, all hundreds of feet long, are white, too. From that perpetual, fearfully steep field of frozen snow nothing but ice emerges to fill gullies, cracks and crevices. Up and down. To left, to right. In every direction, at every angle of steepness.

And there the 'Spider' waits.

Every climber who picks his way up the North Face of the Eiger has to cross it. There is no way round it. And even those who moved best and most swiftly up the Face have met their toughest ordeal on the 'Spider'. Someone once compared the whole Face to a gigantic spider's web catching the spider's victims and feeding them to her. This comparison is unfounded, exaggerated, and merely a cheap way of making the flesh creep. Neither the savage wall nor the lovely mountain have deserved this slur. Nor have the climbers; for climbers are not flies and insects stumbling blindly to their fate, but men of vision and courage. All the same, the 'White Spider' seems to me to be a good symbol for the North Face. The climber has to face its perils on the final third of the wall, when he is tired from many hours and days of exhausting climbing and weakened by chilly bivouacs. But there is no rest to be had there, no matter how tired you are.

He who wishes to survive the spate of avalanches which sweep the 'Spider' must realise that there is no escape from this dangerously steep obstacle; he must know how to blend his strength with patience and reflection. Above the 'Spider' begin the overhanging, iced-up exit cracks; that is where sheer strength tells. But here the man who abandons patience and good sense for fear-induced haste will surely finish up like the fly which struggles so long in the spider's web that it is caught through sheer exhaustion.

The 'White Spider' on the Eiger is the extreme test not only of a climber's technical ability, but of his character as well. Later on in life, when fate seemed to spin some spider's web or other across my path, my thoughts often went back to the 'White Spider'. Life itself demanded the same methods, the same qualities, when there no longer seemed to be any possible escape from its difficulties, as had won us a way out of the difficulties of the Eiger's North Face – common-sense, patience and open-eyed courage. Haste born of fear and all the wild stunts arising from it can only end in disaster.

'Death was but "a frail barrier"'

WADE DAVIS

Into the Silence (2012)

Into the Silence is unusual in Scraps as it is written about the travellers, rather than by them; they did not live to tell their own story. It posits the certainty that these men would never have turned back and examines the circumstances of their experiences in the recently-ended world war that may have moulded this disregard for their own lives.

Wade Davis (b. 1953) considers the long argued question of whether or not the thirty-eight-year old, experienced Mallory, with his twenty-two-year-old companion, Sandy Irvine, whose major qualifications for the expedition had been an Oxford rowing Blue and a few outings with the OU Mountaineering Club, might have reached the summit that day in June 1924.

But the final proof lay in the severity of the Second Step. In 1975 a Chinese expedition had secured an aluminum ladder over the steepest and most perilous pitch. Anker's goal was to climb without making use of this artificial aid, facing the challenge just as Mallory would have done in 1924. The initial ascent of some 45 feet he rated as moderately difficult but not extreme: no trouble for Mallory, though possibly beyond Irvine's abilities. But the next pitch, including the crack crossed by the ladder, was vertical rock, formidably difficult. Anker tried but was unable to free-climb it; the position of the ladder obliged him to set one foot on a rung. He later graded it a 'solid 5.10,' a technical rating implying a rock challenge far more difficult than anything being attempted by British climbers in Wales or elsewhere in the 1920s. That Mallory and Irvine might have overcome such a pitch, a climb made doubly perilous by an exposure of 8,000 feet, defied belief. And even had they done so, it was not clear how they could have returned. Conrad and Hahn, like all modern climbers on the Northeast Ridge, counted on rappelling down the Second Step, their rope anchored to a large and prominent boulder at the top of the final pitch. The climbing ropes available to Mallory and Irvine were neither strong nor long enough for such a rappel. Had they surmounted the Second Step, Mallory and Irvine would have been forced, upon their return, to down-climb, an imposing challenge readily acknowledged by Anker, among the top technical rock climbers of the modern era, as being at the limit of his capabilities.

As Anker and Hahn crested the Second Step and began the long and still dangerous climb toward the summit of Everest, they had answered many of the essential questions. Mallory and Irvine had certainly reached the First Step; this would later be confirmed with the discovery in situ of a discarded oxygen cylinder, which Jochem Hemmleb dated positively to 1924. In all likelihood they overcame the First Step but then turned back either at the foot of the Second Step or somewhere along the ridge between the two. Perhaps in failing light or blinded by the squall that swept the mountain that afternoon, Mallory removed his goggles as he attempted to find a route down through the slabs of the Yellow Band. Tied as one, perhaps with Mallory on belay they fell together, not from the height of the Northeast Ridge but from far lower on the North Face, quite possibly within easy reach of their highest camp. Indeed, later expeditions would determine that Mallory had come to rest not three hundred yards from the safety of his Camp VI.

Mallory and Irvine may not have reached the summit of Mount Everest, but they did, on that fateful day, climb higher than any human being before them, reaching heights that would not be attained again for nearly thirty years. That they were able to do so, given all they had endured, is surely achievement enough. 'To tell the truth,' Dave Hahn remarked, 'I have trouble believing they were as high as we know that they were.' And as Conrad Anker noted, there is still one possibility, one scenario by which they might have indeed surmounted the Second Step. Had the very storms that so battered the 1924 expedition, burying the high camps and causing Norton to retreat not once but twice from the North Col, brought heavy snows of similar magnitude to the Northeast Ridge, it is possible that a drift accumulated, large enough, if not to bury the cliffs of the Second Step, at least to create a cone covering the most difficult pitches of rock. Such a scenario did in fact unfold in 1985, albeit in the autumn. Had this been the case, Mallory and Irvine might simply have walked up the snow, traversing the barrier with the very speed and ease that Odell so famously reported. Had this occurred, surely nothing could have held Mallory back. He would have walked on, even to his end, because for him, as for all of his generation, death was but 'a frail barrier' that men crossed, 'smiling and gallant, every day.' They had seen so much of death that life mattered less than the moments of being alive.

'My highest hopes were realised'

JOHN HUNT

The Ascent of Everest (1953)

Hunt, the leader of the 1953 Everest expedition, gave the pen to his colleague Edmund Hillary, the New Zealand summiteer with Tenzing Norgay, to write the chapter of his book that describes their final steps to the highest point on Earth.

As my ice-axe bit into the first steep slope of the ridge, my highest hopes were realised. The snow was crystalline and firm. Two or three rhythmical blows of the ice-axe produced a step large enough even for our oversized High Altitude boots and, the most encouraging feature of all, a firm thrust of the ice-axe would sink it half-way up the shaft, giving a solid and comfortable belay. We moved one at a time. I realised that our margin of safety at this altitude was not great and that we must take every care and precaution. I would cut a forty-foot line of steps, Tenzing belaying me while I worked. Then in turn I would sink my shaft and put a few loops of the rope around it and Tenzing, protected against a breaking step, would move up to me. Then once again as he belayed me I would go on cutting. In a number of places the overhanging ice cornices were very large indeed and in order to escape them I cut a line of steps down to where the snow met the rocks on the west. It was a great thrill to look straight down this enormous rock face and to see, 8,000 feet below us, the tiny tents of Camp IV in the Western Cwm. Scrambling on the rocks and cutting handholds in the snow, we were able to shuffle past these difficult portions.

On one of these occasions I noted that Tenzing, who had been going quite well, had suddenly slowed up considerably and seemed to be breathing with difficulty. The Sherpas had little idea of the workings of an oxygen set and from past experience I immediately suspected his oxygen supply. I noticed that hanging from the exhaust tube of his oxygen mask were icicles, and on closer examination found that this tube, some two inches in diameter, was completely blocked with ice. I was able to clear it out and gave him much-needed relief. On checking my own set I found that the same thing was occurring, though it had not reached the stage to have caused me any discomfort. From then on I kept a much closer check on this problem.

The weather for Everest seemed practically perfect. Insulated as we were in all our down clothing and windproofs, we suffered no discomfort from cold or wind. However, on one occasion I removed my sunglasses to examine more closely a difficult section of the ridge but was very soon blinded by the fine snow driven by the bitter wind and hastily replaced them. I went on cutting steps. To my surprise I was enjoying the climb as much as I had ever enjoyed a fine ridge in my own New Zealand Alps.

After an hour's steady going we reached the foot of the most formidable-looking problem on the ridge – a rock step some forty feet high. We had known of the existence of this step from aerial photographs and had also seen it through our binoculars from Thyangboche.

We realised that at this altitude it might well spell the difference between success and failure. The rock itself, smooth and almost holdless, might have been an interesting Sunday afternoon problem to a group of expert rock climbers in the Lake District, but here it was a barrier beyond our feeble strength to overcome. I could see no way of turning it on the steep rock bluff on the west, but fortunately another possibility of tackling it still remained. On its east side was another great cornice, and running up the full forty feet of the step was a narrow crack between the cornice and the rock. Leaving Tenzing to belay me as best he could, I jammed my way into this crack, then kicking backwards with my crampons I sank their spikes deep into the frozen snow behind me and levered myself off the ground. Taking advantage of every little rock hold and all the force of knee, shoulder, and arms I could muster, I literally cramponed backwards up the crack, with a fervent prayer that the cornice would remain attached to the rock. Despite the considerable effort involved, my progress although slow was steady, and as Tenzing paid out the rope I inched my way upwards until I could finally reach over the top of the rock and drag myself out of the crack on to a wide ledge. For a few moments I lay regaining my breath and for the first time really felt the fierce determination that nothing now could stop us reaching the top. I took a firm stance on the ledge and signalled to Tenzing to come on up. As I heaved hard on the rope Tenzing wriggled his way up the crack and finally collapsed exhausted at the top like a giant fish when it has just been hauled from the sea after a terrible struggle.

I checked both our oxygen sets and roughly calculated our flow rates. Everything seemed to be going well. Probably owing to the strain imposed on him by the trouble with his oxygen set, Tenzing had been moving rather slowly but he was climbing safely, and this was the major consideration. His only comment on my enquiring of his condition was to smile and wave along the ridge. We were going so well at three litres per minute that I was determined now if necessary to cut down our flow rate to two litres per minute if the extra endurance was required.

The ridge continued as before. Giant cornices on the right, steep rock slopes on the left. I went on cutting steps on the narrow strip of snow. The ridge curved away to the right and we had no idea where the top was. As I cut around the back of one hump, another higher one would swing into view. Time was passing and the ridge seemed never-ending. In one place, where the angle of the ridge had eased off, I tried cramponing without cutting steps, hoping this would save time, but I quickly realised that our margin of safety on these steep slopes at this altitude was too small, so I went on step-cutting. I was beginning to tire a little now. I had been cutting steps continuously for two hours, and Tenzing, too, was moving very slowly. As I chipped steps around still another corner, I wondered rather dully just how long we could keep it up. Our original zest had now quite gone and it was turning more into a grim struggle. I then realised that the ridge ahead, instead of still monotonously rising, now dropped sharply away, and far below I could see the North Col and the Rongbuk glacier. I looked upwards to see a narrow snow ridge running up to a snowy summit. A few more whacks of the ice-axe in the firm snow and we stood on top.

My initial feelings were of relief – relief that there were no more steps to cut – no more ridges to traverse and no more humps to tantalise us with hopes of success. I looked at Tenzing and in spite of the balaclava, goggles and oxygen mask all encrusted with long icicles that concealed his face, there was no disguising his infectious grin of pure delight as he looked all around him. We shook hands and then Tenzing threw his arm around my shoulders and we thumped each other on the back until we were almost breathless. It was 11.30 a.m.

'The great question was: would the mountain go?'

W. E. BOWMAN

The Ascent of Rum Doodle (1956)

Yogistan, then as now, was neither big nor rich; indeed, it was ranked by the United Nations as number 153 in terms of gross domestic product out of not many more listed. It is also not easily accessible, being landlocked and 153 miles from the nearest other country. But it is home to Rum Doodle, a mountain which had to be climbed 'because it is there'.

W. E. Bowman was a civil engineer from Guildford who had never climbed a mountain of any size but enjoyed hill walking in the Lake District. I have been unable to trace any of his family members to secure permission to reprint this passage and to tell them how much entertainment their relative has provided.

We spent a hungry and uncomfortable night in the station waiting room, for until the dispute with the Bang was settled our equipment could not be unloaded, and in the absence of Constant we dared not risk a night in the local hotel. At daybreak I walked over to the train, to find Constant and the Bang still at it. The former explained to me that the Yogistani word for three was identical with the word for thirty, except for a kind of snort in the middle. It was, of course, impossible to convey this snort by telegram, and the Bang had chosen to interpret the message as ordering 30,000 porters. The 30,000 were making a considerable noise outside, and Constant told me that they were demanding food and a month's pay. He was afraid that if we refused they would loot the train.

There was nothing for it but to meet their demands. The 30,000 were fed – at considerable trouble and expense – and three days later we were able to set off with the chosen 3,000 on our 500 mile journey. The 375 boys who completed our force were recruited on the spot. Boys are in plentiful supply in Yogistan; it appears that their mothers are glad to get rid of them.

The journey to the Rum Doodle massif was uneventful. We travelled along a series of river gorges deeply cut between precipitous ridges which rose to heights of 30,000 feet and more. Sometimes we crossed from one valley to another over passes some 20,000 feet above sea level, dropping again to river beds elevated a mere 153 feet or so.

The steepness of the valleys was such that the vegetation ranged from tropical to arctic within the distance of a mile, and our botanists were in their element. I am no naturalist myself, but I tried to show an intelligent interest in the work of the others, encouraging them to come to me with their discoveries. I am indebted to them for what small knowledge I possess in this field.

The lower slopes were gay with Facetia and Persiflage, just then at their best, and the nostrils were continually assailed with the disturbing smell of Rodentia. Nostalgia, which flourishes everywhere but at home, was plentiful, as was the universal Wantonia. Higher up, dark belts of Suspicia and Melancholia gave place to the last grassy slopes below the snow line, where nothing was seen growing but an occasional solitary Excentricular, or old-fashioned Manspride.

The fauna, too, was a constant delight. The scapegoat was, of course, common, as were the platitude and the long-tailed bore. The weak-willed sloth was often met, and sometimes after dark I would catch sight of slinking shadows which Burley identified as the miserable hang-dog. One afternoon Shute, in great excitement, pointed out to me a disreputable-looking creature which he said was a shaggy dog. Burley swore that it was not a shaggy dog at all but a hairy disgrace; but this may have been intended for one of his peculiar jokes. Burley's sense of humour is rather weak. He told me one day that he was being followed by a lurking suspicion, which was obviously absurd. But he is a good fellow.

We were naturally all agog to catch sight of the Atrocious Snowman, about whom so much has been written. This creature was first seen by Thudd in 1928 near the summit of Raw Deedle. He describes it as a man-like creature about seven feet tall covered with blue fur and having three ears. It emitted a thin whistle and ran off with incredible rapidity. The next reported encounter took place during the 1931 Bavarian reconnaissance expedition to Hi Hurdle. On this occasion it was seen by three members at a height of 25,000 feet. Their impressions are largely contradictory, but all agree that the thing wore trousers. In 1933 Orgrind and Stretcher found footprints on a snow slope above the Trundling La, and the following year Moodies heard grunts at 30,000 feet. Nothing further was reported until 1946, when Brewbody was fortunate enough to see the creature at close quarters. It was, he said, completely bare of either fur or hair, and resembled a human being of normal stature. It wore a loincloth and was talking to itself in Rudistani with a strong Birmingham accent. When it caught sight of Brewbody it sprang to the top of a crag and disappeared.

Such was the meagre information gleaned so far, and all were agog to add to it. The most agog among us was Wish, who may have nourished secret dreams of adding the *Eoanthropus Wishi* to mankind's family tree. Wish spent much time above the snow line examining any mark which might prove to be a footprint; but although he heard grunts, whistles, sighs and gurgles, and even, on one occasion, muttering, he found no direct evidence. His enthusiasm weakened appreciably after he had spent a whole rest day tracking footprints for miles across a treacherous mountainside, only to find that he was following a trail laid for him by a porter at Burley's instigation.

The porters were unprepossessing. Mountaineering to them was strictly business. An eight-hour day had been agreed on, for which each received *bohees* five (3 3/4d.). Nothing on earth would persuade them to work longer than this, except money. When not on the march they squatted in groups smoking a villainous tobacco called *stunk*. Their attitude was surly in the extreme; a more desperate-looking crew can hardly be imagined. They were in such contrast to the description which Constant had given us that I was moved to mention the matter to him in a tactful way. He explained that they were used to living above the 20,000 feet line; their good qualities did not begin to appear until this height was reached. He said that they would improve as we got higher, reaching their peak of imperturbability and cheerfulness at 40,000 feet. This was a great relief to me.

. . .

The great question was: would the mountain go? Totter, in 1947, had written: 'The mountain is difficult – severe, even – but it will go.' Later reconnaissance had questioned whether the North Wall itself would go, but the final verdict had been that it would. Totter himself had summed up the prevailing opinion thus: 'Given team spirit and good porters, the mountain will go.' All the world knows now that it did. It is no small part of my satisfaction that we vindicated Totter's opinion.

But as we stood on the Rankling La we were awed by the mighty bastion which reared its majestic head against the cloudless sky. As we stood there, Constant spoke for all of us:

'She stands like a goddess, defying those who would set sacrilegious feet on her unsullied shrine.' There was a murmur of agreement. In that moment we were humbled by the magnitude of the task we had set ourselves, and I for one sent up a fervent prayer that I would not be found wanting in the ordeal that lay before us. In such moments a man feels close to himself.

We stood there, close to ourselves, until sunset, the supreme artist, touched the snowfields of that mighty bastion with rose-tinted brushes and the mountain became a vision such as few human eyes have beheld. In silence we turned and made our way through gathering darkness to our halting-place in the valley.

SIX

<hr />

Ne vaut pas le Voyage

The title is a small bow to the parent of all guide books, the Red Michelin, whose rare three-star restaurants are simply designated *'vaut le voyage'*. The marginally lesser, but still hugely coveted, two-stars simply *mérite un détour* . . . pleasing litotes in an age of promotional hyperbole.

In the following passages either the whole journey or part of it did not merit either the voyage or the detour.

Mark Twain wrote as a journalist to amuse his American home market, always ready for banter at Europe's expense although even Twain was eventually beguiled by Venice. Rudyard Kipling took the chance for a counter-punch a few years later. Redmond O'Hanlon did not get the answer he expected from his friend. John Gimlette expected changes in Paraguay that never occurred.

John Betjeman laments the changes that had occurred to Cornwall in the previous twenty years.

<hr />

'. . . you must ask a surgeon to cut off your penis'

REDMOND O'HANLON

In Trouble Again: A Journey Between the Orinoco and
the Amazon (1988)

Redmond (b. 1947) is a man of legendary bonhomie but also a special
acclaimed expert in natural history, launched apparently by reading
Darwin in bed by torchlight as a schoolboy. He claims to prefer his second-
ary career of filmmaking to writing: 'It's all done for you: no more
privations, no more suffering, never being alone, no chance to get really
depressed, a lot of drinking. Wonderful.' He has a particular talent for
opening chapters. Here he is preparing for an Amazon adventure.

Having spent two months travelling in the primary rain forests of
Borneo, a four-month journey in the country between the Orinoco and
the Amazon would pose, I thought, no particular problem.

I reread my nineteenth-century heroes: the seven volumes of Alexander von Humboldt's *Personal Narrative of Travels to the Equinoctial*
Regions of the New Continent, during the Years 1799–1804 (1814–29); Alfred
Russel Wallace's *A Narrative of Travels on the Amazon and Rio Negro*
(1853); Henry Walter Bates's *The Naturalist on the River Amazon* (1863);
and Richard Spruce's *Notes of a Botanist on the Amazon and Andes* (1908).

There are no leeches that go for you in the Amazon jungles, an absence
which would represent, I felt, a great improvement on life in Borneo. But
then there are much the same amoebic and bacillary dysenteries, yellow
and blackwater and dengue fevers, malaria, cholera, typhoid, rabies, hep-
atitis and tuberculosis – plus one or two very special extras.

There is Chagas' disease, for instance, produced by a protozoon, Tripanozoma crusii, and carried by various species of Assassin bugs which bite you on the face or neck and then, gorged, defecate next to the puncture. When you scratch the resulting itch you rub the droppings and their cargo of protozoa into your bloodstream; between one and twenty years later you begin to die from incurable damage to the heart and brain. Then there is onchocerciasis, river-blindness, transmitted by blackfly and caused by worms which migrate to the eyeball; leishmaniasis, which is a bit like leprosy and is produced by a parasite carried by sandflies (it infects eighty per cent of Brazilian troops on exercise in the jungle in the rainy season): unless treated quickly, it eats away the warm extremities. And then there is the odd exotic, like the fever which erupted in the state of Para in the 1960s, killing seventy-one people, including the research unit sent in to identify it.

The big animals are supposed to be much friendlier than you might imagine. The jaguar kills you with a bite to the head, but only in exceptional circumstances. Two vipers, the fer de lance (up to seven and a half feet long) and the bushmaster (up to twelve feet, the largest in the world), only kill you if you step on them. The anaconda is known to tighten its grip only when you breathe out; the electric eel can only deliver its 640 volts before its breakfast; the piranha only rips you to bits if you are already bleeding, and the Giant catfish merely has a penchant for taking your feet off at the ankle as you do the crawl.

The smaller animals are, on the whole, much more annoying – the mosquitoes, blackfly, tapir-fly, chiggers, ticks, scabies-producing Tunga penetrans and Dermatobia hominis, the human botfly, whose larvae bore into the skin, eat modest amounts of you for forty days, and emerge as inch-long maggots.

But it was the candiru, the toothpick-fish, a tiny catfish adapted for a parasitic life in the gills and cloaca of bigger fish, which swam most persistently into my dreams on troubled nights.

In Borneo, when staying in the longhouses, I learned that going down to the river in the early morning is the polite thing to do – you know you are swimming in the socially correct patch of muddy river when fish nuzzle your pants, wanting you to take them down and produce their breakfast. In the Amazon, on the other hand, should you have too much to drink, say, and inadvertently urinate as you swim, any homeless can-diru, attracted by the smell, will take you for a big fish and swim excitedly up your stream of uric acid, enter your urethra like a worm into its burrow and, raising its gill-covers, stick out a set of retrorse spines. Nothing can be done. The pain, apparently, is spectacular. You must get to a hospital before your bladder bursts; you must ask a surgeon to cut off your penis.

In consultation with my friend at the Radcliffe Hospital in Oxford, Donald Hopkins, the inventor of the haemorrhoid gun, I designed an anti-candiru device: we took a cricket-box, cut out the front panel, and replaced it with a tea-strainer.

Released so brilliantly from this particular fear, I began, in earnest, to panic. Alfred Russel Wallace's resolution seemed the only one possible. Attacked by fever in his dugout on the Rio Negro in 1851, 'I began taking doses of quinine,' he tells us,

. . .

and drinking plentifully cream of tartar water, though I was so weak and apathetic that at times I could hardly muster resolution to move myself to prepare them. It is at such times that one feels the want of a friend . . . for of course it is impossible to get the Indians to do those little things without so much explanation and showing as would require more exertion than doing them oneself – during two days and nights I hardly cared if we sank or swam. While in that apathetic state I was constantly half-thinking, half-dreaming, of all my past life and future hopes, and that they were perhaps all doomed to end here on the Rio Negro. But with returning health those gloomy thoughts passed away, and I again went on, rejoicing in this my last voyage, and looking forward with firm hope to home, sweet home! I however made an inward vow never to travel again in such wild, unpeopled districts without some civilised companion or attendant.

That was the answer: I would persuade the civilised companion of my Borneo journey, the poet James Fenton, to visit the Venezuelan Amazons with me. He would be flattered to be asked. He would be delighted to come.

After supper at the long table in James's kitchen (a map of Borneo still hung on the wall), halfway through a bottle of Glenmorangie, I judged the time was ripe.

'James,' I said, 'you are looking ill. You are working far too hard writing all these reviews. You need a break. Why don't you come to the Amazon with me?'

'Are you listening seriously?'

'Yes.'

'Are you sitting comfortably?'

'Yes.'

'Then I want you to know,' said James, shutting his eyes and pressing his palms up over his face and the top of his bald head, *'that I would not come with you to High Wycombe.'*

'I urgently desire never to see it again'

RUDYARD KIPLING

American Notes (1891)

Rudyard Kipling (1865–1936) lived in Vermont for four years following his marriage in 1892, but he had also visited the USA three years before as part of an extended journey back to England from India, where he was born. His visit to Chicago was part of the earlier journey during which he had also paid an unannounced, but well received, visit to Mark Twain in Elmira, New York.

I have struck a city – a real city – and they call it Chicago.

The other places do not count. San Francisco was a pleasure-resort as well as a city, and Salt Lake was a phenomenon.

This place is the first American city I have encountered. It holds rather more than a million of people with bodies, and stands on the same sort of soil as Calcutta. Having seen it, I urgently desire never to see it again. It is inhabited by savages. Its water is the water of the Hooghly, and its air is dirt. Also it says that it is the 'boss' town of America.

I do not believe that it has anything to do with this country. They told me to go to the Palmer House, which is overmuch gilded and mirrored, and there I found a huge hall of tessellated marble crammed with people talking about money, and spitting about everywhere. Other barbarians charged in and out of this inferno with letters and telegrams in their hands, and yet others shouted at each other. A man who had drunk quite as much as was good for him told me that this was 'the finest hotel in the finest city on God Almighty's earth.' By the way, when an American wishes to indicate the next country or state, he says, 'God A'mighty's earth.' This prevents discussion and flatters his vanity.

Then I went out into the streets, which are long and flat and without end. And verily it is not a good thing to live in the East for any length of time. Your ideas grow to clash with those held by every right-thinking man. I looked down interminable vistas flanked with nine, ten, and fifteen-storied houses, and crowded with men and women, and the show impressed me with a great horror.

Except in London – and I have forgotten what London was like – I had never seen so many white people together, and never such a collection of miserables. There was no color in the street and no beauty – only a maze of wire ropes overhead and dirty stone flagging under foot.

A cab-driver volunteered to show me the glory of the town for so much an hour, and with him I wandered far. He conceived that all this turmoil and squash was a thing to be reverently admired, that it was good to huddle men together in fifteen layers, one atop of the other, and to dig holes in the ground for offices.

He said that Chicago was a live town, and that all the creatures hurrying by me were engaged in business. That is to say they were trying to make some money that they might not die through lack of food to put into their bellies. He took me to canals as black as ink, and filled with untold abominations, and bid me watch the stream of traffic across the bridges.

He then took me into a saloon, and while I drank made me note that the floor was covered with coins sunk in cement. A Hottentot would not have been guilty of this sort of barbarism. The coins made an effect pretty enough, but the man who put them there had no thought of beauty, and, therefore, he was a savage.

Then my cab-driver showed me business blocks gay with signs and studded with fantastic and absurd advertisements of goods, and looking down the long street so adorned, it was as though each vender stood at his door howling – 'For the sake of my money, employ or buy of me, and me only!'

Have you ever seen a crowd at a famine-relief distribution? You know then how the men leap into the air, stretching out their arms above the crowd in the hope of being seen, while the women dolorously slap the stomachs of their children and whimper. I had sooner watch famine relief than the white man engaged in what he calls legitimate competition. The one I understand. The other makes me ill.

And the cabman said that these things were the proof of progress, and by that I knew he had been reading his newspaper, as every intelligent American should. The papers tell their clientele in language fitted to their comprehension that the snarling together of telegraph-wires, the heaving up of houses, and the making of money is progress. . .

. . . Sunday brought me the queerest experiences of all – a revelation of barbarism complete. I found a place that was officially described as a church. It was a circus really, but that the worshippers did not know. There were flowers all about the building, which was fitted up with plush and stained oak and much luxury, including twisted brass candlesticks of severest Gothic design.

To these things and a congregation of savages entered suddenly a wonderful man, completely in the confidence of their God, whom he treated colloquially and exploited very much as a newspaper reporter would exploit a foreign potentate. But, unlike the newspaper reporter, he never allowed his listeners to forget that he, and not He, was the centre of attraction. With a voice of silver and with imagery borrowed from the auction-room, he built up for his hearers a heaven on the lines of the Palmer House (but with all the gilding real gold, and all the plate-glass diamond), and set in the centre of it a loud-voiced, argumentative, very shrewd creation that he called God. One sentence at this point caught my delighted ear. It was apropos of some question of the Judgment, and ran: – 'No! I tell you God doesn't do business that way!'

'we bore down on them with America's greatness until we crushed them . . .'

MARK TWAIN

The Innocents Abroad (1869)

Mark Twain (1835–1910) himself has crossed the Atlantic aboard the Quaker City *with a group of American packet or package tourists in 1867. Twain was in part taking revenge on European writers, including Charles Dickens (*American Notes for General Circulation, *1842), and Frances Trollope (*Domestic Manners of the Americans, *1832), who had dunned aspects of the newly self-confident USA in their own commentary. He loved to blur the line between parody and comment.*

Here he is first in Paris and then Venice, which has been praised enough in Scraps, *and can easily withstand a Mark Twain barb.*

The people of those foreign countries are very, very ignorant. They looked curiously at the costumes we had brought from the wilds of America. They observed that we talked loudly at table sometimes. They noticed that we looked out for expenses, and got what we conveniently could out of a franc, and wondered where in the mischief we came from. In Paris they just simply opened their eyes and stared when we spoke to them in French! We never did succeed in making those idiots understand their own language. One of our passengers said to a shopkeeper in reference to a proposed return to buy a pair of gloves, 'Allong restay trankeel

– may be ve coom Moonday;' and, would you believe it, that shopkeeper, a born Frenchman, had to ask what it was that had been said . . .

The people stared at us everywhere, and we stared at them. We generally made them feel rather small, too, before we got done with them, because we bore down on them with America's greatness until we crushed them.

This Venice, which was a haughty, invincible, magnificent Republic for nearly fourteen hundred years; whose armies compelled the world's applause whenever and wherever they battled; whose navies wellnigh held dominion of the seas, and whose merchant fleets whitened the remotest oceans with their sails and loaded theses piers with the products of every clime, is fallen a prey to poverty, neglect, and melancholy decay. Six hundred years ago, Venice was the Autocrat of Commerce; her mart was the greatest commercial centre, the distributing-house from whence the enormous trade of the Orient was spread abroad over the Western world. Today her piers are deserted, her warehouses are empty, her merchant fleets are vanished, her armies and her navies are but memories. Her glory is departed, and with her crumbling grandeur of wharves and palaces about her she sits among her stagnant lagoons, forlorn and beggared, forgotten of the world. She that in her palmy days commanded the commerce of a hemisphere and made the weal or woe of nations with a beck of her puissant finger is become the humblest among the peoples of the earth, – a peddler of glass-beads for women, and trifling toys and trinkets for school-girls and children.

The venerable Mother of the Republics is scarce a fit subject for flippant speech or the idle gossiping of tourists. It seems a sort of sacrilege to disturb the glamour of old romance that pictures her to us softly from afar off as through a tinted mist, and curtains her ruin and her desolation from our view. One ought, indeed, to turn away from her rags, her poverty and her humiliation, and think of her only as she was when she sank the fleets of Charlemagne; when she humbled Frederick Barbarossa or waved her victorious banners above the battlements of Constantinople.

We reached Venice at eight in the evening, and entered a hearse belonging to the Grand Hotel d'Europe. At any rate, it was more like a hearse than anything else, though to speak the card, it was a gondola. And this was the storied gondola of Venice!—the fairy boat in which the princely cavaliers of the olden times were wont to cleave the waters of the moonlit canals and look the eloquence of love into the soft eyes of patrician beauties, while the gay gondolier in silken doublets touched his guitar and sang as only gondoliers can sing! This the famed gondola and this the gorgeous gondolier!—the one an inky, rusty old canoe with a sable hearse-body clapped on to the middle of it, and the other a mangy, barefooted guttersnipe with a portion of his raiment on exhibition which should have been sacred from public scrutiny. Presently, as he turned a corner and shot his hearse into a dismal ditch between two long rows of towering, untenanted buildings, the gay gondolier began to sing, true to the traditions of his race. I stood it a little while. Then I said:—

'Now, here, Roderigo Gonzales Michael Angelo, I'm a pilgrim, and I'm a stranger, but I am not going to have my feelings lacerated by any such caterwauling as that. If that goes on, one of us has to take water. It is enough that my cherished dreams of Venice had been blighted for ever as to the romantic gondola and the gorgeous gondolier; this system of destruction shall go no further; I will accept the hearse, under pro-test, and you may fly your flag of truce in peace, but here I register a dark and bloody oath that you shan't sing. Another yelp, and overboard you go.'

I began to feel that the old Venice of song and story had departed for ever. But I was too hasty. In a few minutes we swept gracefully out into the Grand Canal, and under the mellow moonlight the Venice of poetry and romance stood revealed. Right from the water's edge rose long lines of stately palaces of marble; gondolas were gliding swiftly hither and thither and disappearing suddenly through unsuspected gates and alleys; ponderous stone bridges threw their shadows athwart the glittering waves. There was life and motion everywhere, and yet everywhere there was a hush, a stealthy sort of stillness, that was suggestive of secret enterprises of bravoes and of lovers; and clad half in moonbeams and half in mysterious shadows, the grim old mansions of the Republic seemed to have an expression about them of having an eye out for such enterprises as these at the same moment. Music came floating over the waters – Venice was complete.

It was a beautiful picture – very soft and dreamy and beautiful. But what was this Venice to compare with the Venice of midnight? Nothing. There was a fête – a grand fête in honour of some saint who had been instrumental in checking the cholera three hundred years ago, and all of Venice was abroad on the water. It was no common affair, for the Venetians did not know how soon they might need the saint's services again, now that the cholera was spreading everywhere. So in one vast space – say a third of a mile wide and two miles long-were collected two thousand gonzolas, and every one of them had from two to ten, twenty, and even thirty coloured lanterns suspended about it, and from four to a dozen occupants. Just as far as the eye could reach, these painted lights were massed together – like a vast garden of many-coloured flowers, except that these blossoms were never still; they were ceaselessly gliding in and out, and mingling together, and seducing you into bewildering attempts to follow their mazy evolutions. Here and there a strong red, green, or blue glare from a rocket that was struggling to get away, splendidly illuminated all the boats around it. Every gondola that swam by us, with its crescents and pyramids and circles of coloured lamps hung aloft, and lighting up the faces of the young and the sweet-scented and lovely below, was a picture; and the reflections of those lights, so long, so slender, so numberless, so many-coloured and so distorted and wrinkled by the waves, was a picture likewise, and one that was enchantingly beautiful. Many and many a party of young ladies and gentlemen had their state gondolas so handsomely decorated, and ate supper on board, bringing their swallow-tailed, white-cravatted varlets to wait upon them, and having their tables tricked out as if for a bridal supper. They had brought along the costly globe lamps from their drawing-rooms, and the lace and silken curtains from the same place, I suppose. And they had also brought pianos and guitars, and they played and sang operas, while the plebeian paper-lanterned gondolas from the suburbs and the back alleys crowded around to stare and listen.

The fête was magnificent. They kept it up the whole night long, and I never enjoyed myself better than I did while it lasted.

This the famed gondola and this the gorgeous gondolier! – the one an inky, rusty old canoe with a sable hearse-body clapped on to the middle of it, and the other a mangy, barefooted guttersnipe with a portion of his raiment on exhibition which should have been sacred from public scrutiny . . .

'All visitors were monitored by a smouldering reptile in reception'

JOHN GIMLETTE

At the Tomb of the Inflatable Pig: Travels in Paraguay (1997)

Paraguay, 'an island surrounded by land', is not an obvious choice for travel literature, and John Gimlette (b. 1963), a London-based barrister when he is not travelling to write, does not have a lot of competition. He disliked and disapproved of so much of it as a young traveller, but is drawn back for more and more. The result is the book with this splendid name.

I stayed at the Hotel Guarani. It was not a great success. The hotel flunkies seemed if anything slightly less interested in my contentment now than they had been when I was an intruder. To get across the swimming pool, I now had to nose my way through a froth of flies. Sometimes, I got lost in the gloomy upper floors of the hotel and found myself in rooms that had been abandoned long ago and that were heaped with dirty plates and sheets and dusty scraps of food. Some years later, the hotel was abandoned altogether, and when I next saw it, it was wreathed in soot and was being slowly devoured by tropical succulents.

I paid a visit to my old hotel, the Hispania. The Mennonites had long gone. Appalled at the new liberal order, 'Mexicans' tried to avoid Asunción now, and besides, the new Korean owners of the *pensión* had painted it white, like an old bridesmaid, and decorated it with parrot feathers and a large photograph of the docks at Seoul. The Anabaptists had drifted elsewhere.

The rains came early. Hot, bright-red water foamed through the streets. An oil tanker crashed in the Plaza de Los Heroes and a guard was mounted over the wreckage, dressed – I thought – like the Afrika Korps.

I took a bus up to Carmelitas to see the house that General Rodriguez was living in. The bus conductress was wearing tights patterned with elongated tigers, leaping up into her knickers. The rain got hotter and more intense.

Rodríguez's house was a worthy tourist attraction because it was the nearest thing that South America had to a Palace of Versailles. I stood in the long wet grass gaping up at the crenellations and turrets. It had a turquoise roof that had been flown in, tile by tile, from France. When someone once asked the old emir how he could enjoy such lavish *bijoux* on $500 a month, he'd wafted away their impertinence: 'I gave up smoking.'

. . .

Apart from the half-dead gerontocrats, there were other, more occasional guests at The Gran Hotel. Twice a week there was a small *técanasta* party in the lobby. I suspected that the ladies were the delicate rump of what had been a larger card circle. They arrived with silvery perms and kidskin gloves and drank tea from china cups and saucers. They conversed in Spanish and played their cards in French, and when the games were over, they slipped their gloves back on and swarthy drivers took them home.

Things were more lively on the weekends. There were the tennis-players, of course, and every Saturday, the ballroom was tinselled up for a ball. It was usually a fifteenth birthday party for a debutante. These weren't like the office girls, but were winsome little slips – tutored in Miami, pastured in Uruguay and heeled in Buenos Aires. They had long cataracts of courtly Spanish names – Caballero, Ibarra, Yegros, Elizeche, Espinoza – which had often been hitched together as evidence of unimpeachable pedigree. They'd be photographed with their parents – bundles of startling tuxedos and organza – and then, as the whisky flowed, they'd all polka and sing in Guarani. It was now chic to be an Indian.

All visitors were monitored by a smouldering reptile in reception. Because her lair was faced – in the Teutonic style – with lumps of rock, she was often difficult to see in the gloom. However, whenever a stranger stepped into the lobby, she was quickly on the scent and her loose-skinned neck craned out of its cave. This being Asunción, most people knew exactly who she was.

'She's a terrible snob,' one friend told me.

'Her father was a minister in the *Stronato*,' said another.

'She's not there working for the salary, she just wants to know what's going on and who everybody is.'

Meanwhile, she devoured their details, mentally weighing up their carats and boring into bank accounts, clambering into their family trees and sniffing their blood for its blueness. She was a sort of social pyragüé, mounted with crimson talons.

She called me 'Monsieur D'Juim au Lait', and I didn't care to correct her.

———

'Farmers started growing bungalows instead of wheat'

JOHN BETJEMAN

Shell Guide to Cornwall (introduction to the 1954 edition)

John Betjeman (1906–84) was the most popular and best known of all the Poets Laureate of the United Kingdom, partly because of the humour and easy accessibility of his poetry, and also because he became a familiar tele-vision personality. The Shell Guides were launched with Betjeman's Cornwall in 1934 and over the next thirty years were to cover most of the British Isles, a new type of guide aimed at the new motorists. Betjeman and his good friend, the artist John Piper, cooperated on several of them.

The passage is also a tribute to one of the most charming of men. He was my sister's friend and sometime employer and as a result it was my luck that he was my guide to Cornwall. I stayed with him and his friend 'Feeble' (Elizabeth Cavendish) at his house at St Enodoc. Even at his most critical he remained affectionate towards almost everyone. We meandered around the golf course together. He would wander off to show me something in the adjacent churchyard or field whilst other golfers waited indulgently behind for us to continue.

When I first came to Cornwall over fifty years ago, as a small boy, we drove the seven miles from the station in a horse-brake, and there was only one motor-car in the parish and this could not attempt the steeper hills. Roads were only partially metalled and in the lesser lanes the rock showed through on the surface. Everyone in the village had oil lamps and candles. A journey to the nearest town and back was a day's expedi-tion. There were still many country people who had never been to London and the story used to be told of one of them who thought the metropolis was all under a glass roof because he never got further than Paddington Station. Visitors to Cornwall, 'foreigners' as they are rightly called by the Cornish, were mostly fishermen, golfers and artists. My own father, in his leisure from business in London, was all three.

. . .

The awakening of the Cornish to the value of the tourist industry came with the railways. The Great Western extended itself into Cornwall and was thought of first in terms of goods traffic – tin, china clay and fish. The London and South-Western, the Great Western's great rival, ran a line into north Cornwall via Okehampton, largely for holiday traffic. Fathers who had come for the fishing and mothers who wanted sea air for their families at cheaper rates and in less plebeian conditions than those provided in Thanet or Brighton came to Cornwall. Monster hotels were built at the beginning of this century to provide for them, such as the King Arthur's Castle at Tintagel, the Poldhu at Mullion and the Metropole at Padstow. Many a terrace of boarding houses arose in seaports which had hitherto thought that their only industry was to be fishing. Newquay and Bude are largely foreigners' creations, and Falmouth, turning the corner westward of Pendennis Castle, built a new seaside town. Simultaneously with the big hotel came the early twentieth-century cult of the old cottage in the country, and picturesque ports like Polperro, St Ives and Looe and Fowey did well. Farmers' wives specialised in Cornish teas and fishermen rowed the 'foreigners' out of the harbour to catch mackerel they would otherwise be catching themselves. Farmers on the sea coast started growing bungalows instead of wheat.

All this tourist industry brought prosperity and security to Cornwall until the appearance of the Duchy was seriously altered by electricity and the motor-car. The Electricity Board has strung the fields, villages and towns of Cornwall with more poles and wires, ill-sited and clumsily arranged, than in any other part of the British Isles. This is partly because even the remotest bungalow on a cliff wants electricity and partly because burying cables in slate or granite is expensive. The motor-car has made the greatest change of all. Roads have been widened, blocks of houses have been taken down in picturesque ports to make way for car parks; petrol stations proliferate; huge hoardings to attract the motorist line the entrances to towns. In the holiday season lorries and cars trailing caravans and boats block lanes never intended for such heavy traffic. The County Planning authorities, hard put to it to find available sites on the coast, have been obliged to introduce caravans and chalets even to the wooded inland valleys. Several stretches of the coast have been rescued by the National Trust or saved, at any rate for their lifetime, by those landowners who can still afford to hold out against the blandishment of 'developers'. The old and beautiful Cornwall is now mostly to be found on foot or in a small car by those skilled in using the 1-inch ordnance survey map. It is partly in search of this Cornwall that this guide book has gone. There is also the consolation that no one yet has discovered how to build houses on the sea.

SEVEN

'. . . let the boy flaunt his genius somewhere'

In chapter three, the authors were travelling tyros, expressing newfound elation in their adventure. In this chapter they have matured and grown with their love of abroad. Now they are at home and comfortable with what they have chosen: Patrick Leigh Fermor in the Peleponnese that was his home for much of his life; Wilfred Thesiger, as content as he would ever be, living with the Madan Arabs in the marshlands of southern Iraq; the much younger and endlessly restless Isabelle Eberhardt, for a moment at complete ease with her life in the unlikely and potentially unfriendly environment of Kedansa, Algeria; Barry Lopez allowing, even willing, himself to be absorbed into the landscape of the Arctic; Ryszard Kapuściński, who came from poverty in Poland: 'I was at home in Africa; food was scarce and everyone was barefoot'.

The title of the chapter comes from a conversation with Alexander Frater (*Chasing the Monsoon*, *Beyond the Blue Horizon*). I sent him an email and added, as a sweetener for his morning coffee, Bruce Chatwin's 'Lament for Afghanistan' (the first passage of this chapter). Within a few minutes he called me and said: 'It's bollocks, Bill, as you well know, at least much of it is.' Then after a suitable pause: 'But we have to let the boy flaunt his genius somewhere'. Alex had managed in just two impromptu comments to sum up with affection the whole genre of travel writing, the sometimes uncomfortable competition between mundane truth and the desire to entertain, as well as the apparently effortless natural talent of Chatwin. He could also have been thinking of Chatwin's great friend Patrick Leigh Fermor.

In this chapter the twentieth-century titans of travel writing flaunt at the very least their talents.

———

'. . . or the whiff of a snow leopard at 14,000 feet'

BRUCE CHATWIN

What Am I Doing Here? (1988)

Chatwin's 'Lament for Afghanistan' is part of his preface to the 1982 Picador edition of Robert Byron's The Road to Oxiana *and is reproduced in* What Am I Doing Here? *The passage is as much a tribute to Byron as it is to Afghanistan. The preface starts with the assertion that 'Anyone who reads around the travel books of the thirties must, in the end, conclude that* Road to Oxiana *is the masterpiece. I write as a partisan, not as a critic. Long ago, I raised it to the status of "sacred text" and thus beyond criticism.'*

But that day will not bring back the things we loved: the high, clear days and the blue icecaps on the mountains; the lines of white poplars fluttering in the wind, and the long white prayer-flags; the fields of asphodels that followed the tulips; or the fat-tailed sheep brindling the hills above Chakcharan, and the ram with a tail so big they had to strap it to a cart. We shall not lie on our backs at the Red Castle and watch the vultures wheeling over the valley where they killed the grandson of Genghiz. We will not read Babur's memoirs in his garden at Istalif and see the blind man smelling his way around the rose bushes. Or sit in the Peace of

Islam with the beggars of Gazar Gagh. We will not stand on the Buddha's head at Bamiyan, upright in his niche like a whale in a dry-dock. We will not sleep in the nomad tent, or scale the Minaret of Jam. And we shall lose the tastes – the hot, coarse, bitter bread; the green tea flavoured with cardamoms; the grapes we cooled in the snow-melt; and the nuts and dried mulberries we munched for altitude sickness. Nor shall we get back the smell of the beanfields, the sweet, resinous smell of deodar wood burning, or the whiff of a snow leopard at 14,000 feet.

'The quiet charm of Kardamyli grew with each passing hour'

PATRICK LEIGH FERMOR

Mani (1958)

Patrick Leigh Fermor (1915–2011) has chanced upon the idea that an old local family, near what became his home at Kardamyli in the Peloponnese, might be the linear descendants of the Palaeologi dynasty, the last and longest ruling dynasty of the Byzantine Empire. Maybe only he could so elegantly juxtapose in one anecdote the village fishermen and the Emperors of Byzantium.

Some readers are uncomfortable with the rococo extravagance of Leigh Fermor's writing in Mani. If so, they could reread, forgetting for a moment that this is a travel book about Greece and instead hear the passage as one would the cadenza of a great soprano. Surely we can 'let the boy flaunt . . .' just because he is so very good at it?

Cooled in summer by the breeze from the gulf, the great screen of the Taygetus shuts out intruding winds from the north and the east; no tramontana can reach it. It is like those Elysian confines of the world where Homer says that life is easiest for men; where no snow falls, no strong winds blow nor rain comes down, but the melodious west wind blows for ever from the sea to bring coolness to those who live there. I was very much tempted to become one of them...

. . .

I woke up the next morning thinking of the Mourtzini and the Palae-ologi. It occurred to me, drinking mountain-tea in the street, that I had forgotten to ask when the Mourtzinos family had died out. 'But it hasn't,' Mr Phalireas said. 'Strati, the last of them, lives just down the road.'

Evstratios Mourtzinos was sitting in his doorway weaving, out of split cane and string, a huge globular fish-trap more complex than any compass design or abstract composition of geometrical wire. The reel of twine revolved on the floor, the thread unwinding between his big toe and its neighbour as the airy sphere turned and shifted in his skilful brown fingers with a dazzling interplay of symmetrical parabolas. The sunlight streamed through the rust-coloured loops and canopies of drying nets, a tang of salt, tar, seaweed and warm cork hung in the air. Cut reeds were stacked in sheaves, two canaries sung in a cage in the rafters, our host's wife was slicing onions into a copper saucepan, Mourtzinos shrugged his shoulders with a smile at my rather absurd questions and his shy and lean face, which brine and the sun's glare had cured to a deep russet, wore an expression of dubious amusement. 'That's what they say,' he said, 'but we don't know anything about it. They are just old stories...' He poured out hospitable glasses of ouzo, and the conversation switched to the difficulties of finding a market for fish: there was so much competition. There is a special delight in this early-morning drinking in Greece.

Old stories, indeed. But supposing every link were verified, each shaky detail proved? Supposing this modest and distinguished looking fisherman were really heir of the Palaeologi, descendant of Constantine XI and of Michael VIII the Liberator, successor to Alexis Comnene and Basil the Bulgar-Slayer and Leo the Isaurian and Justinian and Theodosius and St Constantine the Great? And, for that matter, to Diocletian and Heliogabalus and Marcus Aurelius, to the Antonines, the Flavians, the Claudians and the Julians, all the way back to the Throne of Augustus Caesar on the Palatine, where Romulus had laid the earliest foundations of Rome? ... The generous strength of a second glass of ouzo accelerated these cogitations. It was just the face for a constitutional monarch, if only Byzantium were free. For the sheer luxury of credulity I lulled all scepticism to sleep and, parallel to an unexacting discourse of currents and baits and shoals, a kind of fairy-tale began assembling in my mind: 'Once upon a time, in a far-away land, a poor fisherman and his wife lived by the sea-shore ... One day a stranger from the city of Byzantium knocked on the door and begged for alms. The old couple laid meat and drink before him ...' Here the mood and period painlessly changed into a hypothetic future and the stranger had a queer story to tell: the process of Westernisation in Turkey, the study of European letters, of the classics and the humanities had borne such fruit that the Turks, in token of friendship and historical appropriateness, had decided to give the Byzantine Empire back to the Greeks and withdraw to the Central Asian steppes beyond the Volga from which they originally came, in order to plant their newly-won civilisation in the Mongol wilderness ... The Greeks were streaming back into Constantinople and Asia Minor. Immense flotillas were dropping anchor off Smyrna and Adana and Halicarnassus and Alexandretta. The seaboard villages were coming back to life; joyful concourses of Greeks were streaming into Adrianople, Rhodosto, Broussa, Nicaea, Caesaraea, Iconium, Antioch and Trebizond. The sound of rejoicing rang through eastern Thrace and banners with the Cross and the double-headed eagle and the Four Betas back-to-back were fluttering over Cappadocia and Karamania and Pontus and Bithynia and Paphlagonia and the Taurus mountains . . .

But in the City itself, the throne of the Emperors was vacant . . .

Stratis, our host, had put the fish-trap on the ground to pour out a third round of ouzo. Mrs Mourtzinos chopped up an octopus-tentacle and arranged the cross-sections on a plate. Stratis, to illustrate his tale, was measuring off a distance by placing his right hand in the crook of his left elbow, 'a grey mullet that long,' he was saying, 'weighing five okas if it weighed a dram . . .'

Then, in the rebuilt palace of Blachernae, the search for the heir had begun. What a crackling of parchment and chrysobuls, what clashing of seals and unfolding of scrolls! What furious wagging of beards and flourishes of scholarly forefingers! The Cantacuzeni, though the most authenticated of the claimants, were turned down; they were descendants only from the last emperor but four . . . Dozens of doubtful Palaeologi were sent packing . . . the Stephanopoli de Comnene of Corsica, the Melissino-Comnenes of Athens were regretfully declined. Tactful letters had to be written to the Argyropoli; a polite firmness was needed, too, with the Courtney family of Powderham Castle in Devonshire, kinsmen of Pierre de Courtenai, who, in 1218, was Frankish Emperor of Constantinople; and a Lascaris maniac from Saragossa was constantly hanging about the gates . . . Envoys returned empty-handed from Barbados and the London docks . . . Some Russian families allied to Ivan the Terrible and the Palaeologue Princess Anastasia Tzarogorodskaia had to be considered . . . Then all at once a new casket of documents came to light and a foreign emissary was despatched hot foot to the Peloponnese; over the Taygetus to the forgotten hamlet of Kardamyli . . . By now all doubt had vanished. The Emperor Eustratius leant forward to refill the glasses with ouzo for the fifth time. The Basilissa shooed away a speckled hen which had wandered in-doors after crumbs. On a sunny doorstep, stroking a marmalade cat, sat the small Diadoch and Despot of Mistra.

. . .

Mrs Mourtzinos spooned a couple of onions and potatoes out of the pot, laid them before us and sprinkled them with a pinch of rock salt. 'When we were a couple of hours off Cerigo,' Stratis observed, splashing out the ouzo, 'the wind grew stronger – a real *meltemi* – a roaring *boucadoura*! – so we hauled the sails down, and made everything fast . . .'

There, before the great bronze doors of St Sophia, gigantic in his pontificalia, stood Athenagoras the Oecumenical Patriarch, whom I saw a few months before in the Phanar; surrounded now with all the Patriarchs and Archbishops of the East, the Holy Synod and all the pomp of Orthodoxy in brocade vestments of scarlet and purple and gold and lilac and sea blue and emerald green: a forest of gold pastoral staves topped with their twin coiling serpents, a hundred yard-long beards cascading beneath a hundred onion-mitres crusted with gems; and, as in the old Greek song about the City's fall, the great fane rang with sixty clanging bells and four hundred gongs, with a priest for every bell and a deacon for every priest. The procession advanced, and the coruscating penumbra, the flickering jungle of hanging lamps and the bright groves and the undergrowth of candles swallowed them. Marble and porphyry and lapis-lazuli soared on all sides, a myriad glimmering haloes indicated the entire mosaic hagiography of the Orient and, high above, suspended as though on a chain from heaven and ribbed to its summit like the concavity of an immense celestial umbrella, floated the golden dome. Through the prostrate swarm of his subjects and the fog of incense the imperial theocrat advanced to the iconostasis. The great basilica rang with the anthem of the Cherubim and as the Emperor stood on the right of the Katholikon and the Patriarch on the left, a voice as though from an archangel's mouth sounded from the dome, followed by the fanfare of scores of long shafted trumpets, while across Byzantium the heralds proclaimed the Emperor Eustratius, Servant of God, King of Kings, Most August Caesar and Basileus and Autocrator of Constantinople and New Rome. The whole City was shaken by an unending, ear-splitting roar. Entwined in whorls of incense, the pillars turned in their sockets, and tears of felicity ran down the mosaic Virgin's and the cold ikons' cheeks.

Leaning forward urgently, Strati crossed himself. *'Holy Virgin and all the Saints!'* he said. 'I was never in a worse situation! It was pitch dark and pouring with rain, the mast and the rudder were broken, the bung was lost, and the waves were the size of a house. There I was, on all fours in the bilge water, bailing for life, in the Straits between the Elaphonisi and Cape Malea!'

. . . the whole of Constantinople seemed to be rising on a dazzling golden cloud and the central dome began to revolve as the redoubled clamour of the Byzantines hoisted it aloft. Loud with bells and gongs, with cannon flashing from the walls and a cloud-borne fleet firing long crimson radii of Greek fire, the entire visionary city, turning in faster and faster spirals, sailed to a blinding and unconjecturable zenith . . . The rain had turned to hail, the wind had risen to a scream; the boat had broken and sunk and, through the ink-black storm, Strati was swimming for life towards the thunderous rocks of Laconia. . .

. . . The bottle was empty . . .

The schoolmaster's shadow darkened the doorway. 'You'd better hurry,' he said, 'the caique for Areopolis is just leaving.' We all rose to our feet, upsetting, in our farewells, a basket of freshly cut bait and a couple of tridents which fell to the floor with a clatter. We stepped out into the sobering glare of noon.

'Sometimes when I meditate, the big rocks dance'

PETER MATTHIESSEN

The Snow Leopard (1978)

Here Peter Matthieson (1927–2014) is in north-western Nepal, about half-way between Mount Everest to the east and the pilgrims' mountain, Kailas, to the north. He is there with George Schaller, a zoologist of legendary endurance in the mountains. Matthiessen was warned by a friend: 'the last person who went walking with Schaller came back – or more properly turned back – when his boots were full of blood'. Schaller was one of the very few Westerners ever to have set eyes upon the elusive Himalayan snow leopard. They sought them in the area of Shey Gompa, the 'Crystal Monastery', where the Tibetan Buddhist lamas had decreed sanctuary for the snow leopard.

———

The nights at Shey are rigid, under rigid stars; the fall of a wolf pad on the frozen path might be heard up and down the canyon. But a hard wind comes before the dawn to rattle the tent canvas, and this morning it is clear again, and colder. At daybreak, the White River, just below, is sheathed in ice, with scarcely a murmur from the stream beneath.

The two ravens come to tritons on the gompa roof. *Gorawk, gorawk,* they croak, and this is the name given to them by the sherpas. Amidst the prayer flags and great horns of Tibetan argali, the gorawks greet first light with an odd musical double note – *a-ho* – that emerges as if by miracle from those ragged throats. Before sunrise every day, the great black birds are gone, like the last tatters of departing night.

The sun rising at the head of the White River brings a suffused glow to the tent canvas, and the robin accentor flits away across the frozen yard. At seven, there is breakfast in the cook hut – tea and porridge – and after breakfast on most days I watch sheep with GS, parting company with him after a while, when the sheep lie down, to go off on some expedition of my own. Often I scan the caves and ledges on the far side of Black River in the hope of leopard; I am alert for fossils, wolves, and birds. Sometimes I observe the sky and mountains, and sometimes I sit in meditation, doing my best to empty out my mind, to attain that state in which everything is 'at rest, free, and immortal . . . All things abided eternally as they were in their proper places . . . something infinite behind everything appeared.' (No Buddhist said this, but a seventeenth-century Briton.) And soon all sounds, and all one sees and feels, take on imminence, an immanence, as if the Universe were coming to attention, a Universe of which one is the centre, a Universe that is not the same and yet not different from oneself, even from a scientific point of view: within man as within mountain there are many parts of hydrogen and oxygen, of calcium phosphorus, potassium, and other elements. 'You never enjoy the world aright, till the Sea itself flows in your veins, till you are clothed with the heavens, and crowned with the stars: and perceive yourself to be the sole heir of the whole world, and more than so, because men are in it who are every one sole heirs as well as you.'

I have a meditation place on Somdo mountain, a broken rock outcrop like an altar set into the hillside, protected from all but the south wind by shards of granite and dense thorn. In the full sun it is warm, and its rock crannies give shelter to small stunted plants that cling to this desert mountainside – dead red-brown stalks of a wild buckwheat (*Polygonum*), some shrubby cinquefoil, pale edelweiss, and everlasting, and even a few poor wisps of *Cannabis*. I arrange a rude rock seal as a lookout on the world, set out binoculars in case wild creatures should happen into view, then cross my legs and regulate my breath, until I scarcely breathe at all.

Now the mountains all around me take on life; the Crystal Mountain moves. Soon there comes the murmur of the torrent, from far away below under the ice: it seems impossible that I can hear this sound. Even in windlessness, the sound of rivers comes and goes and falls and rises, like the wind itself. An instinct comes to open outward by letting all life in, just as a flower fills with sun. To burst forth from this old husk and cast one's energy abroad, to fly . . .

Although I am not conscious of emotion, the mind-opening brings a soft mist to my eyes. Then the mist passes, the cold wind clears my head, and body-mind comes and goes on the light air. A sun-filled Buddha. One day I shall meditate in falling snow.

I lower my gaze from the snow peaks to the glistening thorns, the snow patches, the lichens. Though I am blind to it, the Truth is near, in the reality of what I sit on – rocks. These hard rocks instruct my bones in what my brain could never grasp in the Heart Sutra, that 'form is emptiness, and emptiness is form' – the Void, the emptiness of blue-black space, contained in everything. Sometimes when I meditate, the big rocks dance.

———

'Memories of that first visit to the Marshes have never left me. . .'

WILFRED THESIGER

The Marsh Arabs (1964)

In October 1950 Wilfred Thesiger (1910–2003) journeyed on horseback to the marshlands of southern Iraq, north of Basra, where he became the first

recorded outsider to move among the Madan, who lived a waterborne exis-
tence in houses made of reeds, often also built on floating reed beds. For a
large part of the next eight years he lived as a member of the tribe, travel-
ling from village to village by canoe and gradually winning their acceptance.
The book introduced the Madan to the world's attention and predicted
their eventual destruction. This was to come when Saddam Hussein
drained the marshes by destroying the retaining dams because he feared
subversion by the Shia Madan. There are now signs of regeneration.

I was on my way south from Iraqi Kurdistan, where I had gone to try to
recapture the peace of mind I had known in the deserts of Southern
Arabia. There I had lived with the Bedu for five years, and with them
had travelled ten thousand miles across country where no car had ever
been – until seismic parties, the vanguard of modern progress, began to
arrive in search of oil.

In Iraqi Kurdistan, which I had always wanted to visit, I had ridden
from one end of the country to the other, accompanied only by a young
Kurdish servant. The scenery was wild and beautiful, and the Kurds who
lived there still wore the finery of tribal dress – tasselled turbans and
baggy trousers, short jackets and cummerbunds, of every colour
and pattern – hung with daggers and revolvers and crossed with decorated bandoliers, heavy with cartridges. I had slept in terraced villages
that hugged the mountainsides where the flat-roofed houses rose from
the roofs below, and in the black tents of the nomads on bare mountaintops where gentians grew among the grass, and snowdrifts lay
throughout the summer. I had followed tumbling rivers through oak
forests where bears grubbed in the thickets, and I had looked down on a
herd of ibex, threading its way along a three-thousand-foot wall of
rock, while huge griffon vultures swung past, the wind whistling in their
pinions. I had seen the glory of the Kurdish spring, valley-sides covered

with anemones, and mountains crimson with tulips. I had gorged on grapes, freshly picked and warmed by the sun or cooled in a nearby stream.

But having seen Iraqi Kurdistan I had no desire to go back. Travel was too restricted, rather like stalking in a Highland deer forest. Across this stream was Turkey, beyond that watershed lay Persia, where uniformed police waited at the passes demanding visas I did not possess. I was fifty years too late. Half a century earlier I could have gone up through Rowunduz to Urmia, and on to Van, and the only effective hindrance would have been brigands and warring tribes. Admittedly the Marshes, for which I was now bound, covered a smaller area than Iraqi Kurdistan, but they were a world complete in itself, not a fragment of a larger world to the rest of which I was denied access. Besides, being fond of Arabs, it was probable that I could never really like Kurds. Although the landscape appealed to me the people did not. Admittedly I was hampered by not speaking their language, but even had I done so I felt that I should still not have liked them. As people are more important to me than places I decided to return to the Arabs.

Next day we rode on again, southward this time towards the Marshes across the unchanging plain, stopping at midday at some tents to feed ourselves and change horses. Dugald was remounted on a magnificent but restive grey stallion. When I protested that it would be too much for him, the sheikh clearly thought I wanted to ride it myself, and said he had brought it for 'the Consul'. A little later Dugald inadvertently jabbed the stallion with his heel and it bolted. To save himself he dropped the reins and grabbed the pommel with both hands. Our companions started to gallop in pursuit, but, realising that they would only excite it further, I shouted to them to stop. Dugald had already lost both stirrups. It seemed only a matter of time till he came off. The ground was hard and I pictured a ghastly accident, but two miles farther the horse stopped exhausted, with Dugald still clinging to the saddle. When we caught up with him he had dismounted and was looking at his hands. The palms had been scraped raw by the decorative nails in the pommel. 'Now I am bloody well going to walk,' he announced, and no assurances that our horses were quiet would induce him to change his mind and ride one of them.

The sun was still high. Past floods had covered the ground, which was fissured with deep cracks. While the sheikh kept up a flow of remonstrances, Dugald lurched and limped along: 'Oh for God's sake get him to shut up,' he implored me. The sun set and there was still no sign of the Marshes nor of the village for which we were bound. It was dark when we saw lights moving in the distance. The Bazun had warned Maziad bin Hamdan, sheikh of the Al Essa, to expect us, and he had sent out a search party at dusk. They led us to his encampment on the edge of the Marshes. Beyond the tents we could sense rather than see water.

Maziad himself came out to welcome us. A small man, stockily built but standing very upright, he conveyed at once an impression of dignity and authority. The guest tent was lit by a hurricane lamp and filled with men, most of them armed with rifles. They rose as we came in. Maziad showed us to a place opposite the hearth. While we were served with coffee and tea, Maziad asked the conventional questions about our health and journey. Everyone sat very still and upright and no one else spoke. We were in the presence of desert Arabs, who are always formal in public and conscious of their dignity. We fed at last, it seemed hours later, from an enormous platter heaped high with the usual rice and mutton. It was not a delicate meal, but Arabs appreciate quantity rather than quality. We ate first with some old men, and as soon as we had all finished Maziad summoned others by name to take our places. As host, he himself stood until all had finished. They fed in relays and when the last was done he called in children from the dark outside the tent. The smallest, quite naked, cannot have been more than three. They stuffed themselves with the rice that was left and gnawed at bones that had already been picked clean. Then they cleared the dishes, scooping what was left into bowls they had brought with them. The bones were thrown to the dogs. Towards the end, the coffee-man saved a small helping and set it aside on a plate. Maziad now drew a little apart and took his frugal meal, while we were once more served coffee and tea. As host it would not have been seemly for him to eat until the last of his guests had done so, and next day at meal time I watched him standing before his tent to ensure that no one passed by without coming in. Twice daily he killed a sheep for his guests, who might number a hundred. These shepherd tribes still held to the customs, and judged others by the standards, that they had brought with them from the deserts of Arabia.

In the following years I came back many times to Maziad's guest tent, and visited many other encampments of his tribe. During the worst of the summer months, I would escape from the Marshes, borrow horses and move about among the shepherd tribes. I got to know most of them – the Bani Lam, the Bazun, the Al Essa, the Al bu Salih and others. Some would cross the frontier in the spring and move up into the Persian foot-hills, where the new green grass was bright with anemones; others moved down into Saudi Arabia and to the outskirts of Kuwait for the winter, the men and boys herding the sheep and goats, while the black-robed women drove donkeys loaded with tents and poles, carpets, bedding, small wooden chests, cauldrons, dishes and kettles. Often I saw them moving through the mirage across a plain that was as empty as the sea.

After the meal, Maziad showed us to a nearby cabin, neatly built of reeds and matting, where mattresses and colour quilts were spread for us to sleep – an unexpected privacy for which Dugald and I were both grateful. All night the wind, cold off dark water, blew through the lattice, and half asleep I heard waves slapping on a shore.

As I came out into the dawn, I saw, far away across a great sheet of water, the silhouette of a distant land, black against the sunrise. For a moment I had a vision of Hufaidh, the legendary island, which no man may look on and keep his senses; then I realised that I was looking at great reedbeds. A slim, black, high-prowed craft lay beached at my feet – the sheikh's war canoe, waiting to take me into the Marshes. Before the first palaces were built at Ur, men had stepped out into the dawn from such a house, launched a canoe like this, and gone hunting here. Woolley had unearthed their dwellings and models of their boats buried deep under the relics of Sumeria, deeper even than evidence of the Flood. Five thousand years of history were here and the pattern was still unchanged.

Memories of that first visit to the Marshes have never left me: firelight on a half-turned face, the crying of geese, duck flighting in to feed, a boy's voice singing somewhere in the dark, canoes moving in procession down a waterway, the setting sun seen crimson through the smoke of burning reedbeds, narrow waterways that wound still deeper into the Marshes. A naked man in a canoe with a trident in his hand, reed houses built upon water, black, dripping buffaloes that looked as if they had calved from the swamp with the first dry land. Stars reflected in dark water, the croaking of frogs, canoes coming home at evening, peace and continuity, the stillness of a world that never knew an engine. Once again I experienced the longing to share this life, and to be more than a mere spectator.

'Curiosity led me, pure curiosity, the human thrust in time'

FREYA STARK

Ionia: A Quest (1954)

Freya Stark (1883–1993) spent much of her childhood in Asolo in Italy's Veneto. As a young teenager she became intrigued with Arabia after receiving One Thousand and One Nights *as a ninth birthday present. During the late twenties and thirties she travelled much of eastern Persia. She located and explored the Valleys of the Assassins in the mountains between Iraq and Iran. In 1935 she went to the southern Arabian region of Hadramaut, in what is now mainly Yemen, and wrote her Arabian trilogy, for which in part she was to be awarded the Founder's Medal of the Royal Geographical Society. Travel sustained her to live to 110.*

Ionia is an old name for the coastal region of Anatolia, Turkey, near Ismir (Smyrna), so called for the Ionian tribe who lived there during much of the first millennium BC. *Cape Sunium is the promontory to the east of Athens that marks the southeast corner of Attica. The two passages here come from the first chapter, 'Dawn in Ionia', as the author leaves Athens by boat to the east and then Chapter Eighteen, 'Priene'. Priene is the ancient Greek holy city near modern-day Söke in Turkey.*

It was the 4th of September and I watched Cape Sunium fade, lit by a dull western afterglow on one side and by the moon dripping plates of light on the other. The boat was a Turkish boat, the most comfortable I have travelled in across the Mediterranean. She slipped along evenly, and split the smooth surface of the sea as if it were silk. From the horizon, darkening not in a sharp line but indefinitely, like blotting paper, a colour of violets deepened and encompassed our world. There were few passengers; they talked in quiet groups, easy together, each group more separate from the other than in Europe – the millennial intercourse and separateness of the Levant. The Turkish stewards and sailors walked about, with longer arms than most people, and a landsman's walk, and that absence of vanity in clothes which the change to Western costume seems to have produced. They stood aside, bowed the head, and murmured a salutation when an officer passed, with a graceful respect, free of servility, which I was to come to recognise as the charm of Turkish manners.

Two middle-aged women moved about like battleships, so square and broad below; they were built in the Doric order, and made everything look fragile around them. The darkness of violets deepened into night; one listened to the whisper of the sea. What an accurate word, for the sea – to whisper – used by Coleridge who had never known this inhabited, conversational Aegean. Soon, among the surrounding shadows, were shadows of islands; they handed us on from one to another; we were among the Cyclades; their lights, their music floated out like hands to clutch and let go. In the trough of small waves that had risen with the night breeze a fishing boat passed, a glow-worm with dim lanthorn that lit the lower edge of a yellow sail. I turned into my cabin, and lay with my porthole wide open still listening to the voices of the islands, and wondered what I was travelling to find. Curiosity led me, pure, disinterested curiosity, the human thrust in time.

. . .

Eight miles from Söke, a little town blossoming with prosperity and cotton, along a road that once followed (with a few old paving stones left), the ins and outs of the Latmian shore, and now keeps beside the flat delta of Maeander – what remains of Priene lies high up in the sun. I climbed and entered the little city by its eastern gate, and walked along a level, above the ruins of its houses.

The entry to the theatre is so unobtrusive that one scarcely notices it.

Without preparation, it is there. The straight stone shafts that support the proscenium are standing; there is a round base for a statue; a ramp of grey stone slopes down with seats fuming out in something more than a semicircle – the Greek and not the Roman fashion; and one steps suddenly between the seats and the proscenium, into the orchestra, a small grassy space light with daisies, enclosed in a semicircle where six stone arm-chairs for the most important people are evenly spaced with an altar among them. The seats behind rise in their tiers; the narrow shallow steps of gangways cut them at intervals; and I felt that I was inter-rupting – that actors and audience, like a flight of shy birds, had fled in the very instant of my stepping across their threshold with my feet still shod in Time. I felt this with a power and a strangeness not to be described; with tears on my cheeks in a sudden pang of surprise and excitement and wonder; and I lingered in the little theatre as if I were a person in the legend, who is given one glimpse of a world which appears to last for seconds only, though all the expanses of time are packed there.

There was perfect quiet in the theatre. The carvings on the stone were so sharp and delicate that the hand that worked them still seemed alive. They were simple patterns of alternate ivy leaves, placed only where they were required, on the piers of the entrance, on the six chairs with their arm-rests and cushions and footstools cut in stone. There was no seek-ing for praise, through tilings worked upon beyond their own necessities for their effect on other people – where the superfluous begins; for noth-ing here was superfluous. The whole city was built in the flower of the Hellenistic age, and to that its rich austerity belonged.

What was the secret? *Respect* perhaps, so closely tied to love? Respect for what gives itself, and is therefore vulnerable, whether it be a human being or a piece of stone? A gratitude that inspires fastidiousness, a longing to keep intact in its own dignity the object or the being that has helped one to create and to become?

That so subtle a scruple can transmute itself into stone and stay there, is magic; and no conscious effort of the craftsman, nothing but the feeling itself, can leave that mark. Where it exists, it is definite, and every true artist will recognise it across any bridge of time. Without it there is neither sincerity nor greatness. It is a sharing partnership, both giving and taking – a marriage in terms of human life – a tender thankfulness for a benefit received and a forgetfulness of self in the interest of another; and it reaches through the depths of being to that which Heraclitus thought of as Fire and we think of as Love.

'Then the blood in the veins speaks by itself'

ISABELLE EBERHARDT

The Oblivion Seekers; The Breath of Night (1906)

Isabelle Eberhardt (1877–1904) was Swiss-born, but had Russian, German and Jewish parentage. She spoke many languages, to which she would add Arabic in response to the allure of North Africa, which offered an escape from European social norms. Arriving in Algeria in 1897, she espoused the Islamic intellectual discipline of Sufism (although not feeling bound to forgo alcohol and narcotics). Of the many Algerian lovers she had, the one that lasted was a soldier, Slimene Ehnni.

For the remaining seven years of her turbulent, short life she moved between France and Algeria, usually with no money, seldom far from controversy, her lifestyle outraging both domestic French and French colonial society in Algeria. Paul Bowles and Elias Canetti may rank alongside Eberhardt as twentieth-century interpreters of North Africa for outsiders, but she did as much as any to tell of and build the mystique of the Maghreb.

Much of her writing at the end of her life was done in Kenadsa, a place of intense Moslem fanaticism where Europeans were not welcome.

It is the time of evening when the rays of the setting sun pass through an air already cooled by the first breath of night, while the mud walls give off the heat they have stored all during the day. Indoors it is like being in an oven. You must be outside, and feel the touch of the first shadows. And for a long time I lie idly stretched out staring up into the depths of the sky, listening to the last sounds from the *zaouiya* and the *ksar*: doors creaking as they swing heavily shut, the neighing of horses, and the bleat of sheep on the roofs. And the little African donkeys bray, a sound as sad as protracted sobbing. And the sharp thin voices of the black women.

Nearby in the courtyard there is the sound of tambourines and guinbris, making an accompaniment to some very strange vocalisations. These seem less like music than like the cries uttered during lovemaking. Sometimes the voices die down and all is silent. Then the blood in the veins speaks, by itself.

Soon life starts up again. Mats, rugs and sacks appear on the roofs of the slave-quarters. The ear still listens for muffled noises, kitchen sounds, arguments going on in low voices, prayers being murmured. And the sense of smell is jarred by the odors in the smoke that rises from the confusion of black bodies below, where the flames flicker joyously in the braziers. There are other silhouettes in the doorways of the holy men. It is all here, the daily life of the *ksar*, like something I have always known, and yet always new.

Over toward the right, behind the Mellah, there is a patch of wall that remains lighted up until very late. Its reddish surface serves as backdrop for the curious plays of shadow that are projected upon it. At times they move back and forth slowly, and then they seem to go into a furious dance. After all other voices have grown silent and everyone roundabout has gone to sleep, the Aissaoua are still awake. As the night grows perceptibly cooler, the members of that enlightened brotherhood, the *khouan*, pound on the tambourine and draw strident sounds from the oboelike rhaita. They also sing, slowly, as if in a dream. And they dance beside the flaming pots of charcoal, their wet bodies moving to an ever-accelerating tempo. From the fires rise intoxicating fumes of benzoin and myrrh. Through ecstasy they hope to reach the final target of unconsciousness.

I hear something more. When even the Aissaoua have sunk into sleep, I still see moving forms. A breath steals across the terraces, disturbing the calm. I know. I imagine. I hear. There are sighs and catchings of breath out there in the cinnamon-scented night. The heat of rut under the quiet stars. The hot night's languor drives flesh to seek flesh, and desire is reborn. It is terrible to hear teeth grinding in mortal spasms, and lungs making sounds like death-rattles. Agony! I feel like sinking my teeth into the warm earth.

In the morning the west wind arrived suddenly. You could see it coming, raising high spirals of dust, black as smoke. As it moved toward us through the calm air, it made great sighing sounds. And then it was howling like a living thing. I had a fantasy of being lifted up and carried off in the enormous embrace of a winged monster, come to destroy us all. And the sand showered onto the terraces with the steady, small sound of rain.

'I remember the press of light against my face'

BARRY LOPEZ

Arctic Dreams (1986)

The Arctic of Arctic Dreams *is the northern mainland of Alaska, Canada's Northwest Territories, Yukon, Nunavut and Greenland, and in particular the mass of lands and inlets that lie between them. Lopez (b. 1945) is at the vanguard of a new generation of writers who know that their role as reveal-ers of the world to others is all but redundant, given the ubiquity of cameras; his aim is to become one with land around him, to listen to it, and learn from it . . . It may be that historians of travel writing will see* Arctic Dreams *as the outrider for a twenty-first-century school of travel writing. These passages are taken from the preface and from Chapter Three.*

One summer evening I was camped in the western Brooks Range of Alaska with a friend. From the ridge where we had pitched our tent we looked out over tens of square miles of rolling tundra along the southern edge of the calving grounds of the Western Arctic caribou herd. During those days we observed not only caribou and wolves, which we'd come to study, but wolverine and red fox, ground squirrels, delicate-legged whimbrels and aggressive jaegers, all in the unfoldings of their obscure lives. One night we watched in awe as a young grizzly bear tried repeat-edly to force its way past a yearling wolf standing guard alone before a den of young pups. The bear eventually gave up and went on its way. We watched snowy owls and rough-legged hawks hunt and caribou drift like smoke through the valley.

On the evening I am thinking about – it was breezy there on Iling-norak Ridge, and cold; but the late-night sun, small as a kite in the

northern sky, poured forth an energy that burned against my cheek-
bones – it was on that evening that I went on a walk for the first time
among the tundra birds. They all build their nests on the ground, so
their vulnerability is extreme. I gazed down at a single horned lark no
bigger than my fist. She stared back resolute as iron. As I approached,
golden plovers abandoned their nests in hysterical ploys, artfully feign-
ing a broken wing to distract me from the woven grass cups that
couched their pale, darkly speckled eggs. Their eggs glowed with a soft,
pure light, like the window light in a Vermeer painting. I marveled at
this intense and concentrated beauty on the vast table of the plain. I
walked on to find Lapland longspurs as still on their nests as stones,
their dark eyes gleaming. At the nest of two snowy owls I stopped. These
are more formidable animals than plovers. I stood motionless. The wild
glare in their eyes receded. One owl settled back slowly over its three
eggs, with an aura of primitive alertness. The other watched me, and
immediately sought a bond with my eyes if I started to move.

I took to bowing on these evening walks. I would bow slightly with
my hands in my pockets, toward the birds and the evidence of life in
their nests – because of their fecundity, unexpected in this remote
region, and because of the serene arctic light that came down over the
land like breath, like breathing.

I remember the wild, dedicated lives of the birds that night and also
the abandon with which a small herd of caribou crossed the Kokolik
River to the northwest, the incident of only a few moments. They
pranced through like wild mares, kicking up sheets of water across the
evening sun and shaking it off on the far side like huge dogs, a bloom of
spray that glittered in the air around them like grains of mica.

I remember the press of light against my face. The explosive skitter of
calves among grazing caribou. And the warm intensity of the eggs
beneath these resolute birds. Until then, perhaps because the sun was

shining in the very middle of the night, so out of tune with my own customary perception, I had never known how benign sunlight could be. How forgiving. How run through with compassion in a land that bore so eloquently the evidence of centuries of winter.

During those summer days on Ilingnorak Ridge there was no dark night. Darkness never came. The birds were born. They flourished, and then flew south in the wake of the caribou.

. . .

Crossing the tree line to the Far North, one leaves behind the boreal owl clutching its frozen prey to its chest feathers to thaw it. Ahead lies an open, wild landscape, pointed off on the maps with arresting and anomalous names: Brother John Glacier and Cape White Handkerchief, Navy Board Inlet, Teddy Bear Island, and the Zebra Cliffs, Dexterity Fiord, Saint Patrick Canyon, Starvation Cove. Eskimos hunt the ringed seal, still, in the broad bays of the Sons of the Clergy and Royal Astronomical Society Islands.

This is a land where airplanes track icebergs the size of Cleveland and polar bears fly down out of the stars. It is a region like the desert, rich with metaphor, with adumbration. In a simple bow from the waist before the nest of the horned lark, you are able to stake your life, again, in what you dream.

. . .

Tornarssuk
Ursus maritimus

The seascape was almost without color beneath a low gray sky. Scattered ice floes damped any motion of large waves, and fogs and thin snow showers came and went in the still air. The surface of the water was the lacquered black of Japanese wooden boxes.

Three of us stood in the small open boat, about a hundred miles off the northwest coast of Alaska, at the southern edge of the polar pack in the Chukchi Sea. I and two marine scientists were hunting ringed seals that cold September day. In the seal stomachs we found what fish they had been eating; from bottom trawls we learned what the fish they were eating had eaten; and from plankton samplings we learned what the creatures the fish ate were eating.

We had been working at this study of marine food chains for several weeks, moving west in our boat across the north coast of Alaska, from the west end of the Jones Islands to Point Barrow. At Barrow we boarded a 300-foot oceanographic research vessel, the *Oceanographer*, and headed out into the Chukchi Sea. Each morning for the next two weeks our boat was lowered from the deck of this mother vessel and we worked in the sea ice until evening.

We had been hunting seals intensively for three days without success. Twice we had seen a seal, each time for only a split second. We moved slowly, steadily, through the ice floes, without conversation, occasionally raising a pair of field glasses to study a small, dark dot on the water – a piece of ice? A bird? A seal breaking the surface of the water to breathe? It is not so difficult to learn to distinguish among these things, to match a 'search image' in the mind after a few days of tutoring with the shading, shape, and movement that mean *seal*. Waiting in silence, intently attentive, was harder to learn.

We were three good sets of eyes, hunting hard. Nothing. A fog would clear. A snow squall drift through. In the most promising areas of the ice we shut off the engines and drifted with the currents. The ice, despite its occasional vertical relief, only compounded a sense of emptiness in the landscape, a feeling of directionlessness. The floes were like random, silent pieces of the earth. Our compass, turning serenely in its liquid dome, promised, if called upon to do so, to render points on a horizon obliterated in slanting snow and fog.

We drifted and sipped hot liquids, and stared into the quilt-work of grey-white ice and ink-black water. If one of us tensed, the others felt it and were alert. Always we were *hunting*. This particular habitat, the number of cod in the water, the time of the year – everything said ringed seals should be here. But for us they weren't.

Late summer in the sea ice. Eventually the cold, damp air finds its way through insulated boots and wool clothing to your bones. The conscious mind, the mind that knows how long you have been out here, importunes for some measure of comfort. We made a slow, wide turn in the boat, a turn that meant the end of the day. Though we still watched intently, thoughts of the ship were now upon us. Before this, we had camped on the beach in tents; now a hot shower, an evening meal in light clothing at a table, and a way to dry clothes awaited us. In the back of your mind at the end of the day you are very glad for these things.

My friend Bob saw the bear first: an ivory-white head gliding in glassy black water 300 feet ahead, at the apex of a V-wake. We slowed the boat and drew up cautiously to within 30 feet: A male. The great seal hunter himself. About three years old, said Bob.

The bear turned in the water and regarded us with irritation, and then, wary, he veered toward a floe. In a single motion of graceful power he rose from the water to the ice, his back feet catching the ice edge at the end of the movement. Then he stepped forward and shook. Seawater whirled off in flat sheets and a halo of spray. His head lowered, he glared at us with small, dark eyes. Then he crossed the floe and, going down on his forelegs, sliding headfirst, he entered the water on the other side without a splash and swam off.

We found our way to him again through the ice. We were magnetically drawn, in a fundamental but perhaps callow way. Our presence was interference. We approached as slowly as before, and he turned to glower, treading water, opening his mouth: – the gray tongue, the pale violet mouth, the white teeth – to hiss. He paddled away abruptly to a large floe and again catapulted from the water, shook his fur out, and started across the ice to open water on the far side.

We let him go. We watched him, that undeterred walk of authority. 'The farmer,' the whalers had called him, for his 'very agricultural appearance as he stalks leisurely over the furrowed fields of ice.' John Muir, on a visit to these same waters in 1899, said bears move 'as if the country had belonged to them always.'

The polar bear is a creature of arctic edges: he hunts the ice margins, the surface of the water, and the continental shore. The ice bear, he is called. His world forms beneath him in the days of shortening light, and then falls away in the spring. He dives to the ocean floor for mussels and kelp, and soundlessly breaks the water's glassy surface on his return, to study a sleeping seal. Twenty miles from shore he treads water amid schooling fish. The sea bear. In winter, while the grizzly hibernates, the polar bear is out on the sea ice, hunting. In summer his tracks turn up a hundred miles inland, where he has feasted on crowberries and blueberries.

Until a few years ago this resourceful hunter was in a genus by himself: *Thalarctos*. Now he is back where he started, with the grizzly and black bear in the genus *Ursus*, where his genes, if not his behavior, say he belongs.

What was so impressive about the bear we saw that day in the Chukchi was how robust he seemed. At three years of age a bear in this part of the Arctic is likely spending its first summer alone. To feed itself, it has had to learn to hunt, and open pack ice is among the toughest of environments for bears to hunt in. This was September, when most bears are thin, waiting for the formation of sea ice, their hunting platform. In our three days of diligent searching, in this gray and almost featureless landscape of ice remnants so far off the coast, we had seen but two seals. We were transfixed by the young bear. We watched him move off across the ice, into a confusing plane of grays and whites. We were shivering a little and opened a thermos of coffee. A snow shower moved quickly through, and when it cleared we could barely make him out in the black water with field glasses from the rocking boat. A young and successful hunter, at home in his home.

He had found the seals.

***

'The table levitated into the air'

PATRICK LEIGH FERMOR

The Broken Road (2013)

The two masterpieces that told the story of the first part of Patrick Leigh Fermor's walk from the Hook of Holland to Istanbul in 1933, A Time of Gifts *and* Between the Woods and the Water, *were actually written in the early 1960s, after he had begun what eventually became the final part of the trilogy. He agonised over book three for much of the last twenty-five years of his life. The final book was edited and reconstructed for publication by Artemis Cooper and Colin Thubron. Paddy had written most of what became* The Broken Road *without access to his contemporary diaries. These had been left at the house of his Romanian then-girlfriend before the Second World War and were only recovered to him in part some thirty years later when he made a secret trip to visit her. The two versions differed greatly, so that Paddy no doubt found them hard to reconcile.*

Here he is sitting outside a café in Plovdiv, Bulgaria. Storks seem to inspire him; this time it was to create a two hundred and fifty word picture, with which a camera could not compete, and end it with a little universal obituary.

Time for another *slivo* and a couple of roast paprika-pods. A shadow appeared on the awnings further up the lane, gliding across each rectangle of canvas towards my table, sinking in the sag, rising again at the edge, and moving on to the next with a flicker of dislocation, then gliding onwards. As it crossed the stripe of sunlight between two awnings, it threaded the crimson beak of a stork through the air, a few inches above the gap; then came a long white neck, the swell of snowy breast feathers and the six-foot motionless span of its white wings and the tips of the black flight feathers upturned and separated as fingers in the lift of the air current. The white belly followed, tapering, and then, trailing beyond, the fan of its tail and long parallel legs of crimson lacquer, the toes of each of them closed and streamlined, but the whole shape flattening, when the band of sunlight was crossed, into a two-dimensional shadow once more, enormously displayed across the rectangle of cloth, as distinct and nearly as immobile, so languid was its flight, as an emblematic bird on a sail; then sliding across it and along the nearly still corridor of air between the invisible eaves and the chimneys, dipping along the curl of the lane like a sigh of wonder, and at last, a furlong away slowly pivoting, at a gradual tilt, out of sight. A bird of passage like the rest of us.

The passage below is taken from the chapter 'Dancing by the Black Sea'.

It is 1 December 1933. The young Leigh Fermor, alone and at dusk, is trudging the rocky, sparsely inhabited Black Sea coast of Bulgaria, wet and cold and ill-shod, having fallen, back pack and all, into a sea pond, and with little prospect of warmth or shelter for the night. He glimpses a sliver of light from the rocks above. He investigates and finds a cave filled with a disparate group of cutlass-carrying Greek fishermen, Bulgarian shepherds, sheep, dogs, a roaring fire over which lentil stews are cooking and fish frying, and another warming a cauldron of whey. There are leaf beds for slumber, an old broken bagpipe and an instrument 'halfway between lute and mandolin' hanging on the wall. Paddy, with the status of young adventurer from far away, is welcomed and befriended. His own precious raki is added to their alcohol supply, igniting 'a mood of nautico–pastoral wassail' and Greek dancing, led by one of the fishermen, Costa.

On a rock near where I sat was the heavy, low round table that I had eaten from. Revolving past it, Costa leant forward: suddenly the table levitated into the air, sailed past us and pivoted at right angles to his head in a sequence of wide loops, the edge clamped firmly in his mouth and held there by nothing but his teeth buried in the wood. It rotated like a flying carpet, slicing crescents out of the haze of woodsmoke, so fast at some moments that the four glasses on it, the chap-fallen bagpipe with its perforated cow's horn dangling, the raki flask, the knives and spoons, the earthenware saucepan that had held the lentils and the backbones of the two mackerels with their heads and tails hanging over the edge of the tin plate, all dissolved for a few swift revolutions into a circular blur, then redefined themselves, as the pace dwindled, into a still life travelling in wide rings along the cave. As Costa sank gyrating to floor level, firelight lit the table from above, then he soared into the dark so that only the underside glowed. Simultaneously he quickened his pace and reduced the circumference of the circle by rotating faster and faster on the spot, his revolutions striking sparks of astonished applause through the grotto, which quickly rose to an uproar. His head was flung back and his streaming features corrugated with veins and muscles, his balancing arms outflung like those of a dervish until the flying table itself seemed to melt into a vast disc twice its own diameter spinning in the cave's centre at a speed, which should have scattered its whirling still-life into the nether shadows. Slowly the speed slackened. The table was once more a table, looping through the smoke five feet from the floor, sliding out of its own orbit, rotating back to its launching-rock and unhurriedly alighting there with all its impedimenta undisturbed. Not once had the dancer's hands touched it; but, the moment before it resettled in its place, he retrieved the stub of the cigarette he had left burning on the rock, and danced slowly back to the centre with no hint of haste or vertigo, tapping away the long ash with the fourth finger of his upraised left hand. He replaced it in his mouth, gyrated, sank, and unwound into his sober initial steps – the planned anticlimax again! – then having regained his motionless starting point, straight as an arrow and on tip-toe, he broke off, sauntered smoking with lowered lids to the re-established table, picked up his raki glass, took a meditative sip, deaf to the clamour, and subsided unhurriedly among the rest of us.

Of the whole story, Artemis said to me: 'Magnificent, but not a word of it true; then again maybe not a word of it is a lie. It all happened but not there, then or necessarily in that order'. 'Scraps of wool, collected from a barbed wire fence, spun and woven into. . .'

'It is already the end of the journey'

RYSZARD KAPUŚCIŃSKI

The Shadow of the Sun (1998)

Kapuściński was Polish, born in 1932, and grew up at a time when Poles had almost no access to the outside, let alone non-Communist, world. But he was dispatched abroad as a journalist by the Polish Press Agency, first to India, where he taught himself English by reading For Whom the Bell Tolls *with the aid of a dictionary, and in the late 1950s to Africa. Here he was the only Polish correspondent on the continent and therefore had a roving responsibility for fifty countries. He was poorly paid and equipped and, unusually amongst journalists, most comfortable reporting Africa from the level of its less privileged citizens.*

It is already the end of the journey. All that remains now is a brief rest in the shade of a tree, on the way back home. The tree grows in a village called Adofo, which lies near the Blue Nile in the Ethiopian province of Wollega. It is an enormous mango tree, with thick, eternally green foliage. Whoever travels across Africa's plateaux, through the immensity of the Sahel and the savannah, repeatedly sees a startling sight: on the great stretch of sandy, sun-burned ground, on plains covered with parched yellow grasses and sparsely growing, dry, thorny shrubs, there appears every now and then a single, solitary, magnificently branching tree. Its canopy is lush and vibrant, of so intense and saturated a color that it is visible from far away, a pronounced, vivid stain on the horizon. Its leaves, with no apparent trace of wind, move and shimmer. What is this tree doing here, in this dead, moonlike landscape? Why in this precise spot? Why only one? Where does it draw its juices from? Sometimes you will have to travel many kilometers before encountering another one like it.

Perhaps a great many trees used to grow here once, an entire forest that was cut down and burned, and only this one mango tree was left. Everyone from the surrounding area nurtures it, knowing how important it is that it live. A village lies near each one of these solitary trees. Indeed, spotting such a tree from far away, you can head with confidence in its direction, assured that you will find people there, some water, and maybe even something to eat. The tree was saved because without it these people could not live; in this kind of sun, man needs shade to survive, and the tree is that shade's depository and source.

If there is a teacher in the village, the area under the tree serves as the schoolroom. Village children gather here in the mornings. There are no separate classes or age limits. Whoever wants to, comes. The teacher pins to the trunk a piece of paper with the alphabet printed upon it. He points to each letter with a stick, and the children look and repeat after him. They must learn it by heart – they have nothing to write on or with.

When noontime arrives and the sky turns white from the heat, whoever can do so takes shelter in the tree's shade; children, adults, and if there are farm animals in the village, they come too – cows, sheep, goats. It is better to sit out the scorching hours under the tree than in one's own clay house. The houses are cramped and airless, while beneath the tree it is roomy and there is more hope of a breeze.

The afternoons under the tree are very important; it is when the older people gather for a conference. The mango tree is the only place to meet and talk, the village has no larger venue. People assemble eagerly and willingly, because Africans are collectivist by nature, and possess a great need to participate in everything that constitutes communal life. All decisions, such as who should get how much land to farm, are made collectively, and conflicts and disputes are jointly resolved. According to tradition, each resolution must be adopted unanimously. If someone has a differing opinion, the majority must persuade him to change his position. This can drag on endlessly, because the discussions are famously garrulous. If someone in the village is quarreling with someone else, then the court convened beneath the tree will not try to ascertain the truth, or where justice lies, but will set itself the sole task of ending the conflict and conciliating the warring sides, while granting to each that he is in the right.

When the day ends and darkness falls, the meeting is adjourned and everyone goes home. It is impossible to argue in the dark; discussion requires being able to see one's interlocutor's face, to determine whether his words and his eyes are saying the same thing.

Now women and the elderly gather beneath the tree, and children, who are curious about everything. If there is wood, a fire is built. If there is water and mint, a thick, aromatic tea is brewed. Now begins the most pleasant, their favorite, time of day: the retelling of the day's events, stories that mix fact and fiction, the joyous and the frightening. What dark, savage thing was making such a racket in the bushes that morning? What was that strange bird that flew by overhead and suddenly vanished? The children drove a mole into its burrow. They dug up the burrow – the mole wasn't there. What happened to it? As the stories unfold, people start to remember – that once, long ago, the old people used to tell of a strange bird that did indeed fly by and vanish. Someone else recalls that his grandfather used to tell of something dark that had long been making a noise in the bushes. How long ago? As far back as one can remember. Because here the outer reaches of memory are the limits of history. Earlier, there was nothing. Earlier does not exist. History is what is remembered.

Africa, except for the Muslim north, did not know writing, and history here is an oral tradition, legends passed from mouth to mouth, a communal myth created invariably at the base of the mango tree in the evening's profound darkness, in which only the trembling voices of old men resound, because the women and children are silent, raptly listening. That is why the evening hour is so important: it is the time when the community contemplates what it is and whence it came, becomes conscious of its distinctness and otherness, defines its identity. It is the hour for conversing with the ancestors, who have departed yet are nevertheless present, who lead us on through life, and protect us from evil.

In the evening, the quiet beneath the tree is only seemingly so. In reality, the stillness is brimming with the most varied voices, sounds, and whispers. They come from everywhere – from the high branches, from the surrounding bush, from beneath the ground, from the sky. It is best to be close to others at such moments, to feel one another's presence, for this brings comfort and courage. The African always feels endangered. Nature on this continent strikes such monstrous and aggressive poses, dons such vengeful and fearsome masks, sets such traps and ambushes, that man lives with a constant sense of anxiety about tomorrow, in unabating uncertainty and dread. Everything here appears in an inflated, unbridled, hysterically exaggerated form. If there is a storm, then the thunderbolts convulse the entire planet, the lightning tears the sky to shreds; if there is a downpour, then a veritable wall of water pours from the heavens, threatening at any moment now to drown us and pound us into the ground; if there is a drought, then it is one that does not leave a drop of water behind, and we die of thirst. There is nothing here to temper the relations between man and nature – no compromises, no in-between stages, no gradations. Only ceaseless struggle, battle, a fight to the finish. From birth until death, the African is on the front line, sparring with his continent's exceptionally hostile nature, and the mere fact that he is alive and knows how to endure is his greatest triumph.

EIGHT

<hr />

Unexpected Encounters

<hr />

It is the unexpected that has inspired these anecdotes. The traveller opens the door without knowing what will lie behind.

In the 1830s, Alexander Kinglake crossed the closely guarded divide between Europe and the Ottoman Empire, and got more than he expected from his dragoman. Joseph Thomson's objective in 1883 was to cross the Masai lands in Kenya, a notoriously forbidden region for outsiders, and he chanced upon a sight that was barely credible to, and never before seen by Europeans. Jonathan Raban's paean for solitary travel has the conclusion he might have least expected. Ryszard Kapuściński walks into the Congo, crossing the northern border very soon after Congolese independence in 1960. Redmond O'Hanlon, meanwhile, may not next time dismiss so easily the divinings of the féticheuse in Brazzaville.

<hr />

'Conversation with Moostapha Pasha'

<hr />

ALEXANDER KINGLAKE

Eothen: Traces of Travel Brought Home from the East (1844)

<hr />

Alexander Kinglake (1809–91) was a dilettante traveller, who nevertheless was very particular about how he presented himself in writing. It took him many years of rewriting before Eothen *was published in 1844, recording his earlier journeys in the Ottoman Empire and particularly Syria, Palestine and Egypt. Effectively the border between Europe and the Ottoman Empire was then in modern day Serbia between Semlin and Belgrade: 'The two frontier towns are less than a gunshot apart, yet their people hold no communion'. It was the dread of the plague more than political stand-off that enforced the divide. Any, even suspected, transgressors of the quarantine rules were summarily sentenced by a tribunal some fifty yards away, then shot from a similar distance.*

Having managed to cross the border, Kinglake was invited to meet the Pasha. The intermediary was the dragoman or translator.

The Pasha received us with the smooth, kind, gentle manner that belongs to well-bred Osmanlees; then he lightly clapped his hands, and instantly the sound filled all the lower end of the room with slaves; a syllable dropped from his lips; it bowed all heads, and conjured away the attendants like ghosts (their coming and their going was thus swift and quiet, because their feet were bare, and they passed through no door, but only by the yielding folds of a purder). Soon the coffee-bearers appeared, every man carrying separately his tiny cup in a small metal stand; and presently to each of us there came a pipe-bearer – a grave and solemn functionary, who first rested the bowl of the tchibouque at a measured distance on the floor, and then, on this axis, wheeled round the long cherry tube, and gracefully presented it on half-bended knee. Already the fire (well kindled beforehand) was glowing secure in the bowl; and so, when I pressed the amber lip to mine, there was no coyness to conquer – the willing fume came up, and answered my slightest sigh, and followed softly every breath inspired, till it touched me with some faint sense and understanding of Asiatic contentment.

Asiatic contentment! Yet hardly, perhaps, one hour before I had been wanting my bill, and ringing for waiters in a shrill and busy hotel.

In the Ottoman dominions there is scarcely any hereditary influence except that belonging to the family of the Sultan; and wealth, too, is a highly volatile blessing, not easily transmitted to the descendants of the owner. From these causes it results, that the people standing in the place of nobles and gentry, are official personages; and though many (indeed the greater number) of these potentates are humbly born and bred, you will seldom, I think, find them wanting in that polished smoothness of manner and those well-undulating tones which belong to the best Osmanlees. The truth is, that most of the men in authority have risen from their humble station by the arts of the courtier, and they keep in their high estate those gentle powers of fascination to which they owe their success. Yet, unless you can contrive to learn a little of the language, you will be rather bored by your visits of ceremony; the intervention of the dragoman is fatal to the spirit of conversation. I think I should mislead you if I were to attempt to give the substance of any particular conversation with Orientals. A traveller may write and say that 'the Pasha of So-and-so was particularly interested in the vast progress which has been made in the application of steam, and appeared to understand the structure of our machinery – that he remarked upon the gigantic results of our manufacturing industry – showed that he possessed considerable knowledge of our Indian affairs, and of the constitution of the Company, and expressed a lively admiration of the many sterling qualities for which the people of England are distinguished.' But the heap of commonplaces thus quietly attributed to the Pasha will have been founded perhaps on some such talking as this: –

Pasha – The Englishman is welcome; most blessed among hours is this, the hour of his coming.

Dragoman (to the Traveller) – The Pasha pays you his compliments.

Traveller – Give him my best compliments in return, and say I'm delighted to have the honour of seeing him.

Dragoman (to the Pasha) – His Lordship, this Englishman, Lord of London, Scorner of Ireland, Suppressor of France, has quitted his governments, and left his enemies to breathe for a moment, and has crossed the broad waters in strict disguise, with a small but eternally faithful retinue of followers, in order that he might look upon the bright countenance of the Pasha among Pashas – the Pasha of the everlasting Pashalik of Karagholookoldour.

Traveller (to his Dragoman) – What on earth have you been saying about London? The Pasha will be taking me for a mere Cockney. Have not I told you always to say, that I am from a branch of the family of Mudcombe Park, and that I am to be a magistrate for the county of Bedfordshire, only I've not qualified; and that I should have been a deputy-lieutenant, if it had not been for the extraordinary conduct of Lord Mountpromise; and that I was a candidate for Boughton-Soldborough at the last election, and that I should have won easy if my committee had not been bribed. I wish to heaven that if you do say anything about me, you'd tell the simple truth!

Dragoman – [is silent].

Pasha – What says the friendly Lord of London? Is there aught that I can grant him within the Pashalik of Karagholookoldour?

Dragoman (growing sulky and literal) – This friendly Englishman – this branch of Mudcombe – this head purveyor of Boughton-Soldborough – this possible policeman of Bedfordshire – is recounting his achievements and the number of his titles.

Pasha – The end of his honours is more distant than the ends of the earth, and the catalogue of his glorious deeds is brighter than the firmament of heaven.

Dragoman (to the Traveller) – The Pasha congratulates your Excellency.

Traveller – About Boughton-Soldborough? The deuce he does! – but I want to get at his views in relation to the present state of the Ottoman empire. Tell him the Houses of Parliament have met, and that there has been a speech from the Throne pledging England to maintain the integrity of the Sultan's dominions.

Dragoman (to the Pasha) – This branch of Mudcombe, this possible policeman of Bedfordshire, informs your Highness that in England the talking houses have met, and that the integrity of the Sultan's dominions has been assured for ever and ever by a speech from the velvet chair.

Pasha – Wonderful chair! Wonderful houses! – whirr! whirr! all by wheels! – whiz! whiz! all by steam! – wonderful chair! wonderful houses! wonderful people! – whirr! whirr! all by wheels! – whiz! whiz! all by steam!

Traveller (to the Dragoman) – What does the Pasha mean by that whizzing? He does not mean to say, does he, that our Government will ever abandon their pledges to the Sultan?

Dragoman – No, your Excellency, but he says the English talk by wheels and by steam.

Traveller – That's an exaggeration; but say that the English really have carried machinery to great perfection. Tell the Pasha (he'll be struck with that) that whenever we have any disturbances to put down, even at two or three hundred miles from London, we can send troops by the thousand to the scene of action in a few hours.

Dragoman (recovering his temper and freedom of speech) – His Excellency, this Lord of Mudcombe, observes to your Highness, that whenever the Irish, or the French, or the Indians rebel against the English, whole armies of soldiers and brigades of artillery are dropped into a mighty chasm called Euston Square, and, in the biting of a cartridge, they rise up again in Manchester, or Dublin, or Paris, or Delhi, and utterly exterminate the enemies of England from the face of the earth.

Pasha – I know it – I know all; the particulars have been faithfully related to me, and my mind comprehends locomotives. The armies of the English ride upon the vapours of boiling cauldrons, and their horses are flaming coals! – whirr! whirr! all by wheels! – whiz! whiz! all by steam!

Traveller (to his Dragoman) – I wish to have the opinion of an unprejudiced Ottoman gentleman as to the prospects of our English commerce and manufactures; just ask the Pasha to give me his views on the subject.

Pasha (after having received the communication of the Dragoman) – The ships of the English swarm like flies; their printed calicoes cover the whole earth, and by the side of their swords the blades of Damascus are blades of grass. All India is but an item in the ledger-books of the merchants whose lumber-rooms are filled with ancient thrones! – whirr! whirr! all by wheels! – whiz! whiz! all by steam!

Dragoman – The Pasha compliments the cutlery of England, and also the East India Company.

Traveller – The Pasha's right about the cutlery: I tried my scimitar with the common officers' swords belonging to our fellows at Malta, and they cut it like the leaf of a novel. Well (to the Dragoman), tell the Pasha I am exceedingly gratified to find that he entertains such a high opinion of our manufacturing energy, but I should like him to know, though, that we have got something in England besides that. These foreigners are always fancying that we have nothing but ships and railways, and East India Companies; do just tell the Pasha, that our rural districts deserve his attention, and that even within the last two hundred years there has been an evident improvement in the culture of the turnip; and if he does not take any interest about that, at all events you can explain that we have our virtues in the country – that we are a truth-telling people, and, like the Osmanlees, are faithful in the performance of our promises. Oh! and by the by, whilst you are about it, you may as well just say, at the end, that the British yeoman is still, thank God! the British yeoman.

Pasha (after hearing the Dragoman) – It is true, it is true: through all Feringhistan the English are foremost and best; for the Russians are drilled swine, and the Germans are sleeping babes, and the Italians are the servants of songs, and the French are the sons of newspapers, and the Greeks are the weavers of lies, but the English and the Osmanlees are brothers together in righteousness: for the Osmanlees believe in one only God, and cleave to the Koran, and destroy idols; so do the English worship one God, and abominate graven images, and tell the truth, and believe in a book; and though they drink the juice of the grape, yet to say that they worship their prophet as God, or to say that they are eaters of pork, these are lies – lies born of Greeks, and nursed by Jews.

Dragoman – The Pasha compliments the English.

Traveller (rising) – Well, I've had enough of this. Tell the Pasha I am greatly obliged to him for his hospitality, and still more for his kindness in furnishing me with horses, and say that now I must be off.

Pasha (after hearing the Dragoman, and standing up on his divan) – Proud are the sires, and blessed are the dams of the horses, that shall carry his Excellency to the end of his prosperous journey. May the saddle beneath him glide down to the gates of the happy city like a boat swimming on the third river of Paradise! May he sleep the sleep of a child, when his friends are around him; and the while that his enemies are abroad may his eyes flame red through the darkness – more red than the eyes of ten tigers! – farewell! Dragoman – The Pasha wishes your Excellency a pleasant journey. So ends the visit.

'As I stood entranced . . .'

JOSEPH THOMSON

Through Masai Land (1885)

In March 1883, Scottish explorer Joseph Thomson (1858–95) set off from the East African coast to walk to Lake Victoria. Sponsored by the Royal Geographical Society, he was trying to become the first white man to travel through Masai land, a tract of territory little known to outsiders and covering much of the Great Rift Valley, dominated by one of the most warlike tribes in Africa.

Everyone advised Thomson against it. Masai war parties were notorious for their hostility. He was assured that if the warriors didn't kill him, animals or disease certainly would.

Thomson went ahead and claimed to have disarmed Masai aggression by taking out his false teeth and persuading them that he was a witch doctor. He managed to get to Lake Victoria and back unharmed.

Through Masai Land was a publishing success in a Britain that was avid for foreign adventure tales; it is thought to have been the inspiration for Rider Haggard's King Solomon's Mines. *The Thomson heritage lives on throughout East Africa via the species of gazelle that was given his name.*

A short distance from camp I was attracted by a sound like the low roaring of a buffalo, near the top of a steep, wooded slope. As we were short of food, I set off to hunt it up. Peering about for some time to try to spot the exact locality of my game, I was nearly thrown on my beam-ends by a savage growl from a dense patch of tall grass and bamboos.

Looking towards the spot, I saw a fine leopard a few feet in front of me, showing its teeth in a ferocious manner and crouching as if it would spring upon me. Before I could fire it had bounded out of view. Rushing to the top of the ridge to get sight of it again, I was suddenly arrested by an object which fairly took my breath away.

Before me, in the foreground, lay a splendid interchange of grove and glade, of forest and plain, stretching in billowing reaches down to the marshy expanse of Kopè-Kopè. Beyond rose abruptly and very precipitously the black, uninhabited mountains of the Aberdare range. These features, however, were not what had fascinated me. It was something more distant.

Through a rugged and picturesque depression in the range rose a gleaming snow-white peak with sparkling facets, which scintillated with the superb beauty of a colossal diamond. It was, in fact, the very image of a great crystal or sugar-loaf.

At the base of this beautiful peak were two small excrescences like supporters to a monument. From these, at a very slight angle, shaded away a long glittering white line, seen above the dark mass of the Aberdare range like the silver lining of a dark storm-cloud. This peak and silvery line formed the central culminating point of Mount Kenia.

As I stood entranced at this fulfilment of my dearest hopes, I drew a great sigh of satisfaction; and as I said to Brahim, 'Look!' and pointed to the glittering crystal, I am not very sure but there was something like a tear in my eye. But now, even while I stood and gazed, a moisture-laden breeze touched the peak, wove a fleecy mantle, and gradually enshrouded the heaven-like spectacle.

In a few moments there but remained a bank of clouds over the wooded reach of Settima. But I had beheld a vision as if from the Unseen to lure me on.

<hr />

'But I got talking to a stranger'

JONATHAN RABAN

Driving Home: An American Journey (2011)

I have admitted to stealing my title from a Raban essay. British-born, but a resident of Seattle, Washington since 1990, Raban spans both cultures and has acquired the éminence grise *status that his many writing awards confirm. Perversely, he claims not to be really a traveller: 'Dorset for me is remote'. But his many peregrinations, particularly by boat (Coasting, Passage to Juneau, Old Glory: An American Voyage) give contrary evidence. Here he addresses and answers a seminal question: why travel? This essay was first published in the* Sunday Times *in January 1994.*

Bad weather and mishaps have led me to all sorts of curious places, from Port St Mary on the Isle of Man (where I landed up living for a year) to a strange island village in British Columbia, where all the men spoke in the Falls Road accent and responded to me as if I were the Special Branch in oilskins. In my experience, nowhere in the world is more compellingly beautiful than the cluster of houses round the harbour into which you've floundered out of a gale at sea: glorious Grimsby! kindly Pwllheli! merciful Dover! A five-foot swell with a cross-sea breaking over it can make a between-the-wars council house seem a fine piece of architecture, and an open pub a greater wonder than Chartres Cathedral.

The rougher the travel, the more you value the places where you stop and the people you meet there. Most of the glory that has attached itself to legendary destinations like Samarkand, Timbuktu, Mandalay derives, I suspect, from the dangers and miseries of getting to any of them. By the time that the Renaissance traveller at last had the citadel of Samarkand in view, he was in such a state of exhaustion, wonder and relief that he would have been no less ecstatic to find himself within sight of Potter's Bar. It's hard to replicate that sensation now, unless your plane has just made an emergency landing and you've helter-skeltered down the inflatable yellow chute, or you've sailed to Grimsby in a small boat.

I keep on writing *you*. I mean *tu* – the second person insistently singular. For this kind of pure, serendipitous travel is a solitary vice. Going with a companion is cosy, but you might as well be going with a coach party. The marital parliament has to sit in order to debate and settle the issue of lunch. You leave unexplored all the turnings that you would have taken on impulse if you were alone. The stranger doesn't approach you in the dark bar (you're up on the terrace, drinking cappuccino), you don't get off at the wrong station, you don't go netting larks with the retired lieutenant of police. Adapting Clausewitz, travelling in pairs and families is the continuation of staying at home by other means.

Most damagingly of all, in the luck and hap department, you are simply not lonely enough when you travel with companions. 'I was haemorrhaging with loneliness . . ' wrote Edward Hoagland in *African*

Calliope. That captures a mood. For spells of acute loneliness are an essential part of travel. Loneliness makes things happen. It's when you haven't spoken to a soul for days, when your whole being feels possessed by the rage for company, that even the withdrawn social coward feels an invigorating rush of desperate courage. Then you start risking things you wouldn't dare at home. Steeling yourself, you make that call; you go over to the stranger's table; you gratefully accept the dubious invitation. This is how adventures begin. This is why people find themselves waking up in strange beds and don't go home again.

Every journey is a quest of sorts, though few travellers have more than a dim inkling of what it is they're questing for. Most of us leave the house with, at best, a tangible absence in the heart, a void of indeterminate proportions, that we vaguely hope to fill with – what? some person as yet unmet? some life beyond the life we're leading? How can I know what I'm looking for until I see what I've found? But that sense of incompleteness gets us on the move. As the boat slips its moorings, or the familiar city tilts suddenly away, free of the climbing plane, and you remember with a pang the unlocked kitchen window and the unpaid telephone bill, you think, It doesn't matter, everything will be different when I come back; *I will be different when I come back.*

So watch the visitor standing in front of an illuminated estate agent's window in a foreign town, searching surreptitiously for that other life that has somehow escaped her until now. Her face is a study as she scans the laconic poetry of hectares, kitchens, beds and baths. She's raising goats from a tumbledown farmhouse in Provence. She's writing a screenplay in a rented apartment overlooking a Pacific beach in Venice, California. She's opening a small fish restaurant, with living quarters above on the not-as-yet-entirely-spoiled Greek island of Litotes. Travelling, the self goes soft and pliable. You can recast your life in shapes you wouldn't dream of when you're stuck at home.

The good traveller is an inveterate snoop, always ready to poke his nose into other people's business and ask impertinent questions. How much did you have to pay for your ox? How long does it take to learn to play the nose-flute? So how did you come to lose your other leg? The surreal dottiness of phrase-books is a true reflection of the fact that when people go abroad they really do say the weirdest things. But you have to ask some odd questions when you're trying out someone else's life for size. At home, I'm a grump; it's as much as I can do to pass the time of day with the mailman and the checkout clerk. On the road, I am a champion pesterer, milking people for the workaday details of what they do and how they do it, and always the underlying question is *Am I cut out for this, could this life be mine?* So, in imagination, I've been an agricultural-machinery salesman in the Middle East, a barge operator on the Rhine waterway system, a drug smuggler on the Florida Keys, a tuna fisherman in the Cape Verde Islands. I've grown olives in Tuscany and established a salmon farm in the Hebrides.

Worming your way into the skin of a true denizen, you begin to see the landscape itself as a real place and not just as the pretty backdrop to your own holiday. But it is a risky exercise. One day, you'll find a life that seems to be a perfect fit – and you'll be there for good. The world is littered with travellers who asked one question too many, got a satisfactory answer, and never went home again. It happened to me. For the last four years I've been living in a place that I went to visit for a month. But I got talking to a stranger.

'. . . if they wanted to kill me, they would kill me'

RYSZARD KAPUŚCIŃSKI

Travels with Herodotus (2004)

In 1960 Kapuściński was travelling as a roving reporter in the most literal sense of roving, as he rarely had money and had few contacts or introductions. Whereas most journalists court the leaders and decision makers, Kapuściński always sought to understand his destinations at their most basic levels. He was employed by the Polish Press Agency and Polityka *magazine and was certainly the only Polish reporter anywhere on the continent; indeed, it is not quite clear how he ever managed to get the assignment, which lasted for many years.*

His views on travel could be an epigraph for Scraps *as a whole:*

A journey, after all, neither begins when we set out, nor ends when we have reached our doorstep once again. It starts much earlier and is never really over, because the film of memory continues running on inside of us long after we have come to a physical standstill. Indeed, there exists something like the contagion of travel, and the disease is essentially incurable.

Here he has entered the Republic of Congo, as its name then was, without valid papers, from the Central African Republic. It was only a short time after the Belgian colonial authorities had granted independence with no preparation, leaving a country where tribal leaders had much more authority than any central government.

And the country of *Heart of Darkness* was also taking its toll on me, of course, what with the frequent eruption of gunfights, the constant danger of arrest, beatings, and death, and the pervasive climate of uncertainty, ambiguity, and unpredictability. The absolute worst could happen here at any moment and in any place. There was no government, no rule of law and order. The colonial system was collapsing, Belgian administrators were fleeing to Europe, and in their place was emerging a dark, deranged power, which most frequently assumed the guise of drunken Congolese military police.

One could see clearly how dangerous freedom is in the absence of hierarchy and order – or, rather, anarchy in the absence of ethics. Under such circumstances, the forces of evil aggression – all manner of villainy, brutishness, and bestiality – instantly gain the upper hand. And so it was in the Congo, which fell under the rule of these gendarmes. An encounter with any one of them could be deadly.

Here I am walking down the street in the small town of Lisali.

It is sunny, empty, and quiet.

Suddenly, I spot two policemen approaching from the opposite direction. I freeze. But running away makes no sense – there is no place to run to, and, furthermore, it is dreadfully hot and I can barely drag one foot after the other. The gendarmes are in fatigues, with deep helmets which cover half their faces, and bristling with armaments, each carrying an automatic rifle, grenades, knife, flare pistol, truncheon, and a metal implement combining spoon and fork – a portable arsenal. Why do they need it all? I wonder. And there is more. Their imposing silhouettes are also encircled with all kinds of belts and detachable linings, to which are sewn garlands of metal circles, pins, hooks, buckles.

Dressed in shorts and shirts, perhaps they would have seemed pleasant young men, the sort who would greet you politely and pleasantly offer directions if asked. But the uniform and the weaponry altered their nature and stance, and also performed yet another function: rendering difficult, even impossible, any normal human contact. The men walking toward me were not ordinary people to be casually encountered, but dehumanised creatures, extraterrestrials. A new species.

They were drawing nearer and I was dripping with sweat, my legs leaden and getting heavier by the second. The key to the entire situation was that they knew as well as I did that to whatever sentence they might impose there was no appeal. No higher authority, no tribunal. If they wanted to beat me, they would beat me; if they wanted to kill me, they would kill me. I have only ever felt true loneliness in circumstances such as these – when I have stood alone face-to-face with absolute violent power. The world grows empty, silent, depopulated, and finally recedes.

Furthermore, it is not merely two gendarmes and a reporter who are participating in this street scene in a small Congolese town. Also present is a huge swath of world history, which already set us against one another many centuries ago. Here between us stand generations of slave traders; the myrmidons of King Leopold, who cut off the hands and ears of the grandfathers of these policemen; the overseers of cotton and sugar plantations, whips in their hands. The memory of those torments was passed down for years in tribal stories, and the men whom I am about to encounter would have been reared on those tales, on legends ending with a promise of a day of retribution. And today is that day – both they and I know it.

What will happen? We are close already, and getting closer and closer. Finally, they stop. I too stop. And then, from under that mountain of gear and scrap iron, emerges a voice that I will never forget, its tone humble, even pleading:

'Monsieur, avez-vous une cigarette, s'il vous plait?'

———

'One of you', she said slowly in French, 'is very ill, *right now*'

REDMOND O'HANLON

Congo Journey (1996)

Redmond O'Hanlon is an adventurer and also one of the wittiest of all travel writers, but it is his scholarship as a natural scientist that really sets him apart. Here he is in Congo-Brazzaville preparing to launch himself and his new travelling partner (having been deserted by his previous partner, as described in Chapter six) into an upcountry jungle exploration.

In her hut in Poto-Poto, the poor quarter of Brazzaville, the féticheuse, smiling at us, knelt on the floor, drew out a handful of cowrie shells from the cloth bag at her waist, and cast them across the raffia mat.

Lary Shaffer and I, despite ourselves, leaned forward on our wooden stools, studying the meaningless pattern; the shells, obviously much handled, shone like old ivory in the glow of the paraffin lamp. The féticheuse stopped smiling.

'One of you', she said slowly in French, 'is very ill, *right now*.'

The rain seemed to clatter with increased urgency on the corrugated-iron roof. I had the absurd feeling that the other objects in the little breeze-block room – a pile of laundry in a red plastic bucket, a rough double-bed (its mosquito-net suspended from a hook on a cross-beam) – were watching us. It's simply that we're not yet acclimatised, I told myself, we've only been in the Congo for two days: a thought which immediately made the humidity and the heat doubly oppressive.

Lary, still staring at the floor, wiped the blisters of sweat from his forehead and the bridge of his nose. His hand, I noticed, was shaking.

'It's me,' he said, stumbling over his words. 'It's me. I'm the one who's ill. Nine years ago I was in a wheelchair. I have this thing called multiple sclerosis. I forced myself to walk again. One yard one day. Two yards the next. My sight came back. And then last year I cycled across America. Thirty-three days. West to east. Coast to coast. It's okay.'

'A wheelchair?' I said, unable to keep the panic out of my voice.

'I swim forty-five minutes a day. A mile and a quarter. I'm fit. I'm all right. You can see I'm fit. And anyway – I thought I'd rather die in Africa than strip paint in my house in Cornelia Street all summer. There's no problem. There's no worry. No need at all.'

'Please!' said the féticheuse, tossing her head right back and pressing her palms into her eyes. 'You must be quiet. If you talk one to the other I cannot see. And if I cannot see I cannot help you.' And then, 'Here, take these,' she said, opening her eyes, reaching forward, gathering up the shells and giving us three each. 'Hold these against a banknote and breathe your desires into them.'

With my free hand I drew two 1,000 CFA (two pound) notes out of my leg-pocket, gave one to Lary, and crumpled the other over the shells in my cupped palm.

'Now,' she said, 'who is responsible for all this?'

'I am,' I said, puffing out my chest.

'Then tell me – what is it that you really want? What is it that you want most when you are quiet inside? – and don't bother me with anything else, don't tell me the story you prepared for your wives.'

'I hope to go on a great journey through the far northern forests,' I said, liking the sound of the words, 'by dugout to the headwaters of the Motaba where we'll abandon the boats, walk east through the swamp jungle and across the watershed to the Ibenga, take a chance on finding another canoe, and then, if we're lucky, paddle down to the Likouala aux Herbes and walk to the hidden lake, Lake Télé, where Mokélé-mbembé, the Congo dinosaur, is said to live.'

'No! No! No!' sang the féticheuse.

'What's wrong? You think the army won't let us go? You think we'll never get out of Brazzaville?'

'You are not an educated man,' she said, exasperated, rattling the shells in her hand like dice in a box. 'You don't speak your desires. You think them. *I see everything.*'

She snatched my shells and the banknote and threw them hard across the mat; the note spun down like a sycamore seed.

'Your children love you,' she intoned, glancing with contempt at the scatter. 'Your wife loves you.'

I thought: I'll double her fee.

'If you stay for two months,' she said, already turning to Lary, 'the spirits of the forest will not harm you. But if you stay for two months and one day, you will die.'

'But I'm staying for six months!'

'Then you will die,' she said, fixing her attention on Lary with indecent haste and closing her eyes.

He held his shells and 1,000 CFA note in the approved manner and bowed his head. A drop of sweat fell from the end of his nose to the floor. His lips moved.

I realised, with a twinge of disquiet, that the subconscious of this all-American frontiersman (who had personally built three houses for himself at different stages of his life) was fully engaged with something in the room. Lary Shaffer, the emphatically rational Professor of Psychology at the State University of New York at Plattsburgh, was not responding as I thought a scientist should; this specialist in animal behaviour, who had been film cameraman to the Nobel-laureate Niko

Tinbergen at Oxford and written his doctoral thesis on the predation of crabs by Lesser black-backed gulls – this man, I decided, had momentarily lost touch with his own view of the world. But then it dawned on me how presumptuous I'd been: you haven't seen him since you were at university together twenty years ago, I thought, you hardly know him. Or maybe, I comforted myself, it's just that in a mere two days of heat and anxiety and far too much whisky, Africa has got to us.

The féticheuse took Lary's cowries and banknote from him, laid the note carefully at her side, added his shells to her own, spread them across the mat with a gentle roll of her wrists, stared at their pattern – and began to rock backward and forward like a deserted child.

'You think too much,' she said, her voice rising in pitch, becoming startlingly high. 'You have too many worries for one man to bear. You have great problems with your wives. You have led a life broken in many places. Each time you have mended yourself and begun again.'

Lary opened his eyes wide.

'That's right,' he said. 'My mother and then my father died; I got ill; my marriage unravelled; my wife went to live in California with an African American; and the night before I flew out of New York to London to join Redmond and come here I had a phone call – the voice said, "Hi, Daddy, I'm your daughter. It's my birthday. I'm twenty-one. I'm allowed to speak to you." I didn't know. I have a daughter that I've never seen. My only child. I never played with her. I never saw her grow up. Twenty-one years ago I had a row with my girlfriend – we said terrible things to each other and we parted and I went to Oxford and that was that; she never told me.'

We were silent, staring at the floor. The cowrie shell by my boots lay on its tortoise-shaped back, the long slender opening of its underside exposed. It was easy to see, I thought blankly, why a cowrie worn round a woman's neck was supposed to ensure conception and ease childbirth.

I wondered how it had got here: it was a genuine money cowrie, *Cypraea moneta* from the Maldive Islands in the Indian Ocean, perhaps brought to Egypt by an Arab dhow in the thirteenth century, traded along the north coast by Arab merchants, south across the Sahara in a saddle-bag slung on a camel, and then on from one small kingdom to another until it reached Central Africa. Or maybe it arrived in a European slave ship: a stray statistic whined in my skull like a mosquito: in 1520 the Portuguese were paying 6,370 cowries for one man or woman. '6,370,' sang the mosquito, '6,370 . . .'

With a convulsive gesture, Lary pushed both hands up over his head as if trying to scalp himself. A startled gecko moved fast across the wall beside him and stopped, its toes as delicate as ivy tendrils.

He gave me a small wry smile: 'And now,' he said, 'I'm in the sucking Congo.'

The féticheuse retrieved her cowries and the two notes, put them in her bag and got to her feet. We stood up. 'You are full of courage,' she said to Lary, drawing aside the plastic-strip curtain that served as a door to the outer room. 'You have made yourself strong. You are a brave man. You are a good man.' She touched his arm and smiled at him, a smile that lit up her tired eyes and, for a moment, transformed her into a young girl.

NINE

Americans Leaving Home

There are writers from eighteen different countries of birth in *Scraps*. The second largest, after the British contingent, is from the USA. Here, four Americans describe their early or first written adventures. For Jack Kerouac it included his first time outside the USA; for Mark Twain his first long departure from home. Bill Bryson had long since left home and lived in the UK, so he was returning to the USA to write his first book. William Least Heat-Moon was travelling alone for the first time following the breakdown of his first marriage.

'Zut alors! Hey, Jacques, clock those mountains. They look just like my wife's tetons.'

BILL BRYSON

The Lost Continent (1989)

Bill Bryson (b. 1951) set the tone with line one of his first major travel book: 'I come from Des Moines, Iowa. Somebody had to'. He brought travel writing to a wider audience with humour, a challenge to the relative seriousness of the previous generations' travel books. He went on to stretch the genre to an intergalactic scale and mix it with science in A Short History of Nearly Everything.

In the morning I drove to Wyoming, through scenery that looked like an illustration from some marvellous children's book of Western tales – snowy peaks, pine forests, snug farms, a twisting river, a mountain vale with a comely name: Swan Valley. That is the one thing that must be said for the men and women who carved out the West. They certainly knew how to name a place. Just on this corner of the map I could see Soda Springs, Massacre Rocks, Steamboat Mountain, Wind River, Flaming Gorge, Calamity Falls – places whose very names promised adventure and excitement, even if in reality all they contained were a DX gas station and a Tastee-Freez drive-in.

Most of the early settlers in America were oddly inept at devising place-names. They either chose unimaginative, semi-recycled names – New York, New Hampshire, New Jersey, New England – or toadying, kiss-ass names like Virginia, Georgia, Maryland and Jamestown in a generally pitiable attempt to secure favour with some monarch or powdered aristocrat back home. Or else they just accepted the names the Indians told them, not knowing whether Squashaninsect meant 'land of the twinkling lakes' or 'place where Big Chief Thunderclap paused to pass water'.

The Spanish were even worse because they gave everything religious names, so that every place in the south-west is called San this or Santa that. Driving across the south-west is like an 800-mile religious procession. The worst name on the whole continent is the Sangre de Cristo mountains in New Mexico, which means the 'Blood of Christ Mountains'. Have you ever heard of a more inane name for any geographical feature? It was only here in the real West, the land of beaver trappers and mountain men, that a dollop of romance and colour was brought to the business of giving names. And here I was about to enter one of the most beautiful and understatedly romantic of them all: Jackson Hole.

Jackson Hole isn't really a hole at all; it's just the name for a scenic valley that runs from north to south through the Grand Tetons, very probably the most majestic range in the Rockies. With their high white peaks and bluish-grey bases they look like some kind of exotic confection, like blueberry frappés. At the southern edge of Jackson Hole is the small town of Jackson, where I stopped now for lunch. It was a strange place, with an odd combination of bow-legged Yosemite Sams and upmarket stores like Benetton and Ralph Lauren, which are there for the benefit of the many well-heeled tenderfeet who come for the skiing in the winter and to dude ranches in the summer. Every place in town had a Wild West motif – the Antler Motel, the Silver Dollar Saloon, the Hitching Post Lodge. Even the Bank of Jackson, where I went to cash a traveller's cheque, had a stuffed buffalo head on the wall. Yet it all seemed quite natural. Wyoming is the most fiercely Western of all the Western states. It's still a land of cowboys and horses and wide open spaces, a place where a man's gotta do what a man's gotta do, which on the face of it primarily consists of driving around in a pickup truck and being kind of slow. I had never seen so many people in cowboy apparel, and almost everybody owns a gun. Only a couple of weeks before, the state legislature in Cheyenne had introduced a rule that all legislators would henceforth have to check their handguns at the front desk before being allowed into the Statehouse. That's the sort of state Wyoming is.

I drove on to Grand Teton National Park. And there's another arresting name for you. 'Tetons' means 'tits' in French. That's an interesting fact – a topographical titbit, so to speak – that Miss Mucus, my junior high school geography teacher, failed to share with us in the eighth grade. Why do they always keep the most interesting stuff from you in school? If I'd known in high school that Thomas Jefferson kept a black slave to help him deal with sexual tension or that Ulysses S. Grant was a hopeless drunk who couldn't button his own flies without falling over, I would have shown a livelier interest in my lessons, I can assure you.

At any rate, the first French explorers who passed through north-western Wyoming took one look at the mountains and said, 'Zut alors! Hey, Jacques, clock those mountains. They look just like my wife's tetons.' Isn't it typical of the French to reduce everything to a level of sexual vulgarity? Thank goodness they didn't discover the Grand Canyon, that's all I can say. And the remarkable thing is that the Tetons look about as much like tits as ... well, as a frying-pan or a pair of hiking boots. In a word, they don't look like tits at all, except perhaps to desperately lonely men who have been away from home for a very long time. They looked a little bit like tits to me.

'You have seen something worth remembering'

MARK TWAIN

Life on the Mississippi (1883)

Mark Twain (aka Samuel Langhorne Clemens, 1835–1910) has been called both 'the father of American literature' and 'the greatest American humorist of his age'. He was brought up in Missouri on the Mississippi and trained as a steamboat pilot on the river. Life on the Mississippi *is a travel memoir of those days, but written later. It is reputed to be the first book submitted to its publisher in typewritten form.*

I had myself called with the four o'clock watch, mornings, for one cannot see too many summer sunrises on the Mississippi. They are enchanting.

First, there is the eloquence of silence; for a deep hush broods everywhere. Next, there is the haunting sense of loneliness, isolation, remoteness from the worry and bustle of the world. The dawn creeps in stealthily; the solid walls of black forest soften to gray, and vast stretches of the river open up and reveal themselves; the water is glass-smooth, gives off spectral little wreaths of white mist, there is not the faintest breath of wind, nor stir of leaf; the tranquillity is profound and infinitely satisfying. Then a bird pipes up, another follows, and soon the pipings develop into a jubilant riot of music. You see none of the birds; you simply move through an atmosphere of song which seems to sing itself.

When the light has become a little stronger, you have one of the fairest and softest pictures imaginable. You have the intense green of the massed and crowded foliage near by; you see it paling shade by shade in front of you; upon the next projecting cape, a mile off or more, the tint has lightened to the tender young green of spring; the cape beyond that one has almost lost color, and the furthest one, miles away under the horizon, sleeps upon the water a mere dim vapor, and hardly separable from the sky above it and about it. And all this stretch of river is a mirror, and you have the shadowy reflections of the leafage and the curving shores and the receding capes pictured in it. Well, that is all beautiful; soft and rich and beautiful; and when the sun gets well up, and distributes a pink flush here and a powder of gold yonder and a purple haze where it will yield the best effect, you grant that you have seen something that is worth remembering.

We had the Kentucky Bend country in the early morning – scene of a strange and tragic accident in the old times. Captain Poe had a small stern-wheel boat, for years the home of himself and his wife. One night the boat struck a snag in the head of Kentucky Bend, and sank with astonishing suddenness; water already well above the cabin floor when the captain got aft. So he cut into his wife's state-room from above with an ax; she was asleep in the upper berth, the roof a flimsier one than was supposed; the first blow crashed down through the rotten boards and clove her skull.

This bend is all filled up now – result of a cut-off; and the same agent has taken the great and once much-frequented Walnut Bend, and set it away back in a solitude far from the accustomed track of passing steamers.

Helena we visited, and also a town I had not heard of before, it being of recent birth – Arkansas City. It was born of a railway; the Little Rock, Mississippi River and Texas Railroad touches the river there. We asked a passenger who belonged there what sort of a place it was. 'Well,' said he, after considering, and with the air of one who wishes to take time and be accurate, 'It's a hell of a place.' A description which was photographic for exactness. There were several rows and clusters of shabby frame houses, and a supply of mud sufficient to insure the town against a famine in that article for a hundred years; for the overflow had but lately subsided. There were stagnant ponds in the streets, here and there, and a dozen rude scows were scattered about, lying aground wherever they happened to have been when the waters drained off and people could do their visiting and shopping on foot once more.

"'My God!" he cried, slapping the wheel. "It's the world!'"

JACK KEROUAC

On the Road (1957)

Published in 1957, but written a few years earlier, On the Road *was a rite-of-passage book for Americans of the beat generation discovering travel – the first generation that did so en masse. Kerouac was a poet and a novelist;* On the Road *is a travel story converted into novel form. Kerouac introduces himself as the narrator, Sal Paradise, and celebrated beat generation friends such as poet Allen Ginsberg and novelist William Burroughs are also represented in the book.*

Later Kerouac wrote: 'Dean and I were embarked on a journey through post-Whitman America to FIND that America and to FIND the inherent goodness in American man'. Then, with a cultural frisson, they also found abroad, which for them was the nearest abroad they could find, Mexico. 'It's the world!'

Then we turned our faces to Mexico with bashfulness and wonder as those dozens of Mexican cats watched us from under their secret hatbrims in the night. Beyond were music and all-night restaurants with smoke pouring out of the door. 'Whee,' whispered Dean very softly.

'Thassall!' A Mexican official grinned. 'You boys all set. Go ahead. Welcome Mehico. Have good time. Watch you money. Watch you driving. I say this to you personal, I'm Red, everybody call me Red. Ask for Red. Eat good. Don't worry. Everything fine. Is not hard enjoin yourself in Mehico.'

'Yes!' shuddered Dean and off we went across the street into Mexico on soft feet. We left the car parked, and all three of us abreast went down the Spanish street into the middle of the dull brown lights. Old men sat on chairs in the night and looked like Oriental junkies and oracles. No one was actually looking at us, yet everybody was aware of everything we did. We turned sharp left into the smoky lunchroom and went in to music of campo guitars on an American 'thirties jukebox. Shirt-sleeved Mexican cabdrivers and straw-hatted Mexican hipsters sat at stools, devouring shapeless messes of tortillas, beans, tacos, whatnot. We bought three bottles of cold beer – *cerveza* was the name of beer – for about thirty Mexican cents or ten American cents each. We bought packs of Mexican cigarettes for six cents each. We gazed and gazed at our wonderful Mexican money that went so far, and played with it and looked around and smiled at everyone. Behind us lay the whole of America and everything Dean and I had previously known about life, and life on the road. We had finally found the magic land at the end of the road and we never dreamed the extent of the magic. '*Think* of these cats staying up all hours of the night,' whispered Dean. 'And think of this big continent ahead of us with those enormous Sierra Madre mountains we saw in the movies, and the jungles all the way down and a whole desert plateau as big as ours and reaching clear down to Guatemala and God knows where, whoo! What'll we do? What'll we do? Let's move!' We got out and went back to the car. One last glimpse of America across the hot lights of the Rio Grande bridge, and we turned our back and fender to it and roared off.

Instantly we were out in the desert and there wasn't a light or a car for fifty miles across the flats. And just then dawn was coming over the Gulf of Mexico and we began to see the ghostly shapes of yucca cactus and organpipe on all sides. 'What a wild country!' I yelped. Dean and I were completely awake. In Laredo we'd been half dead. Stan, who'd been to foreign countries before, just calmly slept in the back seat. Dean and I had the whole of Mexico before us.

'Now, Sal, we're leaving everything behind us and entering a new and unknown phase of things. All the years and troubles and kicks – and now this! So that we can safely think of nothing else and just go on ahead with our faces stuck out like this, you see, and *understand* the world as, really and genuinely speaking, other Americans haven't done before us – they were here, weren't they? The Mexican war. Cutting across here with cannon.'

'This road,' I told him, 'is also the route of old American outlaws who used to skip over the border and go down to old Monterrey, so if you'll look out on that graying desert and picture the ghost of an old Tombstone hellcat making his lonely exile gallop into the unknown, you'll see further . . .'

'It's the world,' said Dean. 'My God!' he cried, slapping the wheel. 'It's the world! We can go right on to South America if the road goes. Think of it! Son-of-a-*bitch*! Gawd-*damn*!' We rushed on. The dawn spread immediately and we began to see the white sand of the desert and occasional huts in the distance off the road. Dean slowed down to peer at them. 'Real beat huts, man, the kind you only find in Death Valley and much worse. These people don't *bother* with appearances.' The first town ahead that had any consequence on the map was called Sabinas Hidalgo. We looked forward to it eagerly. 'And the road don't look any different than the American road,' cried Dean, 'except one mad thing and if you'll notice, right here, the mileposts are written in kilometers and they click off the distance to Mexico City. See, it's the only city in the entire land, everything points to it.' There were only 767 more miles to that metropolis; in kilometers the figure was over a thousand. 'Damn! I gotta go!' cried Dean. For a while I closed my eyes in utter exhaustion and kept hearing Dean pound the wheel with his fists and say, 'Damn,' and 'What kicks!' and 'Oh, what a land!' and 'Yes!' We arrived at Sabinas Hidalgo, across the desert, at about seven o'clock in the morning. We slowed down completely to see this. We woke up Stan in the back seat. We sat up straight to dig. The main street was muddy and full of holes. On each side were dirty broken-down adobe fronts. Burros walked in the street with packs. Barefoot women watched us from dark doorways. The street was completely crowded with people on foot beginning a new day in the Mexican countryside. Old men with handlebar mustaches stared at us. The sight of three bearded, bedraggled American youths instead of the usual well-dressed tourists was of unusual interest to them. We bounced along over Main Street at ten miles an hour, taking everything in. A group of girls walked directly in front of us. As we bounced by, one of them said, 'Where you going, man?'

I turned to Dean, amazed. 'Did you hear what she said?'

Dean was so astounded he kept on driving slowly and saying, 'Yes, I heard what she said, I certainly damn well did, oh me, oh my, I don't know what to do I'm so excited and sweetened in this morning world. We've finally got to heaven. It couldn't be cooler, it couldn't be grander, it couldn't be *anything*.'

'Well, let's go back and pick em up!' I said.

'Yes,' said Dean and drove right on at five miles an hour. He was knocked out, he didn't have to do the usual things he would have done in America. 'There's millions of them all along the road!' he said. Nevertheless he U-turned and came by the girls again. They were headed for work in the fields; they smiled at us. Dean stared at them with rocky eyes. 'Damn,' he said under his breath. '*Oh!* This is too great to be true. Gurls, gurls. And particularly right now in my stage and condition, Sal, I am digging the interiors of these homes as we pass them – these gone doorways and you look inside and see beds of straw and little brown kids sleeping and stirring to wake, their thoughts congealing from the empty mind of sleep, their selves rising, and the mother's cooking up breakfast in iron pots, and dig them shutters they have for windows and the old men, the old *men* are so cool and grand and not bothered by anything. There's no *suspicion* here, nothing like that. Everybody's cool, everybody looks at you with such straight brown eyes and they don't say anything, just *look*, and in that look all of the human qualities are soft and subdued and still there. Dig all the foolish stories you read about Mexico and the sleeping gringo and all that crap – and crap about greasers and so on – and all it is, people here are straight and kind and don't put down any bull. I'm so amazed by this.' Schooled in the raw road night, Dean was come into the world to see it. He bent over the wheel and looked both ways and rolled along slowly. We stopped for gas the other side of Sabinas Hidalgo. Here a congregation of local straw-hatted ranchers with handlebar mustaches growled and joked in front of antique gas-pumps. Across the fields an old man plodded with a burro in front of his switch stick. The sun rose pure on pure and ancient activities of human life.

'I lay quietly like a small idea in a vacant mind'

WILLIAM LEAST HEAT-MOON

Blue Highways (1982)

Born (more prosaically) William Lewis Trogdon in Kansas City in 1939, Heat-Moon's name derives from his native Indian Osage heritage, Least indicating his position in the family after his brother Little Heat-Moon. In 1982–3, Blue Highways *spent an unprecedented, for a travel book, forty-two weeks on the* New York Times *bestseller list. It chronicles the three months and 13,000 miles that Heat-Moon covered on the back roads (blue roads on the map) of Middle America following his separation from his first wife.*

In Poplar, Montana, where Sitting Bull surrendered six years after the battle of the Little Big Horn, I stopped for groceries. Having resisted a chewing hunger for five days – before meals, after meals, in moments of half-sleep – I gave in to it east of Wolf Point and bought a pound of raisins, a pound of peanuts, and a pound of chocolate nibs and mixed them together. By the time I got across North Dakota the bag was empty, the hunger gone.

U.S. 2 followed the Missouri River for miles. At the High-line town of Culbertson I turned north toward treeless Plentywood, Montana, then went east again down forsaken highway 5, a road virtually on the for-ty-ninth parallel, which is the Canadian border in North Dakota. In a small flourish of hills, the last I was to see for hundreds of miles, on an upthrusted lump sat a cube of concrete with an Air Force radar antenna sweeping the long horizon for untoward blips. A Martello tower of the twentieth century. Below the installation, in the Ice Age land, lay a fine, clear lake. Fingerlings whisked the marsh weed, coots twittered on the surface, and at bankside a muskrat munched greens. It seemed as if I were standing between two worlds. But they were one: a few permuta-tions of life going on about themselves, each thing trying to continue its way.

East of Fortuna, North Dakota, just eight miles south of Saskatche-wan, the high moraine wheat fields took up the whole landscape. There was nothing else, except piles of stones like Viking burial mounds at the verges of tracts and big rock-pickers running steely fingers through the glacial soil of glean stone that freezes had heaved to the surface; behind the machines, the fields looked vacuumed. At a filling station, a man who had farmed the moraine said the great ice sheets had gone away only to get more rock. 'They'll be back. They always come back. What's to stop them?'

The country gave up the glacier hills and flattened to perfection. The road went on, on, on. Straight and straight. Ahead and behind, it ran through me like an arrow. North Dakota up here was a curveless place: not just roads but land, people too, and the flight of birds. Things were angular: fenceposts against the sky, the line if a jaw, the ways of mind, the lay of crops.

The highway, oh, the highway. No place, in theory, is boring of itself. Boredom lies only in the traveler's limited perception and his failure to explore deeply enough. After a while I found my perception limited. The Great Plains, showing so many miles in an immodest exposure of itself, wearied my eyes; the openness was overdrawn. The only mitigation came from potholes, ice sheets had gouged out; there, margins and water were full of stilt-legged birds – godwits, sandpipers, plovers, dowitchers, avocets, yellowlegs – and paddling birds – coots, mallards, canvasbacks, redheads, blue-winged teals, pintails, shovelers, scaups, mergansers, eared grebes, widgeons, Canada geese. Whenever the drone of tread against the pavement began to overcome me, I'd stop and shake the drowsiness among the birds.

You'd think anything giving variety to this near blankness would be prized, yet when a Pleistocene pond got in the way, the road cut right through it, never yielding its straightness to nature. If you fired a rifle down the highway, a mile or so east you'd find the spent slug in the middle of the blacktop.

Here the earth, as if to prove its immensity, empties itself. Gertrude Stein said: 'In the United States there is more space where nobody is than where anybody is. That is what makes America what it is.' The uncluttered stretches of the American West and the deserted miles of roads force a lone traveler to pay attention to them leaving him isolated in them. This squander of land substitutes a sense of self with a sense of place by giving him days of himself until, tiring of his own small compass, he looks for relief to the bigness outside – a grandness that demands attention not just for its scope, but for its age, its diversity, its continual change. The isolating immensity reveals what lies covered in places noisier, busier, more filled up. For me, what I saw revealed was this (only this): a man nearly desperate because his significance had come to lie within his own narrow ambit.

Onward across the appallingly fearless yonder of North Dakota where towns, like the poor verse of Burma Shave signs, came and went quickly; on across fields where farmers planted wheat, rye, barley, and flax, their tractors sowing close to fences marking off missile silos that held Minutemen waiting in the dark underground like seeds of another sort. As daylight went, the men, racing rain and the short growing season, switched on headlights to keep the International Harvesters moving over cropland that miracles of land-grant colleges (cross-pollinated hybrids resistant to everything but growth and petro-chemicals) had changed forever. The farmer's enemy wasn't a radar blip – it was the wild oat.

At last the horizon ruptured at the long hump of Turtle Mountain, obscurely scrubby against the sky, and a pair of silent owls (Indians called them 'hushwings') swooped the dusk to look for telltale movements in the fields.

I needed a hot shower. In Rolla, on the edge of the Turtle Mountain reservation, I stopped at an old house rebuilt into a small hotel. Despite a snarl of a clerk, it looked pleasant; but the floors smelled of disinfectant and the shower was a rusting box at the end of the hall. The nozzle sent one stinging jet of water into my eye, another up my nose, two others over the shower curtain, while most of the water washed down the side to stand icily in the plugged bottom. I lost my temper and banged the shower head. The Neathanderthal remedy.

In a hotel room at the geographical center of North America, a neon sign blinking red through the cold curtains, I lay quietly like a small idea in a vacant mind.

TEN

The Romance of Arabia

The romance of Arabia was nurtured, created even, over the dining tables of members of the western world's geographical societies. Travellers went in search of it and returned to interpret the reality for their readers. Three of these stand out and could be an Arabian library on their own: Doughty, Lawrence and Thesiger. They were each a generation apart, the later ones building on the mystique cultivated by their predecessors and others such as Richard Burton, Harry St John Bridger Philby and Bertram Thomas. All three wanted to convey the Arabia that they admired, and the values and traditions of the Bedu, but also had an eye for their own reputations. All three were probably ill at ease with aspects of themselves or their circumstances, and found in Arabia some welcome anonymity and, despite serious hardship and danger, even refuge.

'I thought the stars were so disposed that I should not go to Arabia'

CHARLES DOUGHTY

Travels in Arabia Deserta (1888)

'The book is not milk for babes' Doughty (1843–1926), who regarded himself as a poet rather than an explorer, wrote in the preface to the first edition.

Indeed it was not, it was a hardly penetrable 1200 page work. It might have been lost and unregarded but for the republication arranged by T. E. Lawrence and with an introduction written by him in 1921. It would not be here in Scraps *but for the impassioned advocacy of Jan Morris (as explained in chapter twenty-three). She told me that she read it in Palestine, having bought it in Steimatzky's Bookshop in Jerusalem. 'One would never read the whole book, too dull. But open any page and you will find a little jewel'. The jewels are the result partly of his knowledge of many diverse subjects, geology, archaeology, all the natural sciences, together with his obsessive interest in taking the English language back to what he saw as the relative linguistic purity of the seventeenth century and beyond. The result is a prose style that has no modern equal; poetic, precise, evocative and strangely archaic.*

The book has been reissued in several progressively less dense editions and under different names: Travels in Arabia Deserta, Wanderings in Arabia *and the most recent and most abridged version* Arabia Deserta *(Bloomsbury 1989) that is illustrated with contemporary photographs, many taken by Gertrude Bell. This passage uses the 1908 edition.*

A new voice hailed me of an old friend when, first returned from the Peninsula, I paced again in that long street of Damascus which is called Straight; and suddenly taking me wondering by the hand, 'Tell me,' said he, 'since thou art here again in the peace and assurance of Allah, whilst we walk as in the former years toward the new blossoming orchards full of the sweet spring as the garden of God, what moved thee, or how couldst thou, take such journeys into the fanatic Arabia?'

It was at the latest hour, when in the same day, and after troubled days of endeavour, I had supposed it impossible. At first I had asked of the *Waly*, Governor of Syria, his license to accompany the *Haj* pilgrims' caravan to the distance of *Medain Salih*. The Waly then privately questioned the British Consulate, an office which is of much regard in these countries. The Consul answered that his was no charge in any such matter: he had as much regard of me, would I take such dangerous ways, as of his old hat.

. . .

Thus rejected by the British Consulate, I dreaded to be turned back altogether if I should visit now certain great personages of Damascus, as the noble Algerian prince *Abd el-Kader*, for whose only word's sake, which I am well assured he would have given, I would have been welcome in all the Haj Road towers occupied by Moorish garrisons, and my life not well-nigh lost amongst them later at Medain Salih.

I went only to the Kurdish Pasha of the Haj, Mohammed Sayid, who two years before had known me as a traveller in the Lands Beyond Jordan, and took me for a well-affected man that did nothing covertly . . . But now he said, 'Well! Would I needs go thither? It might be with the *Jurdy:*' that is the flying provision train which since ancient times is sent down from Syria to relieve the returning pilgrimage at Medain Salih; but commonly lying there only three days, the time would not have sufficed me.

I thought the stars were so disposed that I should not go to Arabia; but, said my Moslem friends, 'the Pasha himself could not forbid any taking this journey with the caravan. And though I were a *Nasrany* – a Christian – what hindered, when I went not down to Mecca and Medina, but to Medain Salih? How is it that I, an honest person, might not go, when there went down every year with the Haj all the desperate types of the town; nay, the most dangerous ribalds of Damascus were already at Muzeyrib, to kill and to spoil upon the skirts of the caravan journeying in the wilderness.'

It was afternoon when a few Arab friends bade me Godspeed, and mounted with my camel bags upon a mule I came riding through Damascus with the Persian, Mohammed Aga, and a small company. As we turned from the long city street, that which in Paul's days was called 'the Straight,' to go up through the *Medan* to the *Boabat-Ullah*, some of the bystanders at the corner, setting upon me with their eyes, said to each other 'Who is this? Eigh!' Another answered half jestingly, 'It is some one belonging to the *Ajamy*' (Persian). From the Boabat (great gate of) Ullah, so named of the passing forth of the great pilgrimage thereat, the high desert lies before us those hundreds of leagues to the Harameyn (two sacred cities); at first a waste plain of gravel and loam upon limestone, for ten or twelve days, and always rising, to *Maan* in the 'mountain of Edom' near to Petra. Twenty-six marches from Muzeyrib is el-Medina, the prophet's city . . . at forty marches is Mecca. There were none now in all the road, by which the last hajjies had passed five days before us. The sun setting, we came to the little out-lying village *Kesmih*: by the road was showed me a white cupola, the sleeping station of the commander of the pilgrimage, *Emir el-Haj*, in the evening of his solemn setting forth from Damascus. We came by a beaten way over the wilderness, paved of old at the crossing of winterstream-beds for the safe passage of the Haj camels, which have no foothold in sliding ground; by some other are seen ruinous bridges – all is now ruinous in the Ottoman Empire. There is a block drift strewed over this wilderness; the like is found, much to our amazement under all climates of the world.

We had sorry night quarters at Kesmih, to lie out, with falling weather, in a filthy field, nor very long to repose.

'you see what a tiny place you occupy in the world'

T. E. LAWRENCE

Seven Pillars of Wisdom (1926)

Despite the unhelpfully grandiose title, Seven Pillars *is the story of Lawrence's (1888–1935) involvement in the Arab Revolt against the Ottomans in the First World War and his travels around Transjordan and Palestine, during which he instigated the revolt and befriended its leaders.*

These are the surprising opening paragraphs, which are in part an apologia or justification for some of what is to come. They were chosen by Wade Davis (Time for Silence) *for reasons explained in Chapter twenty-three.*

Some of the evil of my tale may have been inherent in our circumstances. For years we lived anyhow with one another in the naked desert, under the indifferent heaven. By day the hot sun fermented us; and we were dizzied by the beating wind. At night we were stained by dew, and shamed into pettiness by the innumerable silences of stars. We were a self-centred army without parade or gesture, devoted to freedom, the second of man's creeds, a purpose so ravenous that it devoured all our strength, a hope so transcendent that our earlier ambitions faded in its glare.

As time went by our need to fight for the ideal increased to an unquestioning possession, riding with spur and rein over our doubts. Willy-nilly it became a faith. We had sold ourselves into its slavery, manacled ourselves together in its chain-gang, bowed ourselves to serve its holiness with all our good and ill content. The mentality of ordinary human slaves is terrible – they have lost the world – and we had surrendered, not body alone, but soul to the overmastering greed of victory. By our own act we were drained of morality, of volition, of responsibility, like dead leaves in the wind.

The everlasting battle stripped from us care of our own lives or of others'. We had ropes about our necks, and on our heads prices which showed that the enemy intended hideous tortures for us if we were caught. Each day some of us passed; and the living knew themselves just sentient puppets on God's stage: indeed, our taskmaster was merciless, merciless, so long as our bruised feet could stagger forward on the road. The weak envied those tired enough to die; for success looked so remote, and failure a near and certain, if sharp, release from toil. We lived always in the stretch or sag of nerves, either on the crest or in the trough of waves of feeling. This impotency was bitter to us, and made us live only for the seen horizon, reckless what spite we inflicted or endured, since physical sensation showed itself meanly transient. Gusts of cruelty, perversions, lusts ran lightly over the surface without troubling us; for the moral laws which had seemed to hedge about these silly accidents must be yet fainter words. We had learned that there were pangs too sharp, griefs too deep, ecstasies too high for our finite selves to register. When emotion reached this pitch the mind choked; and memory went white till the circumstances were humdrum once more.

Such exaltation of thought, while it let adrift the spirit, and gave it licence in strange airs, lost it the old patient rule over the body. The body was too coarse to feel the utmost of our sorrows and of our joys. Therefore, we abandoned it as rubbish: we left it below us to march forward, a breathing simulacrum, on its own unaided level, subject to influences from which in normal times our instincts would have shrunk. The men were young and sturdy; and hot flesh and blood unconsciously claimed a right in them and tormented their bellies with strange longings. Our privations and dangers fanned this virile heat, in a climate as racking as can be conceived. We had no shut places to be alone in, no thick clothes to hide our nature. Man in all things lived candidly with man.

The Arab was by nature continent; and the use of universal marriage had nearly abolished irregular courses in his tribes. The public women of the rare settlements we encountered in our months of wandering would have been nothing to our numbers, even had their raddled meat been palatable to a man of healthy parts. In horror of such sordid commerce our youths began indifferently to slake one another's few needs in their own clean bodies – a cold convenience that, by comparison, seemed sexless and even pure. Later, some began to justify this sterile process, and swore that friends quivering together in the yielding sand with intimate hot limbs in supreme embrace, found there hidden in the darkness a sensual co-efficient of the mental passion which was welding our souls and spirits in one flaming effort. Several, thirsting to punish appetites they could not wholly prevent, took a savage pride in degrading the body, and offered themselves fiercely in any habit which promised physical pain or filth.

I was sent to these Arabs as a stranger, unable to think their thoughts or subscribe their beliefs, but charged by duty to lead them forward and to develop to the highest any movement of theirs profitable to England in her war. If I could not assume their character, I could at least conceal my own, and pass among them without evident friction, neither a discord nor a critic but an unnoticed influence. Since I was their fellow, I will not be their apologist or advocate. To-day in my old garments, I could play the bystander, obedient to the sensibilities of our theatre . . .

but it is more honest to record that these ideas and actions then passed naturally. What now looks wanton or sadic seemed in the field inevitable, or just unimportant routine.

Blood was always on our hands: we were licensed to it. Wounding and killing seemed ephemeral pains, so very brief and sore was life with us. With the sorrow of living so great, the sorrow of punishment had to be pitiless. We lived for the day and died for it. When there was reason and desire to punish we wrote our lesson with gun or whip immediately in the sullen flesh of the sufferer, and the case was beyond appeal. The desert did not afford the refined slow penalties of courts and gaols.

Of course our rewards and pleasures were as suddenly sweeping as our troubles; but, to me in particular, they bulked less large. Beduin ways were hard even for those brought up to them, and for strangers terrible: a death in life. When the march or labour ended I had no energy to record sensation, nor while it lasted any leisure to see the spiritual loveliness which sometimes came upon us by the way. In my notes, the cruel rather than the beautiful found place. We no doubt enjoyed more the rare moments of peace and forgetfulness; but I remember more the agony, the terrors, and the mistakes. Our life is not summed up in what I have written (there are things not to be repeated in cold blood for very shame); but what I have written was in and of our life. Pray God that men reading the story will not, for love of the glamour of strangeness, go out to prostitute themselves and their talents in serving another race.

'. . . by missing the oryx I probably saved our lives'

WILFRED THESIGER

Arabian Sands (1959)

Arabian Sands *opens with Wilfred Thesiger reviewing his years in Africa. He was born in Addis Ababa where his father was British consul-general. He returned after his British education to serve in the Sudan Political Service for several years but hankered after the freedom and open spaces of the desert, which he had found during his sojourn with the Danakil in Ethiopia, then the Nuer of the Nile Valley and in Darfur and his trip across the Libyan desert to the Tibesti mountains. 'In the desert I had found a freedom unattainable in civilisation; a life unhampered by possessions, since everything that was not a necessity was an encumbrance. I had found, too, a comradeship inherent in the circumstances, and the belief that tranquility was to be found there. I had learnt the satisfaction which comes from hardship and the pleasure which springs from abstinence: the contentment of a full belly; the richness of meat; the taste of clean water; the ecstasy of surrender when the craving for sleep becomes a torment; the warmth of a fire in the chill of dawn.'*

The rest of the book covers his two crossings of the Empty Quarter of Arabia during 1945–1949. This passage is from the second crossing. He travelled with his long-term companions and guides Bin Kabina and Bin Gabaisha during the first three months of 1949.

After one the most celebrated of twentieth-century adventures they emerge from the desert and arrive at a fishing and pearl diving town on the Arabian Gulf. 'A large castle dominated the small dilapidated town which stretched along the shore. There were a few palms and near them was a well where we watered our camels while some Arabs eyed us curiously, wondering who we were. Then we went over to the castle and sat outside the walls, waiting for the sheiks to wake from their afternoon slumbers.'

Modern travellers know this 'small dilapidated town' as Abu Dhabi.

While Thesiger's accomplishments and place in the history of travel and travel literature are not in doubt, his aloof assurance that he belongs to a club of one as a traveller is never far below the surface.

We travelled through low limestone hills until nearly sunset, and camped in a cleft on their northern side. The Rashid did not trust the Saar whom we had left at Manwakh, so Amair went back along our tracks to keep watch until it was dark, while bin Ghabaisha lay hidden on the cliff above us watching the plain to the north, which was a highway for raiders going east or west. We started again at dawn, after an uneasy watchful night, and soon after sunrise came upon a broad, beaten track, where Murzuk and the Abida had passed two days before.

Bin Kabina and Amair stayed behind to try to identify some of the looted stock by reading the confusion in the sand. We had gone on a couple of miles when they caught up with us, laughing as they chased each other across the plain. They appeared to be in the best of spirits, and I was surprised when bin Kabina told me that he had recognised the tracks of two of his six camels among the spoil. He had left these two animals with his uncle on the steppes. Luckily, Qamaiqam, the splendid camel on which he had crossed the Empty Quarter the year before, and the other three were with his brother at Habarut. He told us which animals they had been able to identify, but said that there had been so many animals that it was only possible to pick out a few that had travelled on the outskirts of the herd. As I listened I thought once again how precarious was the existence of the Bedu. Their way of life naturally made them fatalists; so much was beyond their control. It was impossible for them to provide for a morrow when everything depended on a chance fall of rain or when raiders, sickness, or any one of a hundred chance happenings might at any time leave them destitute, or end their lives. They did what they could, and no people were more self-reliant, but if things went wrong they accepted their fate without bitterness, and with dignity as the will of God.

We rode across gravel steppes which merged imperceptibly into the sands of the Uruq al Zaza. By midday the north-east wind was blowing in tearing gusts, bitter cold but welcome, as it would wipe out our tracks and secure us from pursuit. We pressed on until night, hoping in vain to find grazing, and then groped about in the dark feeling for firewood. Here it was dangerous to light a fire after dark, but we were too cold and hungry to be cautious. We found a small hollow, lit a fire, and sat gratefully round the flames. At dawn we ate some dates, drank a few drops of coffee, and started off as the sun rose.

It was another cold grey day, but there was no wind. We went on foot for the first hour or two, and then each of us, as he felt inclined, pulled down his camel's head, put a foot on her neck, and was lifted up to within easy reach of the saddle. Muhammad was usually the first to mount and I the last, for the longer I walked the shorter time I should have to ride. The others varied their positions, riding astride or kneeling in the saddle, but I could only ride astride, and as the hours crawled by the saddle edge bit deeper into my thighs.

For the next two days we crossed hard, flat, drab-coloured sands, without grazing, and, consequently, had no reason to stop until evening. On the second day, just after we had unloaded, we saw a bull oryx walking straight towards us. To him we were in the eye of the setting sun and he probably mistook us for others of his kind. As only about three Englishmen have shot an Arabian oryx, I whispered to bin Ghabaisha to let me shoot, while the oryx came steadily on. Now he was only a quarter of a mile away, now three hundred yards, and still he came on. The size of a small donkey – I could see his long straight horns, two feet or more in length, his pure white body, and the dark markings on his legs and face. He stopped suspiciously less than two hundred yards away. Bin Kabina whispered to me to shoot. Slowly I pressed the trigger. The oryx spun round and galloped off. Muhammad muttered disgustedly, 'A clean miss,' and bin Kabina said loudly, 'If you had let bin Ghabaisha shoot we should have had meat for supper'; all I could say was 'Damn and blast!'

I little realised at the time that by missing the oryx I probably saved our lives. A year later bin al Kamam joined us on the Trucial Coast. He told us that he had been at Main in the Jauf, when news arrived that the Christian and some Rashid were at Manwakh, preparing to cross the sands. The Governor of the Jauf, Saif al Islam al Hussain, one of the Imam Yahya's sons, sent off two parties of Dahm to kill us. The larger party of twenty occupied some wells on the desert's edge, which they thought we might visit, while the other party of fifteen went into the Sands to pick up our tracks. Bin al Kamam said that he and his companion had been imprisoned to prevent them from escaping and giving us warning. He had been certain that the Dahm would intercept and kill us, and when eventually he saw them riding back across the plain towards the town he was waiting to hear that we were dead. Suddenly he realised that they were riding in silence, instead of singing their war-songs, and that they must have failed to find us. The smaller party reported that they had picked up our tracks, which were two days old; they had followed us for two days, but as we were travelling very fast they had been afraid that they would run out of water before they could overtake us. They said that at our camping places they had seen marks in the sand where we had put down our bags of gold. If I had shot the oryx we should have delayed for a day to dry its meat, and the Dahm would probably have caught up with us. We thought at the time that we were far enough into the Empty Quarter to be safe, and we were not keeping a good look-out. If our pursuers had been from the Yam they would certainly have overtaken us, but the Dahm are afraid of the Sands.

For the next three days we rode across sands where there were only occasional *abal* bushes and a few dry tufts of *ailqi* or *qassis,* the remains of vegetation which had grown after rain four years before. We were now in the Qaimiyat, where parallel dune chains ran from north-east to south-west. These dunes were only about a hundred and fifty feet high, but their steep inclines faced towards us, and the successive floundering ascents exhausted our camels, as they had eaten practically nothing for six days. When we left Manwakh they were very fat, and this gave them reserves on which to draw, but their very fatness distressed them in this heavy sand. They were fresh from pasturage and their backs were soft and unaccustomed to the saddle. Now they were heavily-loaded and doing very long marches. We knew that under such conditions they were certain to develop saddle swellings, which would turn all too easily into ulcers. We would gladly have rested them for a day if we could have found grazing and if our water supply had allowed it. The sheepskins, which I had bought in ignorance, sweated very badly, but we had already finished the water that was in them. Even the goatskins had not been long enough in use to become watertight and we were making constant but ineffectual efforts to check the alarming drip. We passed fresh tracks of oryx and of *rim,* the large white gazelle which is found in the Sands, and knew that if we followed these tracks they would lead us to fresh grazing, but we could not afford to lengthen our journey.

In the afternoon of the sixth day the dune chains turned into gentle downs, but we had already climbed over sixteen of them that day and on one of them a baggage camel collapsed, only moving again when we unloaded her. Bin Kabina's camel went lame in the shoulder, and all the others showed signs of exhaustion. I knew that it would be another ten days before we reached the Hassi and I began to wonder if we should get there.

ELEVEN

'A Book About Himself (Herself) . . .'

'He can interpret so boldly because he is writing a "travel book", that is a book about himself in relation to unfamiliar stimuli.'

This was the critic Paul Fussel's (*Abroad*, 1979) view of D. H. Lawrence. It might apply to most of the *Scraps* writers, but in some cases it is particularly apt. Here Robert Louis Stevenson takes himself and his donkey to the Cévennes in France in a trial for both of them. Around a hundred years later Richard Holmes sets out to retrace the steps of Stevenson and donkey in *Footsteps*. V. S. Naipaul returns to the India of his grandparents and his heritage but without being confident that he belongs either there or in Trinidad, whence he came. Pico Iyer is also testing himself against an alien culture, with eventually the most satisfactory of results. In 2015, Jenny Balfour Paul is conducting an intense relationship with someone who lived in the nineteenth century. But it is Cheryl Strayed in *Wild* who lives most closely, and eventually triumphantly, the Fussel definition.

'I was not English or Indian; I was denied the victories of both'

V. S. NAIPAUL

An Area of Darkness (1964)

Naipaul is one of four Nobel laureates for literature in Scraps. *He was born in Trinidad in 1931 after his grandfather emigrated from India in the 1880s to become an indentured labourer. His father became a journalist and Naipaul won a scholarship to Oxford, where he met his future wife and then sought to establish a literary career. An invitation to present a weekly BBC programme about the Caribbean gave him a platform, and he was commissioned to write a novel. It was* The Mystic Masseur, *and was quickly followed by several others. Aged twenty-nine he visited India for the first time. This journey is* An Area of Darkness; *it reveals him anxious about his identity and cultural heritage, insecure about belonging to any of the three backgrounds of his experience.*

Kashmir was coolness and colour: the yellow mustard fields, the mountains, snow-capped, the milky blue sky in which we rediscovered the drama of clouds. It was men wrapped in brown blankets against the morning mist, the bare footed shepherd boys with caps and covered ears on steep wet rocky slopes. At Qazigund, where we stopped, it was also dust in sunlight, the disorder of a bazaar, a waiting crowd, and a smell in the cold air of charcoal, tobacco, cooking oil, months-old dirt, and human excrement. Grass grew on the mud-packed roofs of cottages – and at last it was clear why, in that story I had read as a child in the 'West Indian Reader', the foolish widow had made her cow climb up to the roof. Buses packed with men with red-dyed beards were going in the direction from which we had come. Another bus came in, halted. The crowd broke, ran forward and pressed in frenzy around a window through which a man with tired eyes held out his thin hand in benediction. He, like the others, was going to Mecca; and among these imprisoning mountains how far away Jeddah seemed, that Arabian pilgrim port dangerous with reefs over which blue water grows turquoise. In smoky kitchen shacks Sikhs with ferocious beards and light eyes, warriors and rulers of an age not long past, sat and cooked. Each foodstall carried an attractive signboard. The heavy white cups were chipped; the tables, out in the open, were covered with oil-cloth in cheap patterns; below them the ground had been softened to mud.

The mountains receded. The valley widened into soft, well-watered fields. The road was lined with poplars and willows drooped on the banks of clear rivulets. Abruptly, at Awantipur, out of a fairy-tale village of sagging wood-framed cottages there rose ruins of grey stone, whose heavy trabeate construction – solid square pillars on a portico, steep stone pediments on a colonnade around a central shrine, massive and clumsy in ruin – caused the mind to go back centuries to ancient worship. They were Hindu ruins, of the eighth century, as we discovered later. But none of the passengers exclaimed, none pointed. They lived among ruins, the Indian earth was rich with ancient sculpture.

. . .

. . . the snow-capped mountains ringed the lake, at whose centre stood Akbar's fort of Hari Parbat; poplars marked the lake-town of Rainawari; and far away, beyond an open stretch of water, on the fresh green lower slopes of the mountains – as though the earth had been washed down through the ages to fill the crevices of rocks – were the Mogul Gardens, with their terraces, their straight lines, their central pavilions, their water-courses dropping from level to level down rippled concrete falls. The Mogul one could accept, and the Hindu. It was this English presence which seemed hardest to accept, in this

mountain-locked valley, this city of hookahs and samovars (so pronounced) where, in a dusty square on Residency Road, was the
caravanserai for Tibetans with their long-legged boots, hats, plaited hair,
their clothes as grimy-grey as their weather-beaten faces, men indistin-
guishable from women.

But we did not take a houseboat. Their relics were still too movingly
personal. Their romance was not mine, and it was impossible to separate
them from their romance. I would have felt an intruder, as I felt in those
district clubs where the billiard rooms were still hung with framed car-
toons of the 1930s, where the libraries had gone derelict, the taste of a
generation frozen, and where on the smoking-room walls were stained
engravings, difficult to see through the reflections of the dusty glass, of
tumultuous horsemen labeled 'Afridis' or 'Baluchis'. Indians could walk
among these relics with ease; the romance had always been partly theirs
and now they had inherited it fully. I was not English or Indian; I was
denied the victories of both.

'A prick, and she broke forth into a gallant little trotlet'

ROBERT LOUIS STEVENSON

Travels with a Donkey in the Cévennes (1879)

*Stevenson was twenty-seven when he made a two-week ramble across the
Cévennes region of France with his donkey Modestine. He had by then
persuaded his father that he should not follow the family tradition and
become a lawyer, even though he had a law degree from Edinburgh University. He had just met Fanny, who was to become his wife and whom he*

followed to California the next year, where he was to scratch a living with some writing until Treasure Island, Kidnapped, *and* The Strange Case of Dr Jekyll and Mr Hyde *earned him international renown a few years later.*

The sleeping-room was furnished with two beds. I had one; and I will own I was a little abashed to find a young man and his wife and child in the act of mounting into the other. This was my first experience of the sort; and if I am always to feel equally silly and extraneous, I pray God it be my last as well. I kept my eyes to myself, and know nothing of the woman except that she had beautiful arms, and seemed no whit embarrassed by my appearance. As a matter of fact, the situation was more trying to me than to the pair. A pair keep each other in countenance; it is the single gentleman who has to blush. But I could not help attributing my sentiments to the husband, and sought to conciliate his tolerance with a cup of brandy from my flask. He told me that he was a cooper of Calais travelling to St Etienne in search of work, and that in his spare moments he followed the fatal calling of a maker of matches. Me he readily enough divined to be a brandy merchant.

I was up first in the morning (Monday, September 23rd), and hastened my toilette guiltily, so as to leave a clear field for madam, the cooper's wife. I drank a bowl of milk, and set off to explore the neighbourhood of Bouchet. It was perishing cold, a grey, windy, wintry morning; misty clouds flew fast and low; the wind piped over the naked platform; and the only speck of colour was away behind Mount Mézenc and the eastern hills, where the sky still wore the orange of the dawn.

It was five in the morning, and four thousand feet above the sea; and I had to bury my hands in my pockets and trot. People were trooping out to the labours of the field by twos and threes, and all turned round to stare upon the stranger. I had seen them coming back last night, I saw them going afield again; and there was the life of Bouchet in a nutshell.

When I came back to the inn for a bit of breakfast, the landlady was in the kitchen combing out her daughter's hair; and I made her my compliments upon its beauty.

'Oh no,' said the mother; 'it is not so beautiful as it ought to be. Look, it is too fine.'

Thus does a wise peasantry console itself under adverse physical circumstances, and, by a startling democratic process, the defects of the majority decide the type of beauty.

'And where,' said I, 'is monsieur?'

'The master of the house is upstairs,' she answered, 'making you a goad.'

Blessed be the man who invented goads! Blessed the innkeeper of Bouchet St Nicolas, who introduced me to their use! This plain wand, with an eighth of an inch of pin, was indeed a sceptre when he put it in my hands. Thenceforward Modestine was my slave. A prick, and she passed the most inviting stable door. A prick, and she broke forth into a gallant little trotlet that devoured the miles. It was not a remarkable speed, when all was said; and we took four hours to cover ten miles at the best of it. But what a heavenly change since yesterday! No more wielding of the ugly cudgel; no more flailing with an aching arm; no more broadsword exercise, but a discreet and gentlemanly fence. And what although now and then a drop of blood should appear on Modestine's mouse-coloured wedge-like rump? I should have preferred it otherwise, indeed; but yesterday's exploits had purged my heart of all humanity. The perverse little devil, since she would not be taken with kindness, must even go with pricking.

'To learn by heart has more than one meaning'

RICHARD HOLMES

Footsteps: Adventures of a Romantic Biographer (1985)

... around a hundred years later, Richard Holmes (b. 1945) decided to retrace the routes taken by some of his biographical subjects including Robert Louis Stevenson and live some new adventures of his own.

I woke at 5 a.m. in a glowing mist, my green sleeping-bag blackened with the dew, for the whole plateau of the Velay is above two thousand feet. I made a fire with twigs gathered the night before, and set water to boil for coffee, in a *petit pois* tin with wire twisted round it as a handle. Then I went down to the Loire, here little more than a stream, and sat naked in a pool cleaning my teeth. Behind me the sun came out and the woodfire smoke turned blue. I felt rapturous and slightly mad.

I reached Le Monastier two hours later, in the local grocer's van, one of those square Citroëns like a corrugated garden privy, which smelt of camembert and apples. Monsieur Crèspy, chauffeur and patron, examined my pack and soaking bag as we jounced along through rolling uplands. Our conversation took place in a sort of no-man's-land of irregular French. M. Crèspy's patois and Midi twang battled for meaning against my stonewall classroom phrases. After initial skirmishing, he adopted a firm line of attack.

'You are walking on foot?' he said, leaning back into the depths of the van with one arm and presenting me with a huge yellow pear.

'Yes, yes. I am searching for *un Ecossais*, a Scotsman, a writer, who walked on foot through all this beautiful country.'

'He is a friend of yours? You have lost him?' enquired M. Crèspy with a little frown.

'No, no. Well . . . Yes. You see, I want to find him.' My chin streamed hopelessly with pear juice.

M. Crèspy nodded encouragingly: 'The pear is good, n'est-ce pas?'

'Yes, it is very good.'

The Citroën lurched round a bend and plunged down towards a rocky valley, broken with trees and scattered stone farmhouses, with pink tiled roofs and goats tethered in small bright pastures where the sun struck and steamed. The spire of a church, perched on the far hillside, pointed the horizon.

'There is Le Monastier. Look! Perhaps your friend is waiting for you,' said M. Crèspy with great confidence.

'No, no, I don't think so,' I said. But it was exactly what I hoped.

I rummaged in my rucksack. 'You see, here is his book. It tells the story of his walk on foot.'

M. Crèspy peered at the little brown volume, and the Citroën swung back and forth across the road, the sound of rolling fruit growing thunderous behind us. I hastily propped the book up on the dashboard, being careful not to cover the St Christophe medal or the picture of Our Lady mounted above a cone of paper flowers. I ran my finger down the sketch map on the title page: Le Monastier, Pradelles, Langogne, Notre Dame des Neiges, Montagne du Goulet, Pic de Finiels, Le Pont-de-Montvert, Florac, Gorges du Tarn, St Jean-du-Gard – to me already magic names, a litany of hills and rivers, with a lone figure striding along them, laughing, beckoning, even mocking: follow! follow!

M. Crèspy considered the map, and then my face, then the map again, and changed gear with a reflective air. 'It is far, it is far.'

'Yes,' I said, 'it is two hundred and twenty kilometres.'

M. Crèspy raised a finger from the steering wheel. 'And you, you are Scottish then?'

'No, no. I am English. My friend – that is to say, Mr Stevenson – was Scottish. He walked on foot with a donkey. He slept à la *belle étoile*. He . . .'

'Ah, *that!*' broke in M. Crèspy with a shout, taking both hands from the steering wheel, and striking his forehead. 'I understand, I understand! You are on the traces of Monsieur Robert Louis Steamson. Bravo, bravo!'

'Yes, yes, I am following his paces!'

We both laughed and the Citroën proceeded by divine guidance. 'I understand, I understand,' repeated M. Crèspy. And I believe he was the first person who ever did.

Robert Louis Stevenson came to Le Monastier in September 1878. He was twenty-seven, spoke good French, and had already spent several summers abroad; near Fontainebleau, and on the canals of Holland, paddling a canoe with a friend. The experience had produced his first book, *An Inland Voyage*, which despite its whimsical style captured an attitude to travel that enthralled me, a child of the Sixties.

'I take it, in short, that I was about as near Nirvana as would be convenient in practical life; and if this be so, I make the Buddhists my sincere compliments . . . It may be best figured by supposing yourself to get dead drunk, and yet keep sober to enjoy it . . . A pity to go to the expense of laudanum, when here is a better paradise for nothing! This frame of mind was the great exploit of our voyage, take it all in all. It was the farthest piece of travel accomplished.'

A few days later. . .

I lay on the rock all morning in the hot sun, listening to the call of pee-wits and the sounds of the river.

I found that Stevenson wrote that day in his journal:

'Why anyone should desire to go to Cheylard or to Luc is more than my much inventing spirit can embrace. For my part, I travel not to go anywhere, but to go; I travel for travel's sake. And to write about it afterwards, if only the public will be so condescending as to read. But the great affair is to move; to feel the needs and hitches of life a little more nearly; to get down off this feather bed of civilisation, and to find the globe granite underfoot and strewn with cutting flints.'

It is one of his most memorable formulations, and I learnt it by heart. At night I would mumble it to myself, almost like a prayer, in the solitariness of my sleeping-bag. Again, I took it quite literally, on trust. Or rather, I was compelled to take it – this, I felt, is what I had to do; though if anyone had asked me why I could not have explained. The fact that Stevenson was also making something of a profession of his bohemian wanderings, and deliberately searching for picturesque copy, did not occur to me at first. (He did not use that sentence about his reading public in the published version of his *Travels*; it revealed his hand too clearly.) But I now think that my critical innocence allowed me to learn other things, far more important, about the personal life that is hidden in, and below, the printed page. To learn by heart has more than one meaning.

'Everything had been there that night'

PICO IYER

The Lady and the Monk (1991)

In 1991 Pico Iyer (b. 1957) spent a year in Kyoto, Japan, living in a temple, intent on writing of his spiritual experiences as he witnessed four seasons in the city.

The charming but untold sequel to the episode is that Sachiko, Pico Iyer's guide and the lady of the title, eventually becomes his wife. He explained this whilst discussing his own choices for Scraps, *ending with the comment 'and she is lying here beside me right here in my Tokyo bedroom'.*

On the final day of summer, Sachiko took me to Arashiyama to watch the cormorant boats. The night was navy blue and gold when we arrived, a lone torch burning against the dark blue hills. On the top of the distant mountains sat a round white moon. Along the riverbank, red lanterns shivered in the faint, chill breeze, their echoes wavering red in the reflecting water. A single pagoda, lonely as a plover's cry, jutted up into the heavens. A solitary canoeist pulled himself soundless through the dark.

Far in the distance, car lights glided silently across the Togetsu Bridge; in a teahouse nearby, the upswept coiffure of a geisha flashed briefly in an upstairs window. Occasionally above the water, a firework shot up into the dark, and then, with a quiet hiss, streamed down in a sad, slow extravagance of gold.

There was a sense of elegy about the river tonight, the smell of spent fireworks, the faintest hint of autumn chill, the happy, clapping songs of summer's final parties.

Cool in her summer kimono, Sachiko led me over the bridge to where the boats knocked against the dock, lanterns along their sides bearing the faint outline of cormorants. Stepping behind her in a boat and steadying myself, I saw the moon shivering in a row of silver lanterns. Without a sound, our boat set off across the lake, the darkness deepening above the dark-blue hills. The boats, with their criss-crossing of lanterns, looked eerie now, and ghostly in the gathering dark, their white globes doubled in the rippling water. From across the water came the dull thud of an oar. The teahouses cast reflections, red and white and blue, across the rippling water.

And so we drifted through the night, approaching, then receding from, the other silent boats. Occasionally, an open cormorant punt came past, torches burning at its prow, scattering sparks across the dark. For a moment in the torchlight, the aged fishermen's faces were lit up, in a flash of Rembrandt gold, and then, as soon, their wrinkled features and medieval grass-skirt forms vanished again into the dark.

Another boat glided past, ringing with the laughs of company men lined up around a long, low table, served strange delicacies by white-faced geisha. A firework shivered off in the dark, and then came down in a shower of white and gold and pink. The torches singed the water gold. Every now and then, a bird plunged down into the water, emerging with a fish within its beak.

'This place before, I little goodbye ceremony,' said Sachiko, face whitened in the dark. Behind her, the lanterned boats were slow and soundless in the night. 'I not know this. But he say he want only friend.' Her voice trailed off into the dreamy dark. A boat bumped up against us, and the gold reflections blurred and shivered in the water.

Along the bank came the sudden sound of children laughing. A grandfather bent down to light a firework for his toddler, and it veered off into the sky, a shooting soundless bird, then slowly came back down again. Across the water, the lone canoeist pulled his way in from the shadowed, distant mountains.

'Summer soon finish,' she said softly. 'Soon weather little cold again. Tonight last summer party.' Thoughts turn to autumn and to separation. In the distance, the sound of ancient folk songs, and of grandmas dancing.

It was only later, after I had left Japan, that I realised that everything had been there that night: the lanterned dark, the moon above the mountains, the dreamlike maiden in kimono. There was the Heian version I had sought since childhood. And yet, by now, it was so much part of my life that I had not even seen it till it was gone.

'. . . the whole escapade had a Thomas-like edge'.

JENNY BALFOUR PAUL

Deeper Than Indigo (2015)

Jenny Balfour Paul's gap year diary (with the dateline Bamiyan, Afghanistan 1970) records: 'I think the wanderlust has entered my blood. Time is non-existent, life is chaotic. I have never been happier.' But it was to be many years later, following the death of her academic/diplomat husband, Glencairn, before she would again travel independently. By then she shared with Thomas Machell, her nineteenth-century 'forgotten explorer', a fascination with indigo, its uses and its manufacture. She chanced upon his long lost diaries, meticulously written and illustrated. As she learns more about him and the insecurities that led him to wander and investigate, the relationship becomes deeper, all but a love affair divided only by a century. Here she follows Machell's route back to Britain by boat from Calcutta.

At last, on 22nd December, the Arabian headland of Ras el Hed is sighted, but the ship is becalmed and off-course. Tom is grumpy on Christmas Eve but at last a breeze springs up and the Hamoody makes Muscat harbour. During the long voyage from Calcutta he has got on well with the crew, but grown sick of the skipper and is ready for a change. He has, however, become close friends with Razumea, the First Mate.

Once ashore, Thomas keeps up his oriental disguise, enjoying an English officer's surprise when this long-bearded Arab suddenly addresses him in perfect English. Thomas is impressed by Muscat, sketching the harbour around three sides of a page. When I went there myself I wrote: 'Muscat must have been enchanting in the past but the old buildings are being bulldozed and replaced in a wink by hideous concrete villas.' 'I wandered about the place,' writes Tom, 'took a peep into the palace diwan where the Imam's son was holding court, had a look at the dilapidated forts and the place down which they pitch their criminals which smashes them to pieces, a Portuguese invention.' He notes the popularity of the Imam, 'who lives mainly in Zanzibar,' the well stocked bazaar and the importance of the port with its 'continual interchange of goods – Cloths, Rice and Spices from India and China, Coffee, Dates and Salt from Arabia, silks, carpets, tobacco and spices from Persia and also a great abundance of pearls from the Persian Gulf and slaves from the coast of Africa.'

I too enjoyed Oman and its people, and Thomas would be amused to hear why and how I was smuggled into Muscat in 1995. Keen to record Oman's last indigo dyers, I couldn't get the obligatory 'No Objection

Certificate' to enter the country because I was a woman and my reason weird. However, I hitched a lift to next-door Sharjah when its Ruler's private plane flew to UK to fetch various Exeter University figures, including Glencairn, for a fundraising trip to Oman. From Sharjah five members of the party got permission to enter Oman, and when they set off for Muscat, again on the Ruler's plane, I sneaked on board as stow-away. On arrival in Muscat I hung back in dark corners of the airport while the party whizzed off in shiny cars to see the Finance Minister. However, their meeting ended in a row, so the party retreated in a huff back to the waiting plane and immediately took off for Sharjah, aban-doning me as a lost cause, which suited me fine. Though penniless, I found my way into Muscat city, cadged some funds, and made contact with Gigi Crocker, a weaver, living in Salalah, with whom I had been corresponding. She drove six hundred miles in her jeep to meet me in Nizwa oasis and we had a splendid adventure in the central desert and its Eden-like date gardens, with Gigi's Bedouin friends, Oman's last indigo dyers (one of whom has since staged a revival, Thomas and Susan Bosence please note) and of course the local djinns. I eventually returned to UK having borrowed money for the airfare from a trusting Omani banker. Tom would have applauded the reason for the trip and looking back the whole escapade had a Thomas-like edge.

He leaves Muscat on New Year's Eve 1847 in self-imposed discomfort. On learning that the wind is in the wrong direction for sailing north up the Persian Gulf he has decided instead 'to go round by the Red Sea'. He writes: 'I suppose we shall get to Suez in about two months "Inshallah". It will be a very interesting trip and I shall have a good opportunity to improve my Arabic.' He has just boarded a baghla type of dhow that he describes as 'a vile high-sterned antique looking craft that appeared to have been built on the model of everything that should be avoided.' He continues: 'The mosquitoes were very troublesome thanks to the dates with which the Futel Khair was partly loaded, the rest of her cargo consisting of Tobacco from Shiraz and rugs and beautiful carpets from Bushire. She was so lumber'd up that there was not space for a fisherman's walk which as all the world knows is only "three strides and overboard". I moved my traps as close aft as possible (there was no place for me below decks) and as the night closed in I rolled myself up in my horse blanket and with my weapons at hand I lay down to sleep with one eye open and the other shut.'

'"Hello, Oregon cows," I called to them'

CHERYL STRAYED

Wild (2012)

Cheryl (b. 1968) chose the name Strayed on getting a divorce at twenty-six, because she felt that she had done so. The straying, including a drug habit, followed the death of her mother and the disintegration of her marriage, her personal and her financial life. She chanced to read ('I'd been standing in line at an outdoor store waiting to purchase a foldable shovel when I picked up a book called The Pacific Crest Trail, Volume 1: California*') of the 2,700 mile Pacific Crest Trail along the high peaks of California, Oregon and Washington. Impulsively she decided to attempt the whole trek alone, and take the chance that the pieces of her disordered life might be reassembled.*

Here Cheryl and Monster (her overweight encumbrance of a backpack) have arrived at the Oregon state line, 700 miles north of their starting point in the Mojave Desert. Her body has been mutilated, but much else has been mended.

I woke in the darkness on my second-to-last night in California to the sound of wind whipping the branches of the trees and the tap-tapping of rain against my tent. It had been so dry all summer long that I'd stopped putting the rain cover on, sleeping with only a wide pane of mesh between the sky and me. I scrambled barefoot into the dark to pull my rain cover over my tent, shivering, though it was early August. It had been in the nineties for weeks, sometimes even reaching a hundred, but with the wind and the rain, the weather had suddenly shifted. Back in my tent, I put on my fleece leggings and anorak, crawled into my sleeping bag, and zipped it all the way up to my chin, cinching its hood tight around my head. When I woke at six, the little thermometer on my backpack said that it was 37 degrees.

I hiked along a high ridgeline in the rain, dressed in most of what I had. Each time I stopped for more than a few minutes, I grew so chilled that my teeth chattered comically until I walked on and began to sweat again. On clear days, my guidebook claimed, Oregon was in view to the north, but I couldn't see anything for the thick fog that obscured anything beyond ten feet. I didn't need to see Oregon. I could feel it huge before me. I would walk its entire length if I made it all the way to the Bridge of the Gods. Who would I be if I did? Who would I be if I didn't?

Midmorning, Stacy appeared out of the mist, walking southbound on the trail. We'd hiked away from Seiad Valley together the day before, after spending a night with Rex and the couples. In the morning Rex had caught a bus back to his real life, while the rest of us walked on, splitting up a few hours out. I was fairly certain I wouldn't see the couples on the trail again, but Stacy and I had made plans to meet up in Ashland, where she was going to lay over for a few days waiting for her friend Dee to arrive before they began their hike through Oregon. Seeing her now startled me, as if she were part woman, part ghost.

'I'm heading back to Seiad Valley,' she said, and explained that she was cold, her feet were blistered, and her down sleeping bag had gotten drenched the night before and she had no hope of drying it out before nightfall. 'I'm taking a bus to Ashland,' she said. 'Come find me at the hostel when you get there.'

I hugged her before she walked away, the fog enveloping her again in seconds.

The next morning I woke earlier than normal, the sky, the palest gray. It had stopped raining and the air had warmed up. I felt excited as I strapped on Monster and walked away from my camp: these were my last miles in California.

I was less than a mile away from the border when a branch that hung along the edge of the trail caught on my William J. Crockett bracelet and sent it flying off into the dense brush. I scanned the rocks and bushes and trees, panicky, knowing as I pushed into the weeds that it was a lost cause. I wouldn't find the bracelet. I hadn't seen where it had gone. It had only made the faintest ping as it flew away from me. It seemed absurd that I'd lose the bracelet at this very moment, a clear omen of trouble ahead. I tried to twist it around in my mind and make the loss represent something good – a symbol of things I didn't need anymore, perhaps, of lightening the figurative load – but then that idea flattened out and I thought only of William J. Crockett himself, the man from Minnesota who'd been about my age when he died in Vietnam, whose remains had never been found, whose family no doubt still grieved him. My bracelet wasn't anything but a symbol of the life he lost too young. The universe had simply taken it into its hungry, ruthless maw.

There was nothing to do but go on.

I reached the border only minutes later, stopping to take it in: California and Oregon, an end and a beginning pressed up against each other. For such a momentous spot, it didn't look all that momentous. There was only a brown metal box that held a trail register and a sign that said WASHINGTON: 498 MILES – no mention of Oregon itself.

But I knew what those 498 miles were. I'd been in California two months, but it seemed like I'd aged years since I'd stood on Tehachapi Pass alone with Monster and imagined reaching this spot. I went to the metal box, pulled out the trail register, and paged through it, reading the entries from the previous weeks. There were notes from a few people whose names I'd never seen and others from people I hadn't met, but whom I knew because I'd been trailing them all summer. The most recent entries were from the couples – John and Sarah, Helen and Sam. Beneath their jubilant entries, I wrote my own, so overwhelmed with emotion that I opted to be concise: 'I made it!' Oregon. Oregon. *Oregon*.

I was here. I walked into it, catching views of the peaks of majestic Mount Shasta to the south and the lower but sterner Mount McLoughlin to the north. I hiked high on a ridgeline, coming to short icy patches of snow that I crossed with the help of my ski pole. I could see cows grazing in the high green meadows not far below me, their big square bells clanking as they moved. 'Hello, Oregon cows,' I called to them.

TWELVE

The Cities of Italy

Among cities, as an inspiration for travel writers, there are few to challenge those of Italy; so often it is for Venice, Rome, Florence and Siena that writers have reserved their most enduring passages. Jan Morris (*Among the Cities* and many others) has written about almost every great city around the world, but it is no coincidence that *Venice* remains her most celebrated book. For Italo Calvino the stature of Venice was above argument. For Goethe, visiting Rome was a rite of passage: 'All the dreams of my youth have come to life'. Writing about Rome two centuries later, Facaros and Pauls put this adulation into perspective and in the process quote Goethe in different mood. Norman Lewis is in Naples in 1944 in a military role.

'There is still one [city] of which you never speak.'

ITALO CALVINO

Invisible Cities (1972)

In Invisible Cities *Calvino (1923-1985) speculates a conversation between the travelling Marco Polo and the aging Emperor, Kublai Khan. Polo describes to the Emperor cities of the world that he claims to be part of the Khan's expanding Empire.*

'There is still one of which you never speak.'

Marco Polo bowed his head.

'Venice,' the Khan said.

Marco smiled. 'What else do you believe I have been talking to you about?'

The Emperor did not turn a hair. 'And yet I have never heard you mention that name.'

And Polo said: 'Every time I describe a city I am saying something about Venice.'

———————

'There's the lust and dark wine of Venice'

JAN MORRIS

Venice (1960)

Jan, as James Morris, became one the most celebrated of journalists when he was assigned by The Times *to record the Hunt expedition to climb Everest in 1953; he was responsible for secreting the news of its success from the world so that it could be announced by* The Times *alone on the morning of Queen Elizabeth II's Coronation on 2 June 1953. The story is told in* Coronation Everest.

In 1972, having had five children, he and his wife Elizabeth went to Morocco together and James had what he called 'that so-called sex change thing'. In her quizzical memoir Conundrum *she sought to explain her need for the transition.*

Jan clings to the claim that she is not a travel writer because her subject is usually cities; 'that is not travel'. Her many readers might not agree.

The allure of Venice, though, is distinct from art and architecture. There is something curiously sensual to it, if not actually sexual. 'Venice casts about you', as a nineteenth-century Frenchman put it, 'a charm as tender as the charm of woman. Other cities have admirers. Venice alone has lovers'. James Howell assured his readers, in the seventeenth century, that if once they knew the rare beauty of the Virgin City, they would 'quickly make love to her'. And Elizabeth Barrett Browning expressed some of this libidinous or perhaps narcotic rapture when she wrote that 'nothing is like it, nothing equal to it, not a second Venice in the world'. Today the place is loud with motor boats, tawdry with tourism, far from virginal: but when I lean from my window in the early morning, when the air is sea-fresh and the day unsullied, when there is a soft plash of oars beneath my terrace, and the distant hum of a ship's turbines, when the first sun gleams on the golden angel of the Campanile, and the shadows slowly stir along the dark line of the palaces – then a queer delicious yearning still overcomes me, as though some creature of unattainable desirability is passing by outside.

I think this is partly a matter of organic design. Venice is a wonderfully compact and functional whole: rounded, small, complete, four-square in the heart of its sickle lagoon like an old golden monster in a pond. Corbusier described the city as an object lesson for town planners. The variegated parts of Venice have been mellowed and diffused, like the two old palaces on the Grand Canal whose roofs intimately overlap above a minute alley-way. Her architecture is a synthesis of styles – eastern and western, Gothic, Renaissance, Baroque – so that Ruskin could call the Doge's Palace the central building of the world. Her canals and streets fit neatly into one another, like the well-machined parts of an engine. Her symbols are simple but catching, like advertisers' images – the sleek winged lions, the golden horses, the Doge in his peaked hat, the twin pillars on the Molo, the ramrod Campanile, the lordly swing of the Grand Canal, the cobra-prows of the gondolas, rearing in the lamplight. Her slogans are exciting and memorable – 'Viva San Marco!' 'Lord of a Quarter and a Half-Quarter', 'Pax Tibi Marce', 'Morto o Vivo', 'Com' era, dov' era'. Venice has the feeling of a disbanded but still brilliant corporation, with the true ring and dazzle of capitalism to her ambiance. You feel, as you stand upon the high arch of the Rialto, that you can somehow capture the whole of her instantly in your mind – the whole of her history, all her meaning, every nuance of her beauty: and although her treasures are inexhaustible, in a way you are right, for Venice is a highly concentrated extract of her own reputation.

It is partly a matter of light. The Venetian painters were preeminent in their mastery of chiaroscuro, and Venice has always been a translucent city, a place of ravishing sunsets and iridescent mornings, monochromatic though its long winters can seem. Once it was vivid with gilded facades and frescoes – the Doge's Palace used to glow with gold, vermilion and blue – and here and there, on decomposing walls or leprous carvings you may still see faint lingering glimmers of the city's lost colour. Even now, when the Venetians hang out their flags and carpets in celebration, put up their gay sunshades, light their fairy-lamps, water the geraniums in their window-boxes, sail their bright pleasure-boats into the lagoon – even now it can be, at its sunlit best, a gaudy kind of place. The atmosphere, too, is remarkable for a capricious clarity, confusing one's sense of distance and proportion, and sometimes etching skylines and facades with uncanny precision. The city is alive with *trompe-l'oeil*, natural and artificial – deceits of perspective, odd foreshortenings, distortions and hallucinations. Sometimes its prospects seem crudely one-dimensional, like pantomime sets; sometimes they seem exaggeratedly deep, as though the buildings were artificially separated, to allow actors to appear between them, or to give an illusion of urban distance. The lagoon swims in misty mirages. If you take a boat into the Basin of St Mark, and sail towards the Grand Canal, it is almost eerie to watch the various layers of the Piazza pass each other in slow movement: all sense of depth is lost, and all the great structures, the pillars and the towers, seem flat and wafer-thin, like the cardboard stage properties that are inserted, one behind the other, through the roofs of toy theatres.

It is partly a matter of texture. Venice is a place of voluptuous materials, her buildings inlaid with marbles and porphyries, cipollino, verd-antico, jasper, marmo greco, polished granite and alabaster. She is instinct with soft seductive textiles, like the silks that Wagner hung around his bedrooms – the velvets, taffetas, damasks and satins that her merchants brought home from the East, in the days when all the ravishing delicacies of the Orient passed this way in a cloud of spice. When the rain streams down the marble facades of the Basilica, the very slabs seem covered in some breathtaking brocade. Even the waters of Venice sometimes look like shot silk. Even the floor of the Piazza feels yielding, when the moonlight shines upon it. Even the mud is womb-like and unguent.

The Venetian allure is partly a matter of movement. Venice has lost her silken dreamy spell, but her motion is still soothing and seductive. She is still a dappled city, tremulous and flickering, where the sunlight shimmers gently beneath the bridges, and the shadows shift slowly along the promenades. There is nothing harsh or brutal about the movement of Venice. The gondola is a vehicle of beautiful locomotion, the smaller craft of the canals move with a staccato daintiness, and often you see the upper-works of a liner in stately passage behind the chimneys. There are several places in Venice where, looking across a canal, you may catch a momentary glimpse of people as they pass the openings in an arcade: their movement seems oddly smooth and effortless, and sometimes an old woman glides past enshrouded in black tasselled shawls, and sometimes a priest strides silently by in a liquefaction of cassocks. The women of Venice walk with ship-like grace, swayed only by the gentle wobbling of their ankles. The monks and nuns of Venice flit noiselessly about its streets, as though they had no feet beneath their habits, one progressed in a convenient state of levitation. The policemen of the Piazza parade slowly, easily, magisterially. The sails of the lagoon laze the long days away, all but motionless on the horizon. The chief verger of the Basilica, when he sees a woman in trousers approaching the fane, or a short-sleeved dress, raises his silver stick in a masterly unhurried gesture of dismissal, his worldly-wise beadle's face shaking slowly to and fro beneath its cockade. The crowds that mill through the narrow shopping streets do so with a leisurely, greasy animation: and in the winter it is pleasant to sit in a warm wine shop and watch through the window the passing cavalcade of umbrellas, some high, some low, manoeuvring and jostling courteously for position, raised, lowered or slanted to fit between one another, like the chips of a mosaic or a set of cogs.

And in the last analysis, the glory of the place lies in the grand fact of Venice herself: the brilliance and strangeness of her history, the wide melancholy lagoon that surrounds her, the convoluted sea-splendour that keeps her, to this day, unique among the cities. When at last you leave these waters, pack away your straw hat and swinging out to sea, all the old dazzle of Venice will linger in your mind; and her smell of mud, incense, fish, age, filth and velvet will hang around your nostrils; and the soft lap of her back-canals will echo in your ears; and wherever you go in life you will feel somewhere over your shoulder, a pink, castellated, shimmering presence, the domes and riggings and crooked pinnacles of the Serenissima.

There's romance for you! There's the lust and dark wine of Venice! No wonder George Eliot's husband fell into the Grand Canal.

'All the dreams of my youth have come to life'

JOHANN WOLFGANG VON GOETHE

Italian Journey (1816, based on journeys taken in 1786–8)

Goethe was an intellectual polymath on an outstanding scale, and still found time to be a lawyer, statesman and diplomat for his adoptive home, the Duchy of Saxe-Weimar. The author of Faust *and* The Sorrows of Young Werther *was also a poet and philosopher who influenced much of the literature and music of the nineteenth century. He was one of the most revered natural scientists of his day, esteemed as geologist, geological specimen collector and biologist. 'As to what I have done as a poet . . . I take no pride in it . . . But that I am the only person who knows the truth in the difficult science of colours – of that, I say, I am not a little proud . . .'*

Rome, 1 November 1786

At last I can break my silence and send my friends a joyful greeting. I hope they will forgive me for my secretiveness and my almost subterranean journey to this country. Even to myself, I hardly dared admit where I was going and all the way I was still afraid I might be dreaming; it was not till I had passed through the Porta del Popolo that I was certain it was true, that I really was in Rome.

Let me say this: here in Rome, in the presence of all those objects which I never expected to see by myself, you are constantly in my thoughts. It was only when I realised that everyone at home was chained, body and soul, to the north, and all desire to visit these parts had vanished, that, drawn by an irresistible need, I made up my mind to undertake this long, solitary journey to the hub of the world.

Now that this need has been satisfied, my friends and my native land have once again become very dear to my heart, and my desire to return very keen, all the keener because I am convinced that the many treasures I shall bring home with me will serve both myself and others as a guide and an education for a lifetime.

Now, at last, I have arrived in the First City of the world! Had I seen it fifteen years ago with an intelligent man to guide me, I should have called myself lucky, but, since I was destined to visit it alone and trust to my own eyes, I am happy, at least, to have been granted this joy so late in life.

Across the mountains of the Tirol I fled rather than travelled. Vicenza, Padua and Venice I saw thoroughly, Ferrara, Cento, Bologna casually, and Florence hardly at all. My desire to reach Rome quickly was growing stronger every minute until nothing could have induced me to make more stops, so that I spent only three hours there. Now I have arrived, I have calmed down and feel as if I had found a peace that will last for my whole life. Because, if I may say so, as soon as one sees with one's own eyes the whole which one had hitherto only known in fragments and chaotically, a new life begins.

All the dreams of my youth have come to life; the first engravings I remember – my father hung views of Rome in the hall – I now see in reality, and everything I have known for so long through paintings, drawings, etchings, woodcuts, plaster casts and cork models is now assembled before me. Wherever I walk, I come upon familiar objects in an unfamiliar world; everything is just as I imagined it, yet everything is new. It is the same with my observations and ideas. I have not had a single idea which was entirely new or surprising, but my old ideas have become so much more firm, vital and coherent that they could be called new.

When Pygmalion's Galatea, whom he had fashioned exactly after his dreams, endowing her with as much reality and existence as an artist can, finally came up to him and said: 'Here I am,' how different was the living woman from the sculptured stone.

Besides, for me it is morally salutary to be living in the midst of a sensual people about whom so much has been said and written, and whom every foreigner judges by the standard he brings with him. I can excuse those who criticise and disapprove of them because their life is so far removed from ours that it is difficult and expensive for a foreigner to have dealings with them.

'... the FSO had assembled the town's notables and lectured them in Latin'

NORMAN LEWIS

Naples '44 (1978)

Lewis (1912–2006) was son of a pharmacist, and a grammar school boy, which set him apart from contemporaries such as Greene, Fleming and Byron. Lewis was much the most prolific travel writer of the group. Naples '44 was created from a diary he kept while serving as a sergeant in the Field Security Service of the British Army in Italy in Naples and the surrounding region. Although it may now be his best known book, it was not published until 1978, when many of the others were already in print. The first para-graph comes from his introduction.

The Field Security Service (as it had hastily renamed itself), brand new in its innocence, confronted emergencies that were undreamed of in England and there were no rules to go by. To have received an inkling of the political situation of the country in which we found ourselves would have been useful, but none was given, and we trod the hard road of trial and error. No. 91's first action in Philippeville – after the FSO had assembled the town's notables and lectured them in Latin – was to release from gaol a certain Giuseppe Moreno, who had convinced us that he was a fervent Gaullist victimised for his pro-Allied stand by the Vichy regime. In reality he was the leader of Algeria's emigrant branch of the Sicilian Mafia, and under sentence of death for the murder of a rival. The mistake must have been fairly typical.

November 5

Called for the first time on two new contacts, Ingeniere Losurdo and Avvocato Mosca, and found – no longer to my entire astonishment – that the circumstances of their lives bore an extreme resemblance to those of Lattarullo. Both lived in the Via Chiaia, once the resort of the town's aristocracy, in vast, dark, bare palazzi of which they occupied a single floor. Both palazzi date from the early eighteenth century, and have much-defaced coats of arms over the doorway. Each of them has its dim little porter's lodge, in which sits an identical old woman knitting in the semidarkness, and a courtyard behind heavy doors with its flag-stones rutted with the passage of the carriages of two centuries. There was a trace of embarrassment, a hint of apology, in the manner of both these men as they invited me into rooms which appeared to be virtually unfurnished. In each case I was led through a bare corridor to the salotto, in which a few pieces of furniture had been placed, without any attempt at arrangement, as if in an auction saleroom. They represented, I suspected, the whole contents of the apartment, hastily concentrated in a single room. The wallpaper – which in Naples had once signified pretension and luxury – was in both instances under attack by mould, and the paintwork on the doors and window-frames was cracked and flaking. A faintly vegetable odour noticeable in both palazzi suggested dry-rot. The general impression was one of genteel but very real poverty.

Ingeniere Losurdo and Avvocato Mosca were exactly fitted to their environment, for which reason they bore a striking resemblance to each other, and also to Lattarullo – so much so that they could easily have been members of the same family. I got the impression that they had been too poor to marry, too poor to do anything but defend themselves with considerable tenacity in the struggle to keep up appearances. They all offered an occasional, diffident reference to the fact that they were well-connected. Lattarullo's ancestor fought with Caracciolo in the war against Nelson and the Bourbons, and Mosca was entitled to put Conte on his visiting card, but no longer bothered. They had grand manners, and hearing them talk one sometimes seemed to be listening to Dr Johnson in an Italian translation. Each of these men had gracefully come to terms with a standard of living far lower than that of an average member of the Neapolitan working class.

In Naples one tends to blame all these things on the calamity of war, but after further acquaintance with the city, it becomes clear that this is only half the story and that the phenomenon of my three friends' near-destitution is an old and familiar one. The war has only aggravated their plight. In 1835 Alexander Dumas, who spent some weeks in Naples, wrote of its upper classes that only four families enjoyed great fortunes, that twenty were comfortably off, and the rest had to struggle to make

ends meet. What mattered was to have a well-painted carriage har-
nessed up to a couple of old horses, a coachman in threadbare livery,
and a private box at the San Carlo – where the social life of the town was
largely conducted. People lived in their carriages or in the theatre, but
their houses were barred to visitors, and hermetically sealed, as Dumas
puts it, against foreigners like himself.

He discovered that all but a tiny handful of the ancient families of
Naples lived in straitened circumstances, and this is roughly the situation a century later. They talked in a matter-of-fact and quite convincing
way of the golden days of their families under Imperial Rome, but they
had not enough to eat. The Neapolitan upper-crust of those times con-
sumed only one meal every twenty-four hours; at two in the afternoon
in winter, and at midnight in summer. Their food was almost as poor in
quality and as monotonous as that served to prisoners in gaol: invariably
the equivalent of a few pence' worth of macaroni flavoured with a little
fish, and washed down with Asprino d'Aversa, tasting – according to
Dumas – more like rough cider than wine. By way of an occasional
extravagance one of these pauper-noblemen might force himself to go
without bread or macaroni for a day, and spend what he had saved on an
ice-cream to be eaten splendidly in public, at the fashionable Cafe Don-
zelli.

In those days the only profession open to a young man of good family
was the diplomatic service, and as there were only sixty such posts
offered by the Kingdom of Naples, the ninety per cent of applicants who
were unsuccessful had to endure aristocratic idleness. The twentieth-
century version of this situation as reflected in the somewhat sterile
existences of Lattarullo, Losurdo and Mosca seemed little changed in its
essentials. Nowadays the learned professions have taken the place of
diplomacy, but they are so overcrowded they only provide a living for
less than one man in ten who enters them. Lattarullo and company have

been brought up to the idea that they cannot enter trade, and they are debarred by the same rule from physical creation of any kind. Therefore while others go hungry, they virtually starve.

November 10

The sexual attitudes of Neapolitans never fail to produce new surprises. Today Prince A., now well known to us all and an enthusiastic informant from our first days at the Riviera di Chiaia, visited us with his sister, whom we met for the first time. The Prince is the absentee landlord of a vast estate somewhere in the South, and owns a nearby palace stacked with family portraits and Chinese antiques. He is the head of what is regarded as the second or third noble family of Southern Italy. The Prince is about thirty years of age, and his sister could be twenty-four. Both are remarkably alike in appearance: thin, with extremely pale skin and cold, patrician expressions bordering on severity. The purpose of the visit was to enquire if we could arrange for the sister to enter an army brothel. We explained that there was no such institution in the British Army. 'A pity,' the Prince said. Both of them speak excellent English, learned from an English governess.

'Ah well, Luisa, I suppose if it can't be, it can't be.' They thanked us with polite calm, and departed.

Last week a section member was invited by a female contact to visit the Naples cemetery with her on the coming Sunday afternoon. Informants have to be cultivated in small ways whenever possible, and he was quite prepared to indulge a whim of this kind, in the belief that he would be escorting his friend on a visit to a family tomb, expecting to buy a bunch of chrysanthemums from the stall at the gate. However, hardly were they inside when the lady dragged him behind a tombstone, and then – despite the cold – lay down and pulled up her skirts. He noticed that the cemetery contained a number of other couples in vigorous activity in broad daylight. 'There were more people above ground than under it,' he said. It turned out that the cemetery is the lovers' lane of Naples, and custom is such that one becomes invisible as soon as one passes through the gates. If a visitor runs into anyone he knows neither a sign nor a glance can be exchanged, nor does one recognise any friend encountered on the 133 bus which goes to the cemetery. I have learned that to suggest to a lady a Sunday-afternoon ride on a 133 bus is tantamount to solicitation for immoral purposes.

In recognition of his medical interests in civilian life, Parkinson deals with the doctors of Naples. One of his most valuable contacts is Professore Placella, whose speciality is the restoration of virginity. He boasts that his replacement hymen is much better than the original, and that – costing only 10,000 lire – it takes the most vigorous husband up to three nights to demolish it.

'Faith is made here and believed elsewhere'

DANA FACAROS AND MICHAEL PAULS

Cadogan Guide to Rome (1989)

This could be a late twentieth century Mark Twain, but is in fact the partnership of Dana Facaros and Michael Pauls, originally from Cleveland, Ohio. Together in the 1980s and 1990s they wrote more than twenty titles for the Cadogan Guides series, initially concentrating on Greece and Italy. They were persuaded to move their attentions to what they referred to as the F word, but now have lived there in the Dordogne for about twenty years. In their hands travel guide writing became travel literature, but always veined with humour.

Vatican, curiously, means 'prophecy', for it was on this eighth hill of Rome that King Numa received tips on religion from the Sibyls. But as it was on the wrong side of the Tiber the land was cheap, and Caligula used it to build his personal circus, later known as Nero's; here St Peter was crucified upside down, at his own request, so that his martyrdom would not resemble Christ's. He was buried in a nearby cemetery, on a spot that has been hallowed ever since. It has been the chief residence of Peter's successors for most of the time since the late fourteenth century.

'The Papacy is not other than the Ghost of the Deceased Roman Empire, sitting crowned upon the grave thereof,' said Thomas Hobbes, though since Hobbes this imperial ectoplasm has been confined like an afrit in a magic lamp. Better known as the independent state of Vatican City (pop. around 1,000), it was the papacy's consolation prize negotiated in the 1929 Lateran Concordat. But the temporal power of the popes had been in decline for centuries; the old Papal States by the eighteenth century were the worst run in Europe, kept 'alive only because the earth refuses to swallow them', as Goethe put it.

Unfortunately, thanks to Mussolini, much of the evil of the Papal States has been concentrated in a country the size of a golf course – one where the duffers don't always count all their strokes. For instead of creating a realm of the spirit, as Vatican brochures would like you to believe, members of the Curia who run Vatican City have used its sovereignty (read unaccountability) to create the Corporate Papacy, the world's last real autocracy, with a tiny tax haven all its own. The scandal of Vatican finances, Mafia connections, the laundering of drug money through the Vatican Bank, and the circumstances surrounding the sudden death of John Paul I have been so unsavoury that the government across the

Tiber has responded by steadily decreasing the Church's role in the state, legalising divorce and abortion, making religious instruction optional in schools, taxing Vatican profits from the stock market, and taking away Roman Catholicism's special status as the official religion of Italy. Ask any Roman about it, and you'll get an earful. It's one reason why the city has one of the lowest percentages of church attendance in Italy – 'Faith is made here and believed elsewhere', is an old Roman saying.

Yet as you stroll among the merry crowds of pilgrims and tourists chattering in every known language, remember Boccaccio's story in the *Decameron*, of two friends who live in Paris, one Christian and one Jewish, the former constantly pestering the other to convert. Finally the Jew agrees, on the condition that he first visits Rome, to see if the life and habits of the pope and his cardinals were evidence of the superiority of their faith. The Christian naturally despairs, but off the Jew goes to Rome, returning with the expected tale of a thousand abominations, declaring that the pontiff and the rest were 'doing their level best to reduce the Christian religion to nought and drive it from the face of the earth'. That the faith could survive and prosper with such sharks in charge was enough to convince him that it must indeed be holy and genuine, and he converted immediately.

Vatican City is surrounded by a high wall, designed by Michelangelo; its only public entrances are through St Peter's Square and the Vatican Museums. Swiss Guards (still recruited from the four Catholic cantons), dressed in a scaled-down version of the striped suits designed by either Michelangelo or Raphael, stand ready to smite you with their halberds if you try to push your way in elsewhere. The Vatican has its own stamps and postal service, which make it a tidy profit; it is also, like every postal system in the galaxy, more efficient than the Posta Italiana.

THIRTEEN

Destinations Achieved

These stories have a purpose, an objective which was personally important to the traveller. For the remarkable Frenchwoman, Alexandra David-Néel, the objective was the forbidden city of Lhasa, which no European woman had ever reached. For Colin Thubron it was the spiritual mountain Kailas, a mountain so revered in many religions that it has remained unclimbed, unsullied by humanity – the tradition is to circle it, a strenuous trek at high altitude. Alexander Frater wanted to find the wettest place on earth, just to experience it at the peak of its annual rain season; he found it in the northeast Indian state of Assam.

Curzon's reason for wanting to get to the Wakhan and the Oxus was a love of adventure, but he was also surely conscious of the political kudos to be obtained from exploring his intended destination at the most sensitive conjunction between the then British and Russian areas of influence.

'A murderer and fratricide of more than ordinary activity'

GEORGE NATHANIEL CURZON

The Pamirs and the Source of the Oxus (1996)

The book records Curzon's (1859–1925) three lectures to the Royal Geographical Society in 1896, in which he claimed to have found the source of the River Oxus in the Wakhan Corridor in the Pamir Mountains of what is now Afghanistan.

The future Viceroy of India, already an MP and ex-Minister, took time off to travel, clearly as part of his preparation for higher office. This was the height of the Great Game standoff between the Empire of the Tzars in Russia and the British Raj in India. Curzon chose to explore the most sensitive areas that marked the then hazy delineation between them.

Curzon, via this book, was my guide and impetus in setting out in 2007 to try to rediscover the ice cave that he claims to have found there as the source of the river. It was there, almost exactly as he had described it, a river emerging in full flow from the confluence of three glaciers. The book was still the most detailed and accurate available guide to the Wakhan 112 years later.

No one who has had the good fortune to visit the astonishing Hunza Valley would quarrel with Curzon's florid opening description.

Then in the Hunza Valley, which is undoubtedly one of the most remarkable scenes in the world, Nature seems to exert her supremest energy, and in one chord to exhaust almost every note in her vast and majestic diapason of sound. She shows herself in the same moment tender and savage, radiant and appalling, the relentless spirit that hovers above the ice-towers, and the gentle patroness of the field and orchard, the tutelary deity of the haunts of men.

Never can I forget the abruptness and splendour of the surprise when, shortly after leaving the fort of Chalt, 30 miles beyond Gilgit, there burst upon our view the lordly apparition of the great mountain Rakapushi, lifting, above the boulder-strewn or forest-clad declivities of his lower stature, 18,000 feet of unsullied ice and snow to a total height of 25,550 feet above the sea. I shall always say that next to the sight of Kinchinjunga from beyond Darjiling, this is the finest mountain spectacle that I have seen. Rakapushi is one of the most superbly modelled of mountains. Everywhere visible, as we ascend the valley, he keeps watch and ward over the lower summits, and over the smiling belts of green and orchard-plots below that owe their existence to his glacial bounty. But up above his true and imperial majesty is best revealed. There enormous and shining glaciers fill the hollows of his sides and only upon the needle point of his highest crest is the snow unable to settle.

. . .

And though our eye, aching with the dazzling vision, may seek a transient solace in the restful verdure of the lower and terraced slopes, and may even dip into the deep gorge where the river hums 1,000 feet below our feet, yet it cannot for long resist the enchantment of those glimmering peaks, and ever hankers for the fascination of the summit.

The distance from Gilgit to Hunza is 61 miles, which we covered easily in three days. In former times, and up till the brilliant little campaign in the winter of 1891, by which the British became the practical masters of the country, the road, if it could be so called without a grim jest, consisted in many parts of rocky and ladder-like tracks up the mountainsides, and of narrow galleries, built out with timbers, round the edges of the cliffs. It has since been much improved by the sappers attached to the Gilgit garrison. Outside Baltit, the capital of Hunza, we were met by the Thum, or Mir, or Rajah, as he is variously called, Mohammed Nazim Khan, a young man of about twenty-eight years of age, whom the Indian Government invested with the ruling title after his elder brother, Safdar Ali Khan, a murderer and fratricide of more than ordinary activity, had fled before the British advance in 1891. The Thum was accompanied by his Wazir, Humaiun Beg, the representative of a family in which that dignity has been hereditary for generations, and himself the most agreeable and capable personality in the Hindu Kush states. I visited the Thum in the so-called castle of Baltit, a most picturesque edifice – the model of a feudal baron's stronghold – that rises to a considerable height above the flat-roofed cubes of the town. I was received in a chamber opening on to the roof, where the Russian explorer, Captain Gromchevski, had opened negotiations with Safdar Ali Khan in 1888. To this apartment it was necessary to ascend by a rude ladder, conducting to a hatchway in the floor. This might, he thought, be a primitive mode of entrance; but then the castle of Baltit (so called because it was originally built by Baltis, from Baltistan) is not precisely a Windsor.

. . .

From Baltit Lonnard and I commenced our march to the Pamirs. The distance to the Kilik Pass is about 81 miles, over one of the worst tracks in the world. At a little beyond Baltit the valley of the Hunza river, which from Chalt has pursued an easterly course, turns due north, and the river cuts a deep gash or furrows an uproarious channel along its bottom in its descent from the watershed of the Pamirs. The scenery also changes. In place of the richly cultivated terraces and the abounding orchards of both the Hunza and the Nagar slopes in the lower valley, we find only rare villages and still rarer cultivation, and are in a region of rocks and stones. Big glaciers propel their petrified cascades to the very edge of the river. In many places this required to be forded. Sometimes the road is only conducted round the edge of the precipices that over-hang the torrent by artificial ladders and ledges, built out from the cliff with stones loosely laid upon supports of brushwood and timber jammed into the interstices of the rock. This sounds very dreadful, but in practice is much less alarming, the galleries, though only lasting for a few days, being sufficiently strong at the beginning, and being slightly inclined inwards toward the cliff. In the course of a very few days I underwent the bodily labours of a Parliamentary session, and parted with the superfluous physical accretions of an entire London season. Over this vile stretch of country there are two tracts, the upper or summer track, which avoids the riverbed, then filled with a fierce and swirling torrent, and climbs to the summit of the cliffs, several thousand feet above the water; and the lower or winter track, which can only be pursued when, the melting of the snow by the hot summer suns being over, the current dwindles to a number of fordable channels, across and amid the boulder-piled fringes of which the traveller picks his way. The second track is not commonly available till the beginning of October; but a few cloudy days had sensibly lowered the river, and it was thought that, with the aid of the Thum's people, who accompanied us in large numbers, the route might be found practicable, except in a few places where, to avoid the still swollen stream, we should require to scale the heights. The whole of our baggage, tents, etc., had to be carried on the backs of men, the route being quite impracticable for baggage-animals. We had riding-horses ourselves, but there were many places where these had to be abandoned and swum across the river. I was very favourably impressed with the Hunza men, who were strong, cheerful, and willing, and struck me as both the most masculine and the most agreeable of the Aryan tribes of the Hindu Kush. Those persons who contended that we should do an injury to them, and heap up trouble for ourselves, by inter-fering with their liberty, which, as interpreted by their chiefs, was merely the liberty to harry and plunder and slay their less manly or warlike neighbours, are shown to have talked nonsense, as croakers usually do. The people themselves extracted very little from the raids, the proceeds of which were commonly pocketed by the chiefs; and I have no doubt that many a converted freebooter lent a not unwilling back to the transport of our loads.

'What a wonderful incognito is mine!'

ALEXANDRA DAVID-NÉEL

My Journey to Lhasa (1927)

Alexandra David-Néel (1868–1969) was born in Paris and lived to the age of 101, by which time her exploits had earned her fame in her native France. Her travelling achievements, mainly in Tibet, exceed those of almost all her contemporaries. However, she did not even start adventuring until at least her mid thirties. She had been until then an opera singer and had taken leading roles in Athens and Hanoi as well Paris, before becoming director of the opera in Tunis.

Already a Buddhist scholar and recently married, she left for Tibet aged forty-four and then spent some fourteen years wandering, latterly with her adopted son, Yongden, and often in circumstances of very considerable poverty and discomfort, at the end of which she spoke many local dialects and could pass for a native. Her journey to Lhasa in 1924 was a successor to four previous long journeys in Tibet, but it was the one at the end of which she finally reached the fabled spiritual capital of Tibet. She and Yongden were disguised as arjopas, or beggar pilgrims, who walked and sometimes even prostrated themselves lengthwise on the ground all the way from their villages out on the Tibetan permafrost to the spiritual capital.

A very famous festival takes place each year at Lhasa on the evening of the full moon of the first month. Light wooden structures of a large size are entirely covered with ornaments and images of gods, men, and animals, all made of butter and dyed in different colours. These frail frameworks are called *tormas*. About one hundred of them are erected along the *par kor* – that is to say, the streets that form the middle circle of religious circumambulation around the *Jo khang*, and in front of each one, a large number of butter lamps burn on a small altar. That nocturnal feast is meant to entertain the gods, just as are certain concerts on the roofs of the temples.

The butter *tormas* festival at Lhasa is famous all over Thibet, and even in Mongolia and China. It is no doubt truly glorious, yet, I think the feast is much more beautiful in its sumptuous surrounding at the great Kum Bum lamasery, where I have seen it several times during the years I lived in that monastery. However, I very much enjoyed that part of the New Year merrymaking at Lhasa.

As soon as darkness had come and the lamps were lighted, Yongden and I went to the Par Kor. A dense crowd was there, waiting for the Dalai lama, who was to go round to inspect the tormas. I had more than once seen big Thibetan gatherings, but I had gone through them with servants and other attendants who made a way for me. This was my first experience of being part of the crowd myself.

Groups of sturdy giants, cowmen clad in sheepskin, holding on to one another, ran for joy in the deepest of the throng. Their big fists belaboured the ribs of those whom bad luck had placed in their way. Policemen, armed with long sticks and whips, growing more and more excited as the time of the Dalai lama's coming approached, used their weapons indiscriminately against anybody. In the midst of this tumult, trying our best to guard ourselves against hustling and blows, we spent some lively moments.

At last the arrival of the Lama-King was announced. Then more policemen appeared, followed by soldiers. The knocking, beating, boxing increased. Some women screamed, others laughed. Finally there remained along the walls of the houses that confronted the tormas only a few rows of people, more tightly pressed against one another than tinned sardines. I was amongst them. From time to time a man seated at a ground-floor window, whose view I was blocking, gave me a strong push in the back, but it was of no use whatever. Even had I wished it I could not have moved a single step. Finally he understood this, or my insensibility disarmed him. Anyway, he ceased from using unnecessary violence.

The whole Lhasa garrison was under arms. Infantry and cavalry marched past the dazzling butter edifices, lighted up by thousands of lamps. In a sedan chair covered with yellow brocade, the Dalai lama passed in his turn, attended by the commander-in-chief of the Thibetan army and other high officials. Soldiers marched in the rear. The band struck up an English music-hall tune. Crackers were fired and meagre Bengal lights coloured the procession red and green for a few minutes.

That was all. And the lamaist ruler had gone.

For a long time after the regal cortège had passed, private processions followed: people of rank surrounded by attendants holding Chinese lanterns, high ecclesiastics with clerical followers, the representatives of the Nepal Maharaja, and many others; clergy, nobility, wealthy traders, and their womenfolk all dressed in their best, laughing – all more or less drunk and happy. Their gaiety was contagious. Yongden and I went with the crowd, running, jostling, and pushing like everybody else, enjoying as youngsters might have done the fun of being there in Lhasa, feasting the New Year with the Thibetans.

When at last the time came to go back to our hovel, we noticed on our way that the streets which ought to have been well lighted by the full moon were growing darker and darker. What did it mean? We are tee-totalers, and could not have the same reason as most citizens on that night, for clouded vision. We reached a square, and noticed a black shadow in a corner of the moon. It was the beginning of an eclipse, and soon we heard a noise of drums made by the good people to frighten away the dragon which was trying to swallow the nocturnal luminary! The eclipse was total. I observed it during the night, and it was the most interesting one that I had ever witnessed.

'This is still better than the curtain of sand before the Potala, on the day of our arrival,' said Yongden, jocularly. 'Now your gods are screen-ing the moon so that we shall not be seen too distinctly. I think you had better ask them to stop their kind protection of our incognito. They might put out the sun!'

Whatever may have been the protection with which I was favoured, the day came when the safety of my disguise was again endangered and I had to defend myself in my own way.

I was wandering in the market when a policeman stopped and gazed at me intently. Why? Perhaps he only wondered from what part of Thibet I might hail, but it was better to be prepared for the worst. A new battle was to be fought, and I began it, my heart beating rather quickly, but brave as usual. I chose, amongst the things for sale, an aluminum saucepan, and began to bargain for it with that ridiculous obstinacy shown by the people of the half-wild tribes of the borderland. I offered an absurd price and talked nonsense in a loud voice, hardly stopping to breathe. People around the booths began to laugh and exchange jokes about me. The cowmen and women of the northern solitudes are a habitual subject of mockery for the more civilised people of Lhasa.

'Ah!' said the merchant, laughing, and yet irritated by my continuous twaddle, 'you are a true *dokpa*, there can be no doubt of that!' And all present ridiculed the stupid woman who knew nothing besides her cattle and the grass of the desert. The policeman passed on, amused like everybody else.

I bought the saucepan, and, as I feared being followed, I compelled myself to loiter about the market, playing a comedy of admiration and stupidity before the ugliest and cheapest goods. Then my good luck caused me to fall in with a group of true *dokpas*. I began to talk with them in their own dialect. I had lived in their country some years ago. I spoke of places and men known to them, and they were convinced that I was born in a neighbouring tribe. I have no doubt that, with the quickness of imagination that is peculiar to them, they would, next day, have sworn in all sincerity that they had known me for a long time.

A second incident happened a few days later. A kind of special constable tried to extort money from me; but I managed the affair cleverly enough to give him nothing without disclosing my identity.

Still another policeman hit me with his truncheon because I had trespassed in a place where 'quality' only were admitted, and truly I had to make a great effort to prevent myself from giving a gratuity to that man, so delighted was I with the fun. 'What a wonderful incognito is mine!' I confided to Yongden. 'Now I am even beaten in the street!' And after that I felt completely secure.

'In this heart-stopping moment pilgrims burst into cries'

COLIN THUBRON

To a Mountain in Tibet (2011)

Broad peaked and imposing at 6,700 metres (22,000 feet), Mount Kailas in southwestern Tibet near the Indian and Nepali borders is one of the world's most revered religious sites, sacred to Buddhists, Hindus and the followers of Bon and Jainism. Despite its importance for pilgrims, few reach it because of the cold and difficult journey from any direction. Colin Thubron (b. 1939) tackled it in his seventies.

To a Mountain in Tibet may be his most personal of more than fifteen major travel titles. It reads as a journey made for himself, into which we have the privilege of a glimpse.

A steep road takes our Land Cruisers north. Behind us the Great Himalaya cover the skyline, while ahead opens an orange and sulphur-coloured wilderness where the Karnali withers away. The 25,000-foot massif of Gurla Mandhata, detached from the Himalaya in its own bright climate, comes shouldering down from the east, and my Tibetan driver, whose dashboard swings with the protective photos of lamas, starts softly to sing.

Near the village of Toyo to our west the most formidable nineteenth-century invader of Tibet came to grief. The Indian general Zorawar Singh, marching in the service of a lightly federated Sikh empire, had already conquered Ladakh and Baltistan, establishing one of the borders of modern India, and in spring 1841 he advanced out of Kashmir with some 500 men, seizing forts as he went. Near Taklakot he routed an 8,000-strong Tibetan army, but fatally detached himself with a small contingent to escort his wife back to the safety of Ladakh. On his return, a Sino-Tibetan force cut him off near Toyo, and his detachment was annihilated.

Such were the legends surrounding him that only a golden bullet was said to have brought him down. His corpse was hacked into morsels to be hung up in local households, and even the hair of his body, which covered it 'like eagles' feathers', was plucked out for luck. Every four years, at the great monastery of Shepeling, his enshrined testicle featured in a rare tantric rite; until the artillery of the Cultural Revolution buried it. At Toyo a walled tomb once enclosed the general's filleted bones, but when Indian pilgrims visited in 1999 they found only rubble. Now the Tibetans have reassembled its stones into a rough chorten, looped with flags, where they still murmur mantras to the invader.

As we climb higher, the sky grows light and thin. The streams peeling off Gurla Mandhata spread small, spinach-green pastures before the wilderness returns. We pass a few road builders' camps, and a castle turning to dust. In less than an hour we have ascended 3,000 feet. Here and there a monastery stands in the wastes, and nomad flocks are grazing on nothing under the far mountains. Then at 16,000 feet, where the skyline is decked with cairns and flags, we crest the Thalladong pass and veer to a stupefied halt. We are gazing on a country of planetary strangeness. Beneath us, in a crescent of depthless silence, a huge lake curves empty out of sight. It is utterly still. In the plateau's barren smoothness it makes a hard purity, like some elemental carving, and its colour is almost shocking: a violent peacock blue. There is no bird or wind-touched shrub to start a sound. And in the cleansed stillness high above, floating on foothills so faded that it seems isolated in the sky, shines the cone of Mount Kailas.

In this heart-stopping moment pilgrims burst into cries and prayer.

Even our seasoned trekkers spill from their Land Cruisers to gaze. There seem no colours left in the world but this bare earth-brown, the snows white, and the sheen of mirrored sky. Everything else has been distilled away. The south face of Kailas is fluted with the illusion of a long, vertical stairway, as if for spirits to climb by. It shines fifty miles away in unearthly solitude. Void of any life, the whole region might have survived from some sacred prehistory, shorn of human complication. We have entered holy land.

Yet the lake is only precariously sacred. It is called Rakshas Tal, the lake of demons, and is inhabited by carnivorous Hindu spirits. Only one monastery, demolished in the Cultural Revolution, has ever touched its shores. Pilgrims shun it. Its crescent is imagined, darker and more brooding than the holy lake of Manasarovar nearby, whose circle reflects the sun. It is said to be tormented by winds and ice floes, and to lie above drowned mountains. Its waters were once a dark poison. But a golden fish, swimming by chance out of Manasarovar, carved a channel into Rakshas by which the sunlit lake flowed into the black one and redeemed it. So, to the initiate, the moon-waters of Rakshas Tal become the dark complement – and psychic fulfilment – of Manasarovar.

We come down gently from the pass, and for a sterile moment the waters drop from sight. But minutes later another needle of blue – darker than the first – appears to our east, and we are descending to Manasarovar. As we pass a Hindu guest house, I feel a twinge of alarm that even in these solitudes this holiest of the world's lakes – sacred to one fifth of humankind – might have been polluted or built upon. Then it opens before us, untouched. Its waters yawn with the same fathomless intensity as Rakshas Tal, but the peacock blue has deepened to a well of pure cobalt, edged by snow mountains that overlook it from one horizon to another. At over 15,000 feet it is the highest freshwater lake of its size on earth. Two hundred square miles of water shine in its chain of snows, so that the few pilgrims who circumambulate it must walk for fifty-four miles. No life disturbs its waters as we descend. Only here and there breezes plough the surface with tracks, as if invisible ships had passed a minute before.

In fact no boat may sail here, and no one may fish its waters. There was a time when even hunting in this holy country was unknown. Visitors within living memory encountered bands of wild asses grazing – I glimpsed only one, shy and far away – and marmots and hares would watch innocently close at hand. In the past half-century, this has changed. But even now, as we reach lake level, a skein of geese flies in on an eerie rush of wings, and water birds are strutting and nesting a stone's throw away from where we pitch camp, and speckle the shore for miles.

From here, if you stand among the birds, the whole lake stretches into view. At its southern end the shelving ridges of Gurla Mandhata ebb still snowlit even along the eastern shore, while at the other end, beyond waves of brown foothills, Kailas mushrooms into the blue. These two white summits haunt the lake. Between them its indigo void appears coldly primeval. Tibetans call it Tso Mapham, 'the Unrivalled', or Rinpoche, 'the Precious'. Its hushed stillness seems to freeze it in a jewel-like concentrate of water. In both Buddhist and Hindu scripture the universe is born from such primal matter. A cosmic wind beats the water into worlds, and the god Vishnu, who dreams in the ocean near-eternally, creates diversity out of oneness by a sheer feat of will. Geology itself heightens the lake's strangeness. For Manasarovar is a stranded fragment of the Tethys Sea, almost drained by the upthrust of the Himalaya.

'God's Gift None Can Blot'

ALEXANDER FRATER

Chasing the Monsoon (1990)

Alexander Frater (b. 1937) was drawn to find the wettest place on earth. It is reputed to be Cherrapunji, in the Khasi Hills of Assam, that bit of eastern India that is squeezed into obscurity and complexity of access by Bangladesh to the south and Bhutan to the north. 'Cherra? In July? So far this month they have had 366 inches,' he was told when he announced his plans to go there in the wettest month of the year.

The rust-pitted Ambassador was driven by a bony young man wearing broken sunglasses and terrific winged moustaches. A youth sat with him, to whom the driver spoke unceasingly in the soft, contrite voice of the confessional. The youth carried a bundle of green leaves which he fed to the driver one by one, but otherwise remained mute and listened intently to the monologue.

We headed west down an alley walled by scarlet rhododendrons, then south through the hills towards the Bangladeshi border. An intricate interlocking matrix of creeks and streams divided the landscape into a series of moated islands. When the car suffered one of its routine stalls the air was loud with the splash of running water. At Laitlyngkot, once a place of backyard iron forges where the air rang with the chime of hammers, we stopped at the bazaar for bananas and glasses of sweet tea. The descendants of the iron workers were stocky, composed, self-reliant people who looked you straight in the eye. Drinking my tea beneath an English yew I saw a bus approach, painted with crimson demons and the legend 'God's Gift None Can Blot'. It stopped and the several joining passengers attacked it like rock climbers, swarming on to the roof and settling back to light their pipes.

An Indian official begged a lift to Sohrarim, the next village. He was a soils analyst from Madras and said the Khasis, unable to burn their dead on ground waterlogged by the monsoon, preserved the bodies in local orange-flavoured honey. I told him I had first heard that story when I was five, the problem then being one of brimming graves in marshy burial grounds. He looked at me curiously. 'Was your family here?' he asked.

'No. A friend of the family.'

We passed a quiet, clear river with hornbeam trees on its banks and hornstone rocks in its bed. The road, walled on one side by coal-bearing sandstone, fell away on the other into deep, wooded valleys that reminded me of the Cherrapunji painting. I wondered if there were still tigers down there, and naked nomads pursuing them with bows and arrows. The soils analyst said the nomads were around, all right, but not the tigers. These days the nomads shot wild boar, sloth bears, barking deer and, of course, monkeys, which they ate in large numbers. There were also leopards and, from time to time, marauding elephants.

'In the forest near Rajapara a while back,' he said, 'a big tusker chased a woman to her house, kicked it to pieces and trampled her to death. Nothing could be done. Only one hunter in the village possessed a gun.' Here he gave a sudden high-pitched giggle. 'It was a muzzle-loader, from the nineteenth century. But, alas, he had neither shot nor shell to fit.'

Outside Sohrarim we passed a group of seated women who shouted and gestured. I took this to be a manifestation of social tension, but the soils analyst said they were merely shooing monkeys from their ginger garden. Then he left us and, still dogged by the sound of the driver's soft, unceasing voice, we set off on the final leg to Cherrapunji. The voice had become petulant, underpinned by a singsong note of complaint.

The country ahead began to open up. We tracked along a high grassy escarpment strewn with rocks and scrubby pandanus palms. It had a scoured, comfortless, wind-blasted look, though the walls of the vertiginous gorges tumbling away beneath were so densely forested that, under a hot sun, they seemed upholstered in lustrous green tapestry.

The sun shone brightly on the escarpment too. There wasn't a raindrop within twenty miles and, aggrieved, I looked up at an empty summer sky. The gorges broadened into deep, jungly valleys, and I realised why there were no clouds above. They were all down below, veils of feathery cirrus, islands of domed cumulus, boiling through the valleys like a grounded tropical front. It was destabilising to observe, this inversion of the sky and earth, but beautiful too. Small, perfect rainbows stood along the clouds' route, delineating their highway in lights, even charging them with a brief, glittering opalescence as they drifted by.

The driver suddenly paused in his discourse and pointed ahead. 'Cherra!' he said.

He changed gear and took the car slowly up a steep, winding incline. I craned to see and, at the head of the gradient, 1,300 metres above sea level, I finally laid eyes on the wettest place on earth.

FOURTEEN

So Long as all You Want is a Penguin's Egg

These adventure stories record events where the writers and their companions were at the limits of their abilities to survive. Mungo Park set out to a part of West Africa about which nothing was known to the outside world.

The next three all take place within twenty years of each other during the last few years of the nineteenth century and first of the twentieth, when there was a concentrated period of exploration of the extremes of the planet. Francis Younghusband crossed the Karakorum massif from India into China; Apsley Cherry-Garrard completed 'the worst journey in the world' and rejoined Scott's Antarctic expedition; Ernest Shackleton found South Georgia in his tiny boat and rescued his team members, who had been marooned also in the Antarctic. These are the stories of those who overcame extremis; many others remain unwritten by those who did not.

'I had no alternative, but to lie down and perish'

MUNGO PARK

Travels in the Interior Districts of Africa; Performed Under the Direction and Patronage of the African Association, in the Years 1795, 1796, and 1797 (1799)

Mungo Park (1771–1806) was exploring West Africa and the upper Niger River more than half a century before African exploration made the names of adventurers such as Burton, Speke, Livingstone and Stanley. At the age of twenty-four, he set off into areas then completely unknown to Europeans. Lionised in London upon the publication of Travels, *he shunned the limelight and returned to Selkirk, his place of birth, where he married and had four children before launching his second West African adventure in 1805. He never returned from this, having reputedly been attacked by natives and drowning after crossing 1,000 kilometres of what is now the Gambia, Senegal and Mali, followed by a further 1,500 kilometres by river down the Niger.*

Aug. 25th. – I departed from Kooma, accompanied by two shepherds, who were going towards Sibidooloo. The road was very steep and rocky, and as my horse had hurt his feet much in coming from Bammakoo, he travelled slowly and with great difficulty; for in many places the ascent was so sharp, and the declivities so great, that if he had made one false step, he must inevitably have been dashed to pieces. The shepherds being anxious to proceed, gave themselves little trouble about me or my horse, and kept walking on at a considerable distance. It was about eleven o'clock, as I stopped to drink a little water at a rivulet (my companions being nearly a quarter of a mile before me), that I heard some people calling to each other, and presently a loud screaming, as from a person in great distress. I immediately conjectured that a lion had taken one of the shepherds, and mounted my horse to have a better view of what had happened. The noise, however, ceased; and I rode slowly towards the place from whence I thought it had proceeded, calling out, but without receiving any answer. In a little time, however, I perceived one of the shepherds lying among the long grass near the road; and though I could see no blood upon him, I concluded he was dead. But when I came close to him, he whispered me to stop; telling me that a party of armed men had seized upon his companion, and shot two arrows at himself as he was making his escape. I stopped to consider what course to take, and looking round, saw at a little distance a man sitting on the stump of a tree; I distinguished also the heads of six or seven more, sitting among the grass, with muskets in their hands. I had now no hopes of escaping, and therefore determined to ride forward towards them. As I approached them, I was in hopes they were elephant hunters; and by way of opening the conversation, enquired if they had shot anything; but without returning an answer, one of them ordered me to dismount; and then, as if recollecting himself, waved with his hand for me to proceed. I accordingly rode past, and had with some difficulty crossed a deep rivulet, when I heard somebody holloa; and looking behind, saw those I had taken for elephant hunters running after me, and calling out to me to turn back. I stopped until they were all come up; when they informed me that the king of the Foulahs had sent them on purpose to bring me, my horse, and everything that belonged to me, to Fooladoo, and that therefore I must turn back, and go along with them. Without hesitating a moment, I turned round and followed them, and we travelled together near a quarter of a mile without exchanging a word; when coming to a dark place of the wood, one of them said, in the Mandingo language, 'This will do;' and immediately snatched my hat from my head. Though I was by no means free of apprehension, yet I resolved to show as few signs of fear as possible, and therefore told them, that unless my hat was returned to me, I should proceed no further. But before I had time to receive an answer, another drew his knife, and seizing upon a metal button which remained upon my waistcoat, cut it off, and put it into his pocket. Their intentions were now obvious;

and I thought that the easier they were permitted to rob me of every-thing, the less I had to fear. I therefore allowed them to search my pockets without resistance, and examine every part of my apparel, which they did with the most scrupulous exactness. But observing that I had one waistcoat under another, they insisted that I should cast them both off, and at last, to make sure work, stripped me quite naked. Even my half boots (though the sole of one of them was tied on to my foot with a broken bridle rein) were minutely inspected. Whilst they were examining the plunder, I begged them, with great earnestness, to return my pocket compass; but when I pointed it out to them, as it was lying on the ground, one of the banditti, thinking I was about to take it up, cocked his musket, and swore that he would lay me dead on the spot if I presumed to put my hand upon it. After this, some of them went away with my horse, and the remainder stood considering whether they should leave me quite naked, or allow me something to shelter me from the sun. Humanity at last prevailed; they returned me the worst of the two shirts, and a pair of trousers; and, as they went away, one of them threw back my hat, in the crown of which I kept my memorandums; and this was probably the reason they did not wish to keep it. After they were gone, I sat for some time looking around me with amazement and terror. Whichever way I turned, nothing appeared but danger and diffi-culty. I saw myself in the midst of a vast wilderness in the depth of the rainy season, naked and alone; surrounded by savage animals, and men still more savage. I was five hundred miles from the nearest European settlement. All these circumstances crowded at once on my recollection; and I confess that my spirits began to fail me. I considered my fate as certain, and that I had no alternative, but to lie down and perish. The influence of religion, however, aided and supported me. I reflected that no human prudence or foresight could possibly have averted my present sufferings. I was indeed a stranger in a strange land, yet I was still under the protecting eye of that Providence who has condescended to call himself the stranger's friend. At this moment, painful as my reflections were, the extraordinary beauty of a small moss, in fructification, irresistibly caught my eye. I mention this to show from what trifling circumstances the mind will sometimes derive consolation; for though the whole plant was not larger than the top of one of my fingers, I could not contemplate the delicate conformation of its roots, leaves, and capsula, without admiration. Can that Being (thought I) who planted, watered, and brought to perfection, in this obscure part of the world, a thing which appears of so small importance, look with unconcern upon the situation and sufferings of creatures formed after His own image? – surely not! Reflections like these would not allow me to despair. I started up, and disregarding both hunger and fatigue, travelled forwards, assured that relief was at hand; and I was not disappointed. In a short time I came to a small village, at the entrance of which I overtook the two shepherds who had come with me from Kooma. They were much surprised to see me; for they said they never doubted that the Foulahs, when they had robbed me, had murdered me. Departing from this village, we travelled over several rocky ridges, and at sunset arrived at Sibidooloo, the frontier town of the kingdom of Manding.

'What, however, saved our party was my holding my tongue'

FRANCIS YOUNGHUSBAND

The Heart of a Continent (1896)

It was 1887 and the Raj in India was haunted by fears, probably unfounded, of imminent Russian invasion.

Francis Younghusband, then a twenty-six-year-old captain in the Irish Dragoon Guards, managed to find his way into the elite group that were involved in the Great Game standoff with the Russians in Central Asia. He persuaded his superiors to allow him first to explore Manchuria and then to attempt a pioneering journey across the whole length of China to the Karakorum border with what is now North Pakistan.

Younghusband crossed Eastern China, the Gobi and then south and east of the Tien Shan range, skirted the Taklamakan Desert and reached Kashgar, the hub of Chinese Turkestan. Thence he went south to attempt the crossing of the Karakorum into India. Here, at the critical moment of his journey, he is confronted with crossing the Mustagh Pass.

Matters were therefore approaching a very critical stage, and that was an anxious night for me. I often recall it, and think of our little bivouac in the snow at the foot of the range we had to overcome. The sun sank behind the icy mountains, the bright glow disappeared from them, and they became steely hard while the grey cold of night settled shimmering down upon them. All around was pure white snow and ice, breathing out cold upon us. The little pools and streamlets of water which the heat of the sun had poured off the glacier during the day were now gripped by the frost, which seemed to creep around ourselves too, and huddle us up together. We had no tent to shelter us from the biting streams of air flowing down from the mountain summits, and we had not sufficient fuel to light a fire round which we might lie. We had, indeed, barely enough brushwood to keep up a fire for cooking; but my Chinese servant cooked a simple meal of rice and mutton for us all. We gathered round the fire to eat it hot out of the bowl, and then rolled ourselves up in our sheepskins and went to sleep, with the stars twinkling brightly above, and the frost gripping closer and closer upon us.

Next morning, while it was yet dark, Wali, the guide, awoke us. We each had a drink of tea and some bread, and then we started off to attack the pass. The ponies, with nearly all the baggage, were left behind under the charge of Liu-san, the Chinaman, and some of the older men. All we took with us was a roll of bedding for myself, a sheepskin coat for each man, some native biscuits, tea and a large tea-kettle, and a bottle of brandy. The ascent to the pass was easy but trying, for we were now not far from nineteen thousand feet above sea-level, and at that height, walking uphill through deep snow, one quickly becomes exhausted. We could only take a dozen or twenty steps at a time, and we would then bend over on our sticks and pant as if we had been running hard uphill. We were tantalised, too, by the apparent nearness of the pass. Everything here was on a gigantic scale, and what seemed to be not more than an hour's walk from the camp was in fact a six hours' climb. It was nearly midday when we reached the top of the pass, and what we saw there I have already related in the letter quoted above. There was nothing but a sheer precipice, and those first few moments on the summit of the Mustagh Pass were full of intense anxiety to me. If we could but get over, the crowning success of my expedition would be gained. But the thing seemed to me simply an impossibility. I had had no experience of Alpine climbing, and I had no ice-axes or other mountaineering appliances with me. I had not even any proper boots. All I had for foot-gear were some native boots of soft leather, without nails and without heels – mere leather stockings, in fact – which gave no sort of grip upon an icy surface. How, then, I should ever be able to get down the icy slopes and rocky precipices I now saw before me I could not think; and if it had rested with me alone, the probability is we never should have got over the pass at all.

What, however, saved our party was my holding my tongue. I kept quite silent as I looked over the pass, and waited to hear what the men had to say about it. They meanwhile were looking at me, and, imagining that an Englishman never went back from an enterprise he had once started on, took it as a matter of course that, as I gave no order to go back, I meant to go on. So they set about their preparations for the descent. We had brought an ordinary pickaxe with us, and Wali went on ahead with this, while the rest of us followed one by one behind him, each hanging on to a rope tied round Wali's waist to support him in case he slipped while hewing steps across the ice-slope. This slope was of hard ice, very steep, and, thirty yards or so below the line we took, ended in an ice-fall, which again terminated far beneath in the head of a glacier at the foot of the pass. Wali with his pickaxe hewed a way step by step across the ice-slope, so as to reach the rocky cliff by which we should have to descend on to the glacier below. We slowly edged across the slope after him, but it was hard to keep cool and steady. From where we stood we could see nothing over the end of the slope but the glacier many hundreds of feet below us. Some of the men were so little nervous that they kicked the fragments of ice hewed out by Wali down the slope, and laughed as they saw them hop down it and with one last bound disappear altogether. But an almost sickening feeling came on me as I watched this, for we were standing on a slope as steep as the roof of a house. We had no ice-axes with which to anchor ourselves or give us support; and though I tied handkerchiefs, and the men bits of leather and cloth, round the insteps of our smooth native boots, to give us a little grip on the slippery ice, I could not help feeling that if any one of us had lost his foothold, the rest of us would never have been able to hold him up with the rope, and that in all likelihood the whole party would have been carried away and plunged into the abyss below. Outwardly I kept as cool and cheerful as I could, but inwardly I shuddered at each fresh step I took. The sun was now pouring down on to the ice, and just melted the surface of the steps after they were hewn, so that by the time those of us who were a few paces behind Wali reached a step, the ice was just covered over with water, and this made it still more slippery for our soft leather boots, which had now become almost slimy on the surface. It was under these circumstances that my Ladaki servant Drogpa gave in. He was shaking all over in an exaggerated shiver, and so unsteady, I thought he would slip at any moment, and perhaps carry us all with him. We were but at the beginning of our trials. We had not even begun the actual descent yet, but were merely crossing to a point from which we should make it. It was dangerous to have such a man with us, so I told him he might return to the ponies and go round with them.

At last we reached the far side of the slope, and found ourselves on a projecting piece of rock protruding through the ice. Here we could rest, but only with the prospect of still further difficulties before us. We were at the head of the rocky precipice, the face of which we should have to descend to reach the ice-slopes which extended to the glacier at the foot of the pass. At such heights as those which we had now reached, where the snow and ice lie sometimes hundreds of feet thick, it is only where it is very steep that the bare rock shows through. The cliff we had now to descend was an almost sheer precipice: its only saving feature was that it was rough and rugged, and so afforded some little hold for our hands and feet. Yet even then we seldom got a hold for the whole hand or whole foot. All we generally found was a little ledge, upon which we could grip with the tips of the fingers or side of the foot. The men were most good to me, whenever possible guiding my foot into some secure hold, and often supporting it there with their hands; but at times it was all I could do to summon sufficient courage to let myself down on to the veriest little crevices which had to support me. There was a constant dread, too, that fragments of these ledges might give way with the weight upon them; for the rock was very crumbly, as it generally is when exposed to severe frosts, and once I heard a shout from above, as a huge piece of rock which had been detached came crashing past me, and as nearly as possible hit two of the men who had already got halfway down.

We reached the bottom of the cliff without accident, and then found ourselves at the head of a long ice-slope extending down to the glacier below. Protruding through the ice were three pieces of rock, which would serve us as successive halting-places, and we determined upon taking a line which led by them. We had brought with us every scrap of rope that could be spared from the ponies' gear, and we tied these and all the men's turbans and waist-clothes together into one long rope, by which we let a man down the ice-slope on to the first projecting rock. As he went down he cut steps, and when he had reached the rock we tied the upper end of the rope firmly onto a rock above, and then one by one we came down the slope, hanging on to the rope and making use of the steps which had been cut. This was, therefore, a comparatively easy part of the descent; but one man was as nearly as possible lost. He slipped, fell over on his back, and came sliding down the slope at a frightful pace. Luckily, however, he still managed to keep hold of the rope with one hand, and so kept himself from dashing over the ice-fall at the side of the slope; but when he reached the rock his hand was almost bared of skin, and he was shivering with fright. Wali, however, gave him a sound rating for being so careless, and on the next stage made him do all the hardest part of the work.

The other men got down the slope without mishap, and then came the last man. He, of course, could not have the benefit of a rope to hang on by, for he would have to untie it from the rock and bring it with him. Wali had selected for this, the most dangerous piece of work in the whole descent, the man who had especially troubled me by knocking pieces of ice over the precipice when we were on the ice-slope at the head of the pass. He was one of the slaves I had released at Yarkand; an incessant grumbler, and very rough, but, next to Wali, the

best man I had for any really hard work. He tied the end of the rope round his waist, and then slowly and carefully came down the steps which had been hewn in the slope. We at the end of the rope pulled it in at every step he took, so that if he slipped, though he might fall past us, we should be able to haul in the rope fast, and so perhaps save him from the ice-fall. He reached our rock of refuge in safety, and we then in the same manner descended two more stages of the ice-slope, and finally reached a part where the slope was less steep, and we could proceed without cutting steps the whole way.

At last, just as the sun set, we reached the glacier at the foot of the pass. We were in safety once more. The tension was over, and the last and greatest obstacle in my journey, had been surmounted. Those moments when I stood at the foot of the pass are long to be remembered by me—moments of intense relief, and of deep gratitude for the success that had been granted. Such feelings as mine were now cannot be described in words, but they are known to everyone who has had his heart set on one great object and has accomplished it. I took one last look at the pass, never before or since seen by a European, and then we started away down the glacier to find some bare spot on which to lay our rugs and rest.

'. . . so long as all you want is a penguin's egg'

APSLEY CHERRY-GARRARD

The Worst Journey in the World (1922)

The Worst Journey in the World *tells the story of Captain Robert Falcon Scott's second expedition to the Antarctic in 1911, which ended in the death of Scott and four of his party. The 'worst journey' refers to the side expedition of Apsley Cherry-Garrard (1886–1959) and his small team to Cape Crozier to find the egg of the Emperor penguin for the Natural History Museum in London. The six-week diversion became known as The Winter Journey and took place during the mid-winter period of uninterrupted darkness. The conditions were as bad as any ever faced by human beings who survived in the region.*

This is his introductory passage . . .

Polar exploration is at once the cleanest and most isolated way of having a bad time which has been devised. It is the only form of adventure in which you put on your clothes at Michaelmas and keep them on until Christmas, and, save for a layer of the natural grease of the body, find them as clean as though they were new. It is more lonely than London, more secluded than any monastery, and the post comes but once a year. As men will compare the hardships of France, Palestine, or Mesopotamia, so it would be interesting to contrast the rival claims of the Antarctic as a medium of discomfort. A member of Campbell's party tells me that the trenches at Ypres were a comparative picnic. But until somebody can evolve a standard of endurance I am unable to see how it can be done. Take it all in all, I do not believe anybody on earth has a worse time than an Emperor penguin.

Even now the Antarctic is to the rest of the earth as the Abode of the Gods was to the ancient Chaldees, a precipitous and mammoth land lying far beyond the seas which encircled man's habitation, and nothing is more striking about the exploration of the Southern Polar regions than its absence, for when King Alfred reigned in England the Vikings were navigating the ice-fields of the North; yet when Wellington fought the battle of Waterloo there was still an undiscovered continent in the South.

. . .

Both sexually and socially the polar explorer must make up his mind to be starved. To what extent can hard work, or what may be called dramatic imagination, provide a substitute? Compare our thoughts on the march; our food dreams at night; the primitive way in which the loss of a crumb of biscuit may give a lasting sense of grievance. Night after night I bought big buns and chocolate at a stall on the island platform at Hatfield station, but always woke before I got a mouthful to my lips; some companions who were not so highly strung were more fortunate, and ate their phantom meals.

And the darkness, accompanied it may be almost continually by howling blizzards which prevent you seeing your hand before your face. Life in such surroundings is both mentally and physically cramped; open-air exercise is restricted and in blizzards quite impossible, and you realise how much you lose by your inability to see the world about you when you are out-of-doors. I am told that when confronted by a lunatic or one who under the influence of some great grief or shock contemplates suicide, you should take that man out-of-doors and walk him about: Nature will do the rest. To normal people like ourselves living under abnormal circumstances Nature could do much to lift our thoughts out of the rut of everyday affairs, but she loses much of her healing power when she cannot be seen, but only felt, and when that feeling is intensely uncomfortable.

Somehow in judging polar life you must discount compulsory endurance; and find out what a man can shirk, remembering always that it is a sledging life which is the hardest test. It is because it is so much easier to shirk in civilisation that it is difficult to get a standard of what your average man can do. It does not really matter much whether your man whose work lies in or round the hut shirks a bit or not, just as it does not matter much in civilization; it is just rather a waste of opportunity. But there's precious little shirking in Barrier sledging; a week finds most of us out.

There are many questions which ought to be studied. The effect upon men of going from heat to cold, such as Bowers coming to us from the Persian Gulf; or vice versa of Simpson returning from the Antarctic to India; differences of dry and damp cold; what is a comfortable temperature in the Antarctic and what is it compared to a comfortable temperature in England, the question of women in these temperatures . . . ? The man with the nerves goes farthest. What is the ratio between nervous and physical energy? What is vitality? Why do some things terrify you at one time and not at others? What is this early morning courage? What is the influence of imagination? How far can a man draw on his capital? Whence came Bowers's great heat supply? And my own white beard? and X's blue eyes: for he started from England with brown ones and his mother refused to own him when he came back? Growth and colour change in hair and skin?

There are many reasons which send men to the Poles, and the Intellectual Force uses them all. But the desire for knowledge for its own sake is the one which really counts and there is no field for the collection of knowledge which at the present time can be compared to the Antarctic.

Exploration is the physical expression of the Intellectual Passion.

And I tell you, if you have the desire for knowledge and the power to give it physical expression, go out and explore. If you are a brave man you will do nothing: if you are fearful you may do much, for none but cowards have need to prove their bravery. Some will tell you that you are mad, and nearly all will say, 'What is the use?' For we are a nation of shopkeepers, and no shopkeeper will look at research which does not promise him a financial return within a year. And so you will sledge nearly alone, but those with whom you sledge will not be shopkeepers: that is worth a good deal. If you march your Winter Journeys you will have your reward, so long as all you want is a penguin's egg.

'... happiness irradiated us. The job was nearly done.'

SIR ERNEST SHACKLETON

South (1919)

South recounts the story of a journey so unlikely and dangerous that its chances of success at the outset must have been asymptotic to zero. The Anglo-Irish Shackleton (1874–1922) had already made two Antarctic expeditions before Endurance set sail just five days after the outbreak of the First World War. The journey described in South came about when, five months later, Endurance was frozen fast in an ice floe, eventually sinking in the Weddell Sea. The crew reached Elephant Island in Endurance's lifeboats. With no chance of being rescued, Shackleton elected to make the 620-mile journey across the Southern Ocean, the world's most notoriously dangerous ocean, in an attempt to reach the island of South Georgia in the six-metre open lifeboat, the James Caird.

When daylight came on the morning of the sixth day out we saw and felt that the *James Caird* had lost her resiliency. She was not rising to the oncoming seas. The weight of the ice that had formed in her and upon her during the night was having its effect, and she was becoming more like a log than a boat. The situation called for immediate action. We first broke away the spare oars, which were encased in ice and frozen to the sides of the boat, and threw them overboard. We retained two oars for use when we got inshore. Two of the fur sleeping bags went over the side; they were thoroughly wet, weighing probably 40 lb. each, and they had frozen stiff during the night. Three men constituted the watch below, and when a man went down it was better to turn into the wet bag just vacated by another man than to thaw out a frozen bag with the heat of his unfortunate body. We now had four bags, three in use and one for emergency use in case a member of the party should break down permanently. The reduction of weight relieved the boat to some extent, and vigorous chipping and scraping did more. We had to be very careful not to put axe or knife through the frozen canvas of the decking as we crawled over it, but gradually we got rid of a lot of ice. The *James Caird* lifted to the endless waves as though she lived again.

About 11 a.m. the boat suddenly fell off into the trough of the sea. The painter had parted and the sea anchor had gone. This was serious. The *James Caird* went away to leeward, and we had no chance at all of recovering the anchor and our valuable rope, which had been our only means of keeping the boat's head up to the seas without the risk of hoisting sail in a gale. Now we had to set the sail and trust to its holding. While the *James Caird* rolled heavily in the trough, we beat the frozen canvas until the bulk of the ice had cracked off it and then hoisted it. The frozen gear worked protestingly, but after a struggle our little craft came up to the wind again, and we breathed more freely. Skin frostbites were troubling us, and we had developed large blisters on our fingers and hands. I shall always carry the scar of one of these frostbites on my left hand, which became badly inflamed after the skin had burst and the cold had bitten deeply.

The eighth, ninth, and tenth days of the voyage had few features worthy of special note. The wind blew hard during those days, and the strain of navigating the boat was unceasing, but always we made some advance towards our goal. No bergs showed on our horizon, and we knew that we were clear of the ice fields. Each day brought its little round of troubles, but also compensation in the form of food and grow-ing hope. We felt that we were going to succeed. The odds against us had been great, but we were winning through. We still suffered severely from the cold, for, though the temperature was rising, our vitality was declin-ing owing to shortage of food, exposure, and the necessity of maintaining our cramped positions day and night. I found that it was now absolutely necessary to prepare hot milk for all hands during the night, in order to sustain life till dawn. This meant lighting the Primus lamp in the dark-ness and involved an increased drain on our small store of matches. It was the rule that one match must serve when the Primus was being lit. We had no lamp for the compass and during the early days of the voyage we would strike a match when the steersman wanted to see the course at night; but later the necessity for strict economy impressed itself upon us, and the practice of striking matches at night was stopped. We had one watertight tin of matches. I had stowed away in a pocket, in readiness for a sunny day, a lens from one of the telescopes, but this was of no use during the voyage. The sun seldom shone upon us. The glass of the com-pass got broken one night, and we contrived to mend it with adhesive tape from the medicine-chest. One of the memories that comes to me from those days is of Crean singing at the tiller. He always sang while he was steering, and nobody ever discovered what the song was. It was devoid of tune and as monotonous as the chanting of a Buddhist monk at his prayers; yet somehow it was cheerful. In moments of inspiration Crean would attempt 'The Wearing of the Green.'

On the tenth night Worsley could not straighten his body after his spell at the tiller. He was thoroughly cramped, and we had to drag him beneath the decking and massage him before he could unbend himself and get into a sleeping bag. A hard northwesterly gale came up on the eleventh day (May 5) and shifted to the southwest in the late afternoon. The sky was overcast and occasional snow squalls added to the discomfort produced by a tremendous cross-sea – the worst, I thought, that we had experienced. At midnight I was at the tiller and suddenly noticed a line of clear sky between the south and southwest – I called to the other men that the sky was clearing, and then a moment later I realised that what I had seen was not a rift in the clouds but the white crest of an enormous wave. During twenty-six years' experience of the ocean in all its moods I had not encountered a wave so gigantic. It was a mighty upheaval of the ocean, a thing quite apart from the big white-capped seas that had been our tireless enemies for many days. I shouted, 'For God's sake, hold on! It's got us!' Then came a moment of suspense that seemed drawn out into hours. White surged the foam of the breaking sea around us. We felt our boat lifted and flung forward like a cork in breaking surf. We were in a seething chaos of tortured water; but somehow the boat lived through it, half full of water, sagging to the dead weight and shuddering under the blow. We baled with the energy of men fighting for life, flinging the water over the sides with every receptacle that came to our hands, and after ten minutes of uncertainty we felt the boat renew her life beneath us. She floated again and ceased to lurch drunkenly as though dazed by the attack of the sea. Earnestly we hoped that never again would we encounter such a wave.

The conditions in the boat, uncomfortable before, had been made worse by the deluge of water. All our gear was thoroughly wet again. Our cooking stove had been floating about in the bottom of the boat, and portions of our last hoosh seemed to have permeated everything. Not until 3 a.m., when we were all chilled almost to the limit of endurance, did we manage to get the stove alight and make ourselves hot drinks. The carpenter was suffering particularly, but he showed grit and spirit. Vincent had for the past week ceased to be an active member of the crew, and I could not easily account for his collapse. Physically he was one of the strongest men in the boat. He was a young man, he had served on North Sea trawlers, and he should have been able to bear hardships better than McCarthy, who, not so strong, was always happy.

The weather was better on the following day (May 6), and we got a glimpse of the sun. Worsley's observation showed that we were not more than a hundred miles from the northwest corner of South Georgia. Two more days with a favorable wind and we would sight the promised land. I hoped that there would be no delay, for our supply of water was running very low. The hot drink at night was essential, but I decided that the daily allowance of water must be cut down to half a pint per man. The lumps of ice we had taken aboard had gone long ago. We were dependent upon the water we had brought from Elephant Island, and our thirst was increased by the fact that we were now using the brackish water in the breaker that had been slightly stove in in the surf when the boat was being loaded. Some sea water had entered at that time.

Thirst took possession of us. I dared not permit the allowance of water to be increased since an unfavorable wind might drive us away from the island and lengthen our voyage by many days. Lack of water is always the most severe privation that men can be condemned to endure, and we found, as during our earlier boat voyage, that the salt water in our clothing and the salt spray that lashed our faces made our thirst grow quickly to a burning pain. I had to be very firm in refusing to allow anyone to anticipate the morrow's allowance, which I was sometimes begged to do. We did the necessary work duly and hoped for the land. I had altered the course to the east so as to make sure of our striking the island, which would have been impossible to regain if we had run past the northern end. The course was laid on our scrap of chart for a point some thirty miles down the coast.

That day and the following day passed for us in a sort of nightmare. Our mouths were dry and our tongues were swollen. The wind was still strong and the heavy sea forced us to navigate carefully, but any thought of our peril from the waves was buried beneath the consciousness of our raging thirst. The bright moments were those when we each received our one mug of hot milk during the long, bitter watches of the night. Things were bad for us in those days, but the end was coming. The morning of May 8 broke thick and stormy, with squalls from the northwest. We searched the waters ahead for a sign of land, and though we could see nothing more than had met our eyes for many days, we were cheered by a sense that the goal was near at hand. About ten o'clock that morning we passed a little bit of kelp, a glad signal of the proximity of land. An hour later we saw two shags sitting on a big mass of kelp, and knew then that we must be within ten or fifteen miles of the shore. These birds are as sure an indication of the proximity of land as a lighthouse is, for they never venture far to sea. We gazed ahead with increasing eagerness, and at 12:30 p.m., through a rift in the clouds, McCarthy caught a glimpse of the black cliffs of South Georgia, just fourteen days after our departure from Elephant Island. It was a glad moment. Thirst-ridden, chilled, and weak as we were, happiness irradiated us. The job was nearly done.

Shackleton's conclusion that 'the job was nearly done' does not quite catch the moment. They still had to make the fifty kilometre crossing of South Georgia to find the whaling station on the north side, without knowing the terrain or the route, if there was one, and without any mountain gear.

But they did succeed. The final obstacle on this journey, after they sighted the station below them, was a thirty foot icicled waterfall, through which they had to descend.

We had flung down the adze from the top of the fall and also the log-book and the cooker wrapped in one of our blouses. That was all, except our wet clothes, that we brought out of the Antarctic, which we had entered a year and a half before with well-found ship, full equipment, and high hopes. That was all of tangible things; but in memories we were rich. We had pierced the veneer of outside things. We had 'suffered, starved, and triumphed, grovelled down yet grasped at glory, grown bigger in the bigness of the whole.' We had seen God in His splendours, heard the text that Nature renders. We had reached the naked soul of man.

FIFTEEN

'*I Never Knew of a Morning in Africa When I Woke that I was Not Happy*'

The Africa that here beguiles Ernest Hemingway, Alexandra Fuller, Karen Blixen and Elspeth Huxley is the Africa that is south of the Equator. It is the Africa where things happen in the mornings and then wind down, with the evenings left for reviewing the events of the day. Huxley and Fuller, although sixty years apart, came from England, respectively to Kenya and Rhodesia, as it was then, as the very young children of immigrant farmers. Karen Blixen chose to leave her native Denmark for an African life with her new husband and arrived in Kenya at the beginning of the First World War.

Paul Theroux also came to Africa as a young man, but it was to be a long way into his travel writing career that he returned for the journey described in *Dark Star Safari*.

Hemingway was in his fifties before he was drawn to Africa; the lure was the big game and the hunt.

'Something, or something awful or something wonderful was certain to happen . . .'

ERNEST HEMINGWAY

True at First Light (1999)

True at First Light recorded Hemingway's (1899–1961) journey in 1953–4 with his fourth wife, the journalist Mary Welsh, to whom he had proposed marriage on their third meeting, although not yet fully estranged from the third, Martha Gellhorn. The book was not published until 1999, many years after his death. During the journey they were involved in two plane crashes and were reported as dead. It is possible that the premature obituary reports contributed towards the announcement of his award of the Nobel Prize for Literature in 1954. Hemingway had surely coveted the prize, but refused to travel to Sweden to receive it and said that Isak Dinesen was one of those who deserved it more than he.

Something, or something awful or something wonderful was certain to happen on every day in this part of Africa. Every morning when you woke it was as exciting as though you were going to compete in a downhill ski race or drive a bobsled on a fast run. Something, you knew, would happen and usually before eleven o'clock. I never knew of a morning in Africa when I woke that I was not happy.

———

'. . . before we can in decency ask the giraffes to forgive us our transgressions against them'

KAREN, BARONESS BLIXEN-FINECKE (writing as Isak Dinesen)

Out of Africa (1937)

Karen Blixen (1885–1962) left her native Denmark and joined her Swedish husband in Kenya in 1913. They ran a coffee farm, although soon divorced; her companion became the British hunter-adventurer Denys Finch Hatton. She wrote Out of Africa *in her second language, English. The book is a reminiscence of her triumphs and her sorrows, including the loss of her farm, the death of Finch Hatton, and the disappearance of the simple African way of life she admired.*

In the harbour of Mombasa lay a rusty German cargo-steamer, homeward bound. I passed her in Ali bin Salim's rowing boat with his Swaheli rowers, on my way to the island and back. Upon the deck there stood a tall wooden case, and above the edge of the case rose the heads of two giraffes. They were, Farah, who had been on board the boat, told me, coming from Portuguese East Africa, and were going to Hamburg, to a travelling menagerie.

The giraffes turned their delicate heads from the one side to the other, as if they were surprised, which they might well be. They had not seen the sea before. They could only just have room to stand in the narrow case. The world had suddenly shrunk, changed and closed round them.

They could not know or imagine the degradation to which they were sailing. For they were proud and innocent creatures, gentle amblers of the great plains; they had not the least knowledge of captivity, cold, stench, smoke, and mange, nor of the terrible boredom in a world in which nothing is ever happening.

Crowds, in dark smelly clothes, will be coming in from the wind and sleet of the streets to gaze on the giraffes, and to realise man's superiority over the dumb world. They will point and laugh at the long slim necks when the graceful, patient, smoky-eyed heads are raised over the railings of the menagerie; they look much too long in there. The children will be frightened at the sight and cry, or they will fall in love with the giraffes, and hand them bread. Then the fathers and mothers will think the giraffes nice beasts, and believe that they are giving them a good time.

In the long years before them, will the giraffes sometimes dream of their lost country? Where are they now, where have they gone to, the grass and the thorn-trees, the rivers and water-holes and the blue mountains? The high sweet air over the plains has lifted and withdrawn. Where have the other giraffes gone to, that were side by side with them when they set going, and cantered over the undulating land? They have left them, they have all gone, and it seems that they are never coming back.

In the night where is the full moon?

The giraffes stir, and wake up in the caravan of the menagerie, in their narrow box that smells of rotten straw and beer.

Good-bye, good-bye, I wish for you that you may die on the journey, both of you, so that not one of the little noble heads, that are now raised, surprised, over the edge of the case, against the blue sky of Mombasa, shall be left to turn from one side to the other, all alone, in Hamburg, where no one knows of Africa.

As to us, we shall have to find someone badly transgressing against us, before we can in decency ask the giraffes to forgive us our transgressions against them.

———

'"Kiss each of the four walls of the living-room," Tilly said, "and you will come back for sure"'

ELSPETH HUXLEY

The Flame Trees of Thika: Memories of an African Childhood (1959)

Elspeth Grant (1907–97), as she was until she married Gervas Huxley, was six when her parents moved to Thika in Kiambu County, central Kenya, to farm coffee. Her parents were not well prepared for the life as settler-farmers, but their daughter acquired an enduring love for the country and all that she grew up with during an unconventional childhood.

We set off in an open cart drawn by four whip-scarred little oxen and piled high with equipment and provisions. No medieval knight could have been more closely armoured than were Tilly and I, against the rays of the sun. A mushroom-brimmed hat, built of two thicknesses of heavy felt and lined with red flannel, protected her creamy complexion, a long-sleeved white blouse clasped her by the neck, and a heavy skirt of khaki drill fell to her booted ankles.

I sat beside my mother, only a little less fortified in a pith helmet and a starched cotton dress. The oxen looked very thin and small for such a task but moved off with resignation, if not with speed, from the Norfolk hotel. Everything was dusty; one's feet descended with little plops into a soft, warm, red carpet, a red plume followed every wagon down the street, the dust had filmed over each brittle eucalyptus leaf and stained the seats and backs of rickshaws waiting under the trees.

We were going to Thika, a name on a map where two rivers joined.

Thika in those days – the year was 1913 – was a favourite camp for big-game hunters and beyond it there was only bush and plain. If you went on long enough you would come to mountains and forests no one had mapped and tribes whose languages no one could understand. We were not going as far as that, only two days' journey in the ox-cart to a bit of El Dorado my father had been fortunate enough to buy in the bar of the Norfolk hotel from a man wearing an Old Etonian tie.

The story of her African childhood amongst the Kikuyu ends when the family can no longer sustain their life there and return to Europe.

One of the wives, with wide cheek-bones, eyes like a moth's, and an air of wisdom and sadness, spoke to me in Kikuyu and put into my hand a necklace of blue and white beads.

'These you must take to Europe and wear for us,' Kupanya explained. 'These beads will be like our people, the blue ones are men, the white ones are women, and the children are the spaces in between, and the thread is the river that runs past your father's shamba. If you wear it always, you will come back safely to greet us again.'

I thanked him, and looked for something to give in return, but my pockets yielded only a crumpled handkerchief, a knife, a few beans, and bits of string. I thought perhaps the knife would do and offered it to Kupanya, but he shook his head.

'The traveller does not give a present to those who stay, it is those who remain who give presents to the traveller to help him on his journey, and bring about his safe return.'

. . .

Everything was packed, and loaded into the mule-cart. I had said goodbye to Moyale and Njombo and to many others; I could not believe that in a few moments the house, the garden, the farm, and everything in it would be out of sight and gone, as if on another planet; or that it was beyond my power, beyond anyone's, to freeze it, to catch it in a groove like an old gramophone record and keep repeating the same few minutes over and over, forever.

'Kiss each of the four walls of the living-room,' Tilly said, 'and you will come back for sure.' I did so, and fingered Kupanya's bead necklace with the men, women, and children in it, and felt better. This was only an interlude, like going to Molo, and everything would still be here to greet us when we returned after the war.

'The most idyllic stretch of the Nile I saw . . .'

PAUL THEROUX

Dark Star Safari (2002)

Born in Massachusetts in 1941, Paul Theroux went to Africa with the Peace Corps as a young man, where he became a teacher in Malawi. Dark Star Safari *tells the story of his return to the continent and his overland journey from Cairo to Cape Town. Some of the fun of* Dark Star Safari *stems from his unexpected ability in Malawi to speak the local language, Chichewa. When confronted by an awkward border policeman while trying to re-enter the country, Theroux reminds him of some Chichewa wisdom: 'Matako alaabili tabuli kucumbana' (two buttocks cannot avoid friction).*

Here he is early in the journey and on the Nile and visiting some of the haunts that Gustave Flaubert had written about during his 1849–50 adventures through the Middle East and Egypt.

Some aspects of the touristy Nile cannot have changed much in a hundred years. There are no taxis in Edfu, only pony carts and they clashed and competed for customers, the drivers yelling, flailing their whips, maneuvering their carts, scraping their wheels, and there was something ancient, perhaps timeless, in the way a driver – my Mustafa, say – turned, as the pony trotted towards the temple, and demanded more money, double the price in fact, whining, 'Food for my babies! Food for my horse! Give me, bleeeez!'

The most idyllic stretch of the Nile that I saw, an Egyptian pastoral as serene as any watercolor, lay between Edfu and Esna. Afterwards, when I thought about Egypt I always saw it as it appeared to me that hot afternoon from the deck of the *Philae*. Fifty miles of farms and plowed fields, mud houses and domed mausoleums on hilltops; fishermen in rowboats, in the stream of the river, and donkeys and camels on the banks, loping among the palms. The only sounds were the gurgle of the boat's bow wave, the whine of locusts, and the flop and splash of the fishermen's oars. The sky was cloudless and blue, the land baked the color of biscuits and with the same rough, dry texture, as though these low hills and riverbanks had just come out of the oven. The green was deep and well watered, the river was a mirror of all of this – the sky, the banks, the boats, the animals, a brimming reflection of everything, near and far, an ambitious aquarelle that took in the whole visible peaceful landscape.

Esna had always been a stopping-off place, even when the temple lay buried, 'to its chin,' as one Victorian traveler wrote. The ruination had not made it less popular. The advantage of a mostly buried temple like this was that a visitor had a close-up view of the upper parts of the massive pillars: the great sculpted capitals and the interior ceiling showing papyrus leaves and ferns, grasshoppers, the symbolic garden easily visible, with zodiac signs, the enormous scorpion and the ram-headed god, Khnum, to whom the temple is dedicated.

The young sensualist Flaubert – he was only twenty-seven – went to Esna in search of a celebrated courtesan, Kuchuk Hanem, 'Little Princess', and her famous dance, the 'Dance of the Bee.' Esna at that time was the most vicious town in Egypt, filled with prostitutes who by law had been rounded up and rusticated there from Cairo. Flaubert found Kuchuk Hanem, she danced naked for him, among blindfolded musicians.

The Dance of the Bee has been described as 'essentially a frenzied comic routine in which the dancer, attacked by the bee, has to take all her clothes off.' But in the word bee there is also a distinct allusion, for it is an Arabic euphemism for the clitoris. Flaubert slept with the dancer and minutely recorded in his travel notes the particularities of each copulation, the temperature of her body parts, his own performance ('I felt like a tiger') and even the bedbugs in her bed, which he loved ('I want a touch of bitterness in everything'). In every sense of the word, he anatomised his Egyptian experience and he became an informal guide and role model to me.

At Esna, Flaubert made two memorable entries in his diary. At the temple, while an Arab is measuring the length of one of the exposed columns for him, he notes, 'a yellow cow, on the left, poked her head inside'.

Without that yellow cow we see nothing; with it, the scene is vivid and complete. And leaving Kuchuk's room after the sexual encounter he writes, 'How flattering it would be to one's pride if at the moment of leaving you were sure that you left a memory behind, that she would think of you more than of the others who had been there, that you would remain in her heart!'

But that is a lament, with the foreknowledge that he will be quickly forgotten, for later he concedes that, even as he is 'weaving an aesthetic around her,' the courtesan – well, whore – cannot possibly be thinking of him. He concludes: 'Traveling makes one modest – you see what a tiny place you occupy in the world.'

———

'It was the time of day that hurries too quickly past'

ALEXANDRA FULLER

Scribbling the Cat (2005)

Alexandra Fuller (b. 1969) lived almost all her early years from 1972 in Zimbabwe and Zambia. In Don't Let's Go to the Dogs Tonight *and* Cocktail Hour Under the Tree of Forgetfulness *she relates the upheavals and comedy of family life with an alcoholic mother and a father who made his living managing farms in a period of civil war surrounding the struggles for independence in the old Rhodesias. She eventually left, despite feeling African and tied to Africa. She returned to visit in 2004.* Scribbling the Cat *follows a rough local white African farmer whom she met on that visit, known as K, who had fought in the Rhodesian and Mozambican wars, as he reviews the role he has taken in the fighting and his way of life now as a farmer.*

The first two days passed quietly. Mum and Dad were busy on the farm all morning (fish, if nothing else, seem to breed and grow extravagantly in October) and I stayed up at the camp pretending to write while they were gone. Everything felt entangled by the heat, as if it were able to throw out limb-snagging webs that caught at our ankles, our arms, and even our tongues, making us all slower-moving than usual and more languid of speech.

We woke very early – mashambanzou, the Goba say, 'when the elephants wash' – to take advantage of what little respite from the sun the night might have given us (the earth swallowed heat all day and regurgitated it all night). But by midmorning, when the buffalo beans tossed up stinging hairs from their fruit into the air – hairs that found skin and burrowed into flesh with burning insistence – all activity on the farm came to a halt. Everyone found refuge in the damp shade of the banana plantation, or in the cool gloom of a hut, and slept off the poisonous part of the day, awaking in late afternoon feeling tongue-swollen and bleary. Then, we drank tea and worked for another two or three hours, until sundown approached.

In the evenings – marirangwe, the Goba say, 'when the leopard calls out' – we took cold beers down to the banks of the river and watched the sky turn from a sun-wrecked wash of pale yellow-blue to a vivid display of reds and yellows and lurid, clashing streaks of purple. Doves called and trilled prettily to one another from the fig trees, crickets buzzed in the whispering dry grass, and, from the villages, an intermittent volley of dog barks and the wails of children shattered the air. Hippos, pink and gray humps scattered like rocks off the edges of eddies, occasionally surfaced under a spray of water and honked a warning at the shadowy dugout canoes that skimmed past them.

. . .

I smiled at K. He smiled back. We drank tea. The heat sighed up from the earth and curled around my neck. I waved my cigarette smoke toward some flies that had settled on the edge of the milk jug. 'It's warm, isn't it?'

. . .

I lit another cigarette and kept my hand cupped around it this time.

261

It was the time of day that hurries too quickly past, those elusive, regrettably beautiful moments before night, which are shorter here than anywhere else I have been. The achingly tenuous evening teetered for a moment on the tip of the horizon and then was overcome by night and suddenly the business of returning back to shelter was paramount. It is the time of day the Goba call rubvunzavaeni, 'when visitors ask for lodging.'

SIXTEEN

◦•◦•◦

The Journey is the Destination

Patrick Leigh Fermor, Colin Thubron and Paul Theroux are all quoted elsewhere in *Scraps*. Here Patrick Leigh Fermor is writing about his first youthful travelling steps. Paul Theroux is writing his first travel book, whereas Colin Thubron is already well established, with twenty years of travel writing behind him. For all three in their different ways it is the journey itself rather than the destination that is their subject.

Robert Macfarlane cites Barry Lopez's *Arctic Dreams* as the book that 'changed the course of my life. It turned me into a writer.' Echoing Lopez, Macfarlane's *The Wild Places*, *The Old Ways* and *Landmarks* are part of a new age of travel writing. The omnipresence of cameras has changed the role of the travel writer. Macfarlane shows instead what is under our feet and gives the reader an intimacy with land and landscape, with which a camera could not compete.

Both he and Leigh Fermor are simultaneously travel and philological adventurers. Leigh Fermor's use of vocabulary and historical reference can be luxuriantly flamboyant, such as in *Mani*. Macfarlane introduces a lexicon of rediscovered words and foreign words maybe as a device to make us look again at the familiar. The difference is that Macfarlane is an evangelist of land and language, whereas Leigh Fermor was an epicurean, in life as well as book.

◦•◦•◦

'... dripped and glittered like faces at an ogre's banquet'

PATRICK LEIGH FERMOR

A Time of Gifts (1977)

A Time of Gifts *is the first book of the trilogy that narrates Leigh Fermor's celebrated walk from London to Istanbul. It started on a wet December afternoon from a sheltered archway in what was then Mayfair's red light district, Shepherd Market. Leigh Fermor was just eighteen. He had a prodigious memory for historical and social detail. The book was finally completed four decades later, following the rediscovery of the diaries he had lost in Romania.*

Here the eagerly exuberant Leigh Fermor is taking his very early steps, first in Holland and then a while later into High Germany.

My spirits, already high, steadily rose as I walked. I could scarcely believe that I was really there; alone, that is, on the move, advancing into Europe, surrounded by all this emptiness and change, with a thousand wonders waiting. Because of this, perhaps, the actual doings of the next few days emerge from the general glow in a disjointed and haphazard way. I halted at a signpost to eat a hunk of bread with a yellow wedge of cheese sliced from a red cannon ball by a village grocer. One arm of the signpost pointed to Amsterdam and Utrecht, the other to Dordrecht, Breda and Antwerp and I obeyed the latter. The way followed a river with too swift a current for ice to form, and brambles and hazel and rushes grew thick along the banks. Leaning over a bridge I watched a string of barges gliding downstream underneath me in the wake of a stertorous tug bound for Rotterdam, and a little later an island as slender as a weaver's shuttle divided the current amidstream. A floating reed-fringed spinney, it looked like; a small castle with a steeply-pitched shingle roof and turrets with conical tops emerged romantically from the mesh of the branches. Belfries of a dizzy height were scattered haphazard across the landscape. They were visible for a very long way, and, in the late afternoon, I singled one of them out for a landmark and a goal.

It was dark when I was close enough to see that the tower, and the town of Dordrecht which gathered at its foot, lay on the other bank of a wide river. I had missed the bridge; but a ferry set me down on the other shore soon after dark. Under the jackdaws of the belfry, a busy amphibian town expanded; it was built of weathered brick and topped by joined gables and crowsteps and snow-laden tiles and fragmented by canals and re-knit by bridges. A multitude of anchored barges loaded with timber formed a flimsy extension of the quays and rocked from end to end when bow-waves from passing vessels stirred them. After supper in a waterfront bar, I fell asleep among the beer mugs and when I woke, I couldn't think where I was. Who were these bargees in peaked caps and jerseys and sea-boots? They were playing a sort of whist in a haze of cheroot-smoke and the dog-eared cards they laid down were adorned with goblets and swords and staves; the queens wore spiked crowns and the kings and the knaves were slashed and ostrich-plumed like François I and the Emperor Maximilian. My eyes must have closed again, for in the end someone led me upstairs like a sleep-walker and showed me a bedroom with a low and slanting ceiling and an eiderdown like a giant meringue. I was soon under it. I noticed an oleograph of Queen Wilhelmina at the bed's head and a print of the Synod Dort at the foot before I blew the candle out.

The clip-clop of clogs on the cobblestones – a puzzling sound until I looked out of the window – woke me in the morning. The old landlady of the place accepted payment for my dinner but none for the room:

they had seen I was tired and taken me under their wing. This was the first marvellous instance of a kind hospitality that was to occur again and again on these travels.

. . .

Into High Germany

Apart from that glimpse of tramlines and slush, the mists of the Nibelungenlied might have risen from the Rhine-bed and enveloped the town; and not only Mainz: the same vapours of oblivion have coiled upstream, enveloping Oppenheim, Worms and Mannheim on their way. I spent a night in each of them and only a few scattered fragments remain: a tower or two, a row of gargoyles, some bridges and pinnacles and buttresses and the perspective of an arcade dwindling into the shadows. There is a statue of Luther that can only belong to Worms; but there are cloisters as well and the black-letter pages of a Gutenberg Bible, a picture of St Boniface and a twirl of Jesuit columns. Lamplight shines through shields of crimson glass patterned with gold crescents and outlined in lead; but the arch that framed them has gone. And there are lost faces: a chimney sweep, a walrus moustache, a girl's long fair hair under a tam o'shanter. It is like reconstructing a brontosaur from half an eye socket and a basket full of bones. The cloud lifts at last in the middle of the Ludwigshafen – Mannheim bridge.

After following the Rhine, off and on ever since I had stepped ashore, I was about to leave it for good. The valley had widened after Bingen and opened into the snowy Hessian champaign: the mountains still kept their distance as the river coiled southwards and out of sight. But the Rhine map I unfolded on the balustrade traced its course upstream hundreds of miles and far beyond my range. After Spires and Strasburg, the Black Forest scowled across the water at the blue line of the Vosges. In hungry winters like this, I had been told, wolves came down from the conifers and trotted through the streets. Freiburg came next, then the Swiss border and the falls of Schaffhausen where the river poured from Lake Constance. Beyond, the map finished in an ultimate and unbroken white chaos of glaciers.

On the far side of the bridge I abandoned the Rhine for its tributary and after a few miles alongside the Neckar the steep lights of Heidel-berg assembled. It was dark by the time I climbed the main street and soon softly-lit panes of coloured glass, under the hanging sign of a Red Ox, were beckoning me indoors. With freezing cheeks and hair caked with snow, I clumped into an entrancing haven of oak beams and carving and alcoves and changing floor levels. A jungle of impedimenta encrusted the interior – mugs and bottles and glasses and antlers – the innocent accumulation of years, not stage props of forced conviviality – and the whole place glowed with a universal patina. It was more like a room in a castle and, except for a cat asleep in front of the stove, quite empty.

This was the moment I longed for every day. Settling at a heavy inn-table, thawing and tingling, with wine, bread, and cheese handy and my papers, books and diary all laid out; writing up the day's doings, hunting for words in the dictionary, drawing, struggling with verses, or merely subsiding in a vacuous and contented trance while the snow thawed off my boots. An elderly woman came downstairs and settled by the stove with her sewing. Spotting my stick and rucksack and the puddle of melting snow, she said, with a smile, 'Wer reitet so spat durch Nacht und Wind?' My German, now fifteen days old, was just up to this: 'Who rides so late through night and wind?' But I was puzzled by *reitet*. (How was I to know that it was the first line of Goethe's famous *Erlkonig*, made more famous still by the music of Schubert?) *What, a foreigner?* I knew what to say at this point, and came in on cue ... 'Englischer Student ... zu Fuss nach Konstantinopel' ... I'd got it pat by now. 'Konstantinopel?' she said. '*Ooh Weh!*' O Woe! So far! And in midwinter too. She asked where I would be the day after, on New Year's Eve. Somewhere on the road, I said. 'You can't go wandering about in the snow on Sylvesterabend!' she answered. 'And where are you staying tonight, pray?' I hadn't thought yet. Her husband had come in a little while before and overheard our exchange. 'Stay with us,' he said. 'You must be our guest.'

They were the owner and his wife and their names were Herr and Frau Spengel. Upstairs, on my hostess's orders, I fished out things to be washed – it was my first laundry since London – and handed them over to the maid; wondering as I did so how a German would get on in Oxford if he turned up at the Mitre on a snowy December night.

'I came upon a monkey skeleton, and four bears' paws'

COLIN THUBRON

Behind the Wall: A Journey Through China (1987)

Colin Thubron has said: 'The opening up of China (in the 1980s) stirred me unbearably. It was like discovering a new room in a house in which you had lived all your life.' Behind the Wall, the first of four books about China and Central Asia by the author, is a 10,000-kilometre journey alone around most of China east of Qinghai and Tibet. It won Thubron both the Hawthornden Prize and the Thomas Cook Travel Book Award in 1988.

I walked into the food market with a squeamish certainty of what was coming. Under its covered way the first stalls were pungent with roots and powdered spices. Sacks of medicinal tree-bark lay heaped up like firewood, and the air was drowsy with musk, but when I peered closer I saw that several of these piles were desiccated snakes – coiled skeletons and clouded skins – or smaller snakes dried rigid like sticks. I came upon a monkey skeleton, and four bears' paws. There were cellophane bags brimming with dried seahorses, and python skins folded up like linen.

In shallow bins among the fish-stalls, yellow-headed tortoises scrambled over one another's backs – many already overturned and dead – and strings of frogs dangled for sale in pendants of pulsing gullets and legs. The vendors described their wares as 'fresh', not 'alive'. They weighed and dismembered them as if they were vegetables. Throats were cut and limbs amputated at a casual stroke, turtles tossed about like small change.

Then I entered an arena resembling other countries' pet shops – but here it was a butcher's. From its banked cages rose the piping wails of hundreds of cats and kittens – mere scaffolds of fur-covered bones – which were huddled together in a congeries of ginger and white, or were tied to the cage-tops with gaily coloured string. Customers bought several at a time, the meat on them was so scant. They were weighed in mewing sacks and lugged away.

My revulsion, I knew, was hypocritical. When I passed the huddled quails and pheasants I felt nearly nothing, but the thrushes seemed pitiful and the tiered death-cells of the dulled and hopeless mammals angered me. The only dogs I saw had already been killed and skinned, but six or seven racoons lay with their heads buried in their legs, one still hopelessly suckling its young. In another cage sat a monkey – monkey brains are a delicacy – picking at its bars; in another was a porcupine, most of whose quills had already been pulled out. And once I came across a deer lying on a crate, its head tied up with newspapers from which the nostrils still palpitated.

Then I arrived at the owls. They were chained to their cages in a bedraggled row: two handsome eagle-owls, a group of Scops owls and some tufted grey predators which I did not know. Finally, on a cage beside a brute-faced entrepreneur, perched a barn-owl. With its white culottes and heart-shaped facial disks, it was identical to the north European species. Its head and cream-coloured breast, dusted with black specks, were so soft that I might have been stroking air. In its quaint face the eyes gleamed defiantly. It was beautiful.

The man perhaps knew that foreigners did not buy in the market, and he greeted my questions with boredom. He would have no trouble selling it, he said. (Some peasants believed that to devour a whole owl – feathers and all – was a cure for epilepsy.) Then he saw that I was fingering money. So he tugged out one of the bird's wings, pinched its chest and shoved his fingers into his mouth. 'That's the best part.' For its beauty and its fierceness – and perhaps as a penance for eating wildcat – I paid over the equivalent of £4. Briefly I wondered whether I should have chosen a kitten or a racoon instead, but they would only have been recaptured and eaten. Whereas the owl was a predator, and would survive. The man tied its feet, and I took it away in a carrier-bag. I decided to keep it until I had reached the countryside, and fed it meat on the top of my hotel wardrobe, where it shuffled and snored all night.

. . .

The train crept out of the river delta. For the first time I was leaving the Pacific littoral and entering the mountains and plateaux of the centre, which never stop until they fall into the Gobi fifteen hundred miles to the north, or merge with the Himalaya in the west. In my luxury carriage the four berths were each furnished with a pair of black slippers and a muslin-covered pillow patterned in dainty flowers. I shared it with three plump officials. After lunch they stretched out to nap under orange blankets, like crystallised fruit, and fell importantly asleep. In the neighbouring compartments sat a few Hong Kong Chinese with their look of irritably enduring China, and a group of retired army officers on their way to holiday camp.

As darkness fell I hoped the cadres would retire early to bed. I was waiting for an opportunity to release the owl. It crouched unseen in my carrier-bag, but had defecated nervously in the bottom, and the stench was pervading the carriage. The monkey-faced official beside me was reading *Megatrends: Ten New Directions Transforming Our Country*, but from time to time his nose would wrinkle and he would glance around him nonplussed.

I started conversation with the men opposite, trying to deflect attention from the smell. They turned out to be professional painters and administrators in an art museum, but when I asked one about his feelings for landscape, I realised that I'd gone too far. His gaze detached itself, his smile expanded, and he said nothing. But the official beside him looked appalled, and whispered across to me: 'Mr Kung is now Deputy Director of our museum. You cannot ask such personal things,' while Mr Kung went on smiling smugly in front of him through a mouthful of stained teeth.

This indiscretion drove them both to bed. I climbed into my berth and smuggled meat into the owl's beak. It was growing restless with the night. But the *Megatrends* official was still awake, reposing on his bunk with his head supported on his hand, like the Buddha entering paradise. I killed time by inspecting some pamphlets which the railway attendant had handed me. They were like parodies from fifteen years before. I started 'Raptures of Devotion' – the success-story of a citric acid work team at Nantong Distillery. I began to doze. After a while the loudspeaker in the ceiling emitted 'The Last Rose of Summer' in Mandarin, then went silent and the lights dimmed.

Much later I woke to find the train slowing down and whistling feebly. We were among steep, empty hills. The officials in their blankets lay still as tomb effigies. While the train laboured on a forested incline, I dropped from my bunk and eased open the window. The air came soft and warm. Gingerly I tipped the owl on to the sill. For a second, while its courtier's legs dallied along the ledge, I thought it would not fly. It averted its head from the slipstream. Then, like a giant white moth, it opened its wings and vanished into the night.

I closed the window with relief and turned round. Mr Kung's eyes were open and he was looking at me aghast. I had already disgraced myself with him, and now I had emptied this expensive meal into the dark. He buried his face in his blanket.

'Trains seemed the happiest choice. You could live your life and go long distances'

PAUL THEROUX

The Great Railway Bazaar (1975)

Paul Theroux began the large part of his life that has been devoted to travel writing determined that: 'The travel book was a bore. A bore wrote it and bores read it.' But he changed his mind when offered an advance by his publisher, as he explained in the introduction to his first of many, The Great Railway Bazaar. *'When I wrote it, I was groping around in the dark ... my self assurance in the narrative was sheer bravado. But I knew with delight when I finished this first travel book that I could do it again.'*

The station at Calais was dark, but the Paris Express was floodlit. I was comforted. Lady Glencora says to her friend, 'We can get to the Kurds,

Alice, without getting into a packet again. That, to my way of thinking, is the great comfort of the Continent.' Well, then, to Paris, and the Orient Express, and the Kurds. I boarded and, finding my compartment oppressively full, went to the dining car for a drink. A waiter showed me to a table where a man and woman were tearing their bread rolls apart but not eating them. I tried to order wine. The waiters, hurrying back and forth with trays, ignored my pleading face. The train started up; I looked out the window, and when I turned back to the table I saw that I had been served with a piece of burned fish. The roll-shredding couple explained that I'd have to ask the wine waiter. I looked for him, was served the second course, then saw him and ordered.

'Angus was saying in *The Times* that he did research,' the man said. 'It just doesn't make sense.'

'I suppose Angus has to do research,' said the woman.

'Angus Wilson?' I said.

The man and woman looked at me. The woman was smiling, but the man gave me a rather unfriendly stare. He said, 'Graham Greene wouldn't have to do research.'

'Why not?' I said.

The man sighed. He said, 'He'd know it already.'

'I wish I could agree with you,' I said. 'But I read *As If By Magic* and I say to myself, "Now there's a real agronomist!" Then I read *The Honorary Consul* and the thirty-year-old doctor sounds an awful lot like a seventy-year-old novelist. Mind you, I think it's a good novel. I think you should read it. Wine?'

'No, thank you,' said the woman.

'Graham sent me a copy,' said the man. He spoke to the woman. '*Affectionately, Graham.* That's what he wrote. It's in my bag.'

'He's a lovely man,' said the woman. 'I always like seeing Graham.'

There was a long silence. The dining car rocked the cruets and sauce bottles, the dessert was served with coffee. I had finished my half-bottle of wine and was anxious for another, but the waiters were again busy, reeling past the tables with trays, collecting dirty plates.

'I love trains,' said the woman. 'Did you know the next carriage on is going to be attached to the Orient Express?'

'Yes,' I said. 'As a matter of fact –'

'Ridiculous,' said the man, addressing the small penciled square of paper the waiter had given him. He loaded the saucer with money and led the woman away without another glance at me.

My own meal came to forty-five francs, which I estimated to be about ten dollars. I was horrified, but I had my small revenge. Back in my compartment I realised I had left my newspaper on the table in the dining car. I went back for it, but just as I put my hand on it, the waiter said, '*Qu'est-ce que vous faites?*'

'This is my paper,' I snapped.

'*C'est votre place, cela?*'

'Of course.'

'*Eh bien alors, qu'est-ce que vous avez mangé?*' He seemed to be enjoying the subtlety of his cross-examination.

I said, 'Burned fish. A tiny portion of roast beef. *Courgettes*, burned and soggy, cold potatoes, stale bread, and for this I was charged forty-five, I repeat, *forty-five* –'

He let me have my paper.

'I stopped to look out over one of the last great wild spaces of Britain'

ROBERT MACFARLANE

The Old Ways (2012)

The Old Ways *is subtitled* A Journey on Foot. *It leads us, sometimes bare-foot, along the old pathways of Britain (plus a little of Sichuan) to see the land as it was when the paths were first used. Among these old ways there is the Icknield Way, meandering along topographically sensible lines from Norfolk to Dorset, and the Broomway, an offshore pathway at Foulness traversable only at low tide, known as the deadliest path in Britain for the number of travellers lost to the incoming tide.*

Here Macfarlane is on Lewis in the Outer Hebrides seeking a part-lost path; its 'elusive nature was appropriate to the terrain through which it ran'. His guide was Finlay MacLeod, who is described as novelist, natural-ist, seal summoner, sometime selkie-singer, eloquent in Gaelic and English.

Everywhere we went, people knew Finlay. They stopped their cars on the moor roads and scrolled down their windows to talk with him, or downed tools on peat-banks to raise hands of greeting. It was like trav-elling with the Queen. 'It must take you a long time to get anywhere,' I said.

Eventually, late on a windy sunlit day, he drove me down the thin west-coast road that leads from the great sands of Uig through the croft-ing township of Breanish to Mealasta, where the road petered out. All that survived of Mealasta was a ground-plan of stones, but it felt oddly like the blueprint of a future village, rather than the trace of a near-vanished one.

The road ended at a wide cove called Camus Mol Linis: the Bay of the Boulders of Linis. I hugged Finlay goodbye, and he drove off north, waving out of the window as he went. I walked onto the little peninsula that jutted south of the bay, and found a smear of grass on which to pitch my tent. The peninsula was a *beirgh*, or *a' bheirgh*, a loan-word from the Norse that designates 'a promontory or point with a bare, usually vertical rock-face, and often with a narrow neck'. Its cliffs were pinkish with feldspar. Inland, near Griomabhal, I could see a golden eagle, its primaries extended like delicate fingers, roaming on a late-day hunt. A tern beat upwind: scissory wings, its black head seemingly eyeless, its movement within the air veery and unpredictable as a pitcher's knuckle-ball. Creamy waves moshed and milked on the beach and rocks, making rafts of floating foam just offshore and sending spray shooting above the level of the tent. Wave-surged infralittoral rock, tide-swept circalittoral rock, micro-terrains of lichen and moss. Far out to sea there were breaches in the cloud through which sun fell.

I boiled up a cup of tea and sat drinking it and eating a slab of cake, glad to be alone and in such a place. A seal surfaced – a fine-featured female, ten yards to my north. I tried to sing a seal song that Finlay had taught me a year or two previously, but it turned out that I couldn't remember either the tune or the words, so I switched to early English folk music, a Vaughan Williams setting of one of Robert Louis Stevenson's 'Songs of Travel'. The seal ducked its head under water and out again three times, as if rinsing its ears clean of the noise. I changed to the only other song I could remember – 'Paradise City' by Guns 'n' Roses. The seal dived and never came back. I felt rather embarrassed.

The sun set over the Atlantic. The water a sea-silver that scorched the eye, and within the burn of the sea's metal the hard black back of an island, resilient in the fire, and through it all the sound of gull-cry and wave-suck, the sense of rock rough underhand, machair finely lined as needlepoint, and about the brinks other aspects of the moment of record: the iodine tang of seaweed, and a sense of peninsularity – of the land both sloping away and fading out at its edges.

A sea mist crept up the coast, cutting visibility to fifty yards, so that my narrow-necked cape of rock seemed to have become an island. It felt as if anything might be going on under the mist's cover, and soon I experienced the peculiar illusion, with a light westerly wind moving across my face from the sea, that I was on board a boat beating outwards into the ocean and that I would wake the next morning far out into the North Atlantic. Then in a meteorological magic trick – like whipping away the tablecloth and leaving the crockery standing – the mist dispersed to reveal a cloudless sky and the coastline still intact. Inland was the half-dome of Griomabhal, and near it hung Jupiter again, bright as a lantern, while clouds juddered westwards across the moon.

It was the next morning that I followed the deer tracks up into the glen of stones that ran beneath Griomabhal's north face, with the wind rushing from the east. I searched the glen for almost two hours, moving inland and uphill, losing hope of finding the path.

Right beneath the north face, where the rock dropped 500 feet sheer to the moor, was a pool called the Dubh Loch – the Black Lake – by whose shore I rested. Tar-black water, emerald reeds in the shallows. The surface of the loch was being stirred by the wind in vortical patterns, rotating in sympathy with the wind-shear flows coming down off the north face of Griomabhal. This was a miniature cyclone-alley. Griomabhal's summit was finally cloud-free, and looking up its face, with the clouds posting far overhead, the mountain seemed to be toppling onto me. The face was tracked laterally with seams of quartz, hundreds of yards long, standing out like the veins on a weightlifter's arms. I glanced uphill and into the wind to pick my next line – and there was Manus's path.

Click. Alignment. Blur resolving into comprehension. The pattern standing clear: a cairn sequence, subtle but evident, running up from near the Dubh Loch shore. The form of the cairns was the *rudhan*, the three-bricked stack, though there were also single stones standing like fingers and pointing the way. I jumped up from my resting stone and followed Manus's path, eastwards over the slopes of gneiss. Mostly, the cairns were thirty or fifty yards apart. But near the pass, where the ground flattened off, I found seventeen cairns, each no further than ten yards from the next. Malky had been right: Manus's path really was a Richard Long sculpture, created long before Long, and similar in form to his *A Line in the Himalaya*s. I stepped into the path of the cairns and looked along it. One end pointed off towards the summit of the pass. The other ran toward Mealasta, dropping out of sight over a shoulder of gneiss. Above me, ravens muttered their hexes.

At last I reached the crest of the pass beneath Griomabhal's north face. I stopped to look out over one of the last great wild spaces of Britain – the deer forests of South Lewis and North Harris, hundreds of square miles of (privately owned) moor, river, loch and mountain. The cairn stones at the pass were decisive, and they led the eye and the foot down over the back of Griomabhal and toward the wilderness of the moor.

I was grateful to the *rudhan* for their guidance, and followed them steeply down towards the head of Loch Hamnaway. The sun was breaking through the cloud, bringing a redness to the moor. I stopped to drink at a river pool, its water bronze and gold. In its shallows I could see several rough white pebbles of quartz, and I recalled a word that Finlay had taught me, one of the many poetically precise terms that Hebridean Gaelic possesses to designate the features of the moor landscape. '*Eig*' referred, Finlay said, to 'the quartz crystals on the bed of moorland stream-pools that catch and reflect moonlight, and therefore draw migrating salmon to them in the late summer and autumn.'

SEVENTEEN

Opium and Kif Dens

Isabelle Eberhardt, fired with the zeal of the new convert to Islam and entranced by the Maghreb, and young journalist Jon Swain investigate the stimulants of their new surroundings. Fifty years apart the two young travellers express the thrill of new found liberation abroad as they set out on very different courses in life, and death in the case of Isabelle.

'I have discovered a kif den'

ISABELLE EBERHARDT

The Oblivion Seekers (1906)

Few travellers have achieved fame and notoriety as fast as Isabelle Eberhardt. She was just twenty-seven when she was drowned in a flash flood at Ain Sefra, Algeria, in 1904. By that point she had challenged the sexual mores of her adoptive as well as her native country, and had established repute as a writer, a spy, an agitator and a sexual libertine, some of which was deserved. Her new adherence to Islamic Sufism did not go so far as to prevent her exploring the kif smoking dens of Kenadsa, then part of Morocco, subsequently absorbed into Algeria.

In this ksar, where the people have no place to meet but the public square or the earthen benches along the foot of the ramparts on the road to Bechar, here where there is not even a café, I have discovered a kif den.

It is in a partially ruined house behind the Mellah, a long hall lighted by a single eye in the ceiling of twisted and smoke-blackened beams. The walls are black, ribbed with lighter-colored cracks that look like open wounds. The floor has been made by pounding the earth, but it is soft and dusty. Seldom swept, it is covered with pomegranate rinds and assorted refuse.

The place serves as a shelter for Moroccan vagabonds, for nomads, and for every sort of person of dubious intent and questionable appearance. The house seems to belong to no one; as at a disreputable hotel, you spend a few badly-advised nights there and go on. It is a natural setting for picturesque and theatrical events, like the antechamber of the room where the crime was committed.

In one corner lies a clean reed mat, with some cushions from Fez in embroidered leather. On the mat, a large decorated chest which serves as a table. A rosebush with little pale pink blooms, surrounded by a bouquet of garden herbs, all standing in water inside one of those wide earthen jars from the Tell. Further on, a copper kettle on a tripod, two or three teapots, a large basket of dried Indian hemp. The little group of kif-smokers requires no other decoration, no other mise-en-scene. They are people who like their pleasure.

On a rude perch of palm branches, a captive falcon, tied by one leg.

The strangers, the wanderers who haunt this retreat sometimes mix with the kif-smokers, notwithstanding the fact that the latter are a very closed little community into which entry is made difficult. But the smokers themselves are travellers who carry their dreams with them across the countries of Islam, worshippers of the hallucinating smoke.

The men who happen to meet here at Kenadsa are among the most highly educated in the land.

Hadj Idriss, a tall thin Filali, deeply sunburned, with a sweet face that lights up from within, is one of these rootless ones without family or specific trade, so common in the Moslem world. For twenty-five years he has been wandering from city to city, working or begging, depending on the situation. He plays the guinbri, with its carved wooden neck and its two thick strings fastened to the shell of a tortoise. Hadj Idriss has a deep clear voice, ideal for singing the old Andaluz ballads, so full of tender melancholy.

Si Mohammed Behaouri, a Moroccan from Meknès, pale-complexioned and with caressing eyes, is a young poet wandering across Morocco and southern Algeria in search of native legends and literature. To keep alive, he composes and recites verse on the delights and horrors of love.

Another is from the Djebel Zerhoun, a doctor and witch-doctor, small, dry, muscular, his skin tanned by the Sudanese sun under which he has journeyed for many years following caravans to and fro, from the coast of Senegal to Timbuctoo. All day long he keeps busy, slowly pouring out medicine and thumbing through old Moghrebi books of magic.

Chance brought them here to Kenadsa. Soon they will set out again, in different directions and on different trails, moving unconcernedly toward the fulfillment of their separate destinies. But it was community of taste that gathered them together in this smoky refuge, where they pass the slow hours of a life without cares.

At the end of the afternoon a slanting pink ray of light falls from the eye in the ceiling into the darkness of the room. The kif-smokers move in and form groups. Each wears a sprig of sweet basil in his turban. Squatting along the wall on the mat, they smoke their little pipes of baked red earth, filled with Indian hemp and powdered Moroccan tobacco.

Hadj Idriss stuffs the bowls and distributes them, after having carefully wiped the mouthpiece on his cheek as a gesture of politeness. When his own pipe is empty, he picks out the little red ball of ash and puts it into his mouth – he does not feel it burning him – then, once his pipe is refilled, he uses the still red-hot cinder to relight the little fire. For hours at a time he does not once let it go out. He has a keen and penetrating intelligence, softened by being constantly in a state of semi-exaltation; his dreams are nourished on the narcotic smoke.

The seekers of oblivion sing and clap their hands lazily; their dream-voices ring out late into the night, in the dim light of the mica-paned lantern. Then little by little the voices fall, grow muffled, the words are slower. Finally the smokers are quiet, and merely stare at the flowers in ecstasy. They are epicureans, voluptuaries; perhaps they are sages. Even in the darkest purlieu of Morocco's underworld such men can reach the magic horizon where they are free to build their dream-palaces of delight.

***

'Sometimes a man can lose his heart to a place'

JON SWAIN

River of Time (1996)

Having had a brief flirtation with the French Foreign Legion, Jon Swain (b. 1948) was working in Paris for the English desk of Agence France Presse when he got the chance to move to Phnom Penh as its correspondent. It is hard to imagine a better posting for a twenty-five-year-old, single, aspiring journalist than Indo-China in 1970, with few firm responsibilities, no immediate boss and the right to roam.

Jon wrote to me when he heard that I wanted to reprint this passage: 'I am at this moment sitting in a soulless hotel in Johannesburg so hearing that you are using the section on the 482 fumerie opened a window on my past that has been closed for a while. I allowed myself to be transported back and could visualise being present in the fumerie again with a pang of longing because, of course, it no longer exists, nor does sweet Chantal who always made me so welcome to smoke a pipe or two, escape from the war and dream.'

I felt I had entered a beautiful garden . . . I forgot about Paris and began a love affair with Indo-China, to which I have been faithful ever since . . . I stepped into an enchanting world of tropical scents, the evening silence broken only by a bevy of girls in the cyclos who crowded round offering to pass the night with us.

'Indo-China is like a beautiful woman; she overwhelms you and you never quite understand why,' his companion said with unashamed tenderness. 'Sometimes a man can lose his heart to a place, one that lures him back again and again.'

. . .

In those hard-bitten days, a number of us smoked opium. It seemed natural to do so after a day at the front. Opium had been legal in Indo-China just a few years before, and while it was now officially prohibited, was still widely smoked among the French colonels. The most famous *fumerie* in Phnom Penh was Madame Chum's. Madame Chum, a one-time mistress of a former president of the national assembly, was Cambodia's Opium Queen. She ran the *fumerie* for more than thirty years, until her death in September 1970, aged sixty-seven, and earned a small fortune from the pipe-dreams of others.

Madame Chum sent her two children, a boy and a girl, to France to be educated. She also adopted a host of abandoned Cambodian children as her own, paying for their food, housing and education from her profits. Her generosity made her as well known for welfare work as for opium and she was accorded a national funeral, her body wrapped in a white cloth, holding three lotus flowers as an offering to the Buddha. People said she had never forgotten how she suffered when she was young and poor and had made a vow to help others all she could. I wrote her obituary for AFP and was pleased when *Le Figaro* published it in full.

Her *fumerie*, in a residential part of town near the Independence Monument, was used mainly by the French. They were jealously protective of it and resented other westerners smoking there. When it was briefly closed at the outbreak of war by the authorities, one of the women who worked for Madame Chum decided to do away with the friction this resentment had caused and opened her own den. Her name was Chantal.

The den was called 482 after the side street in which her wooden house on stilts was located. To reach it we pedalled by cyclo through the curfew-stilled streets, past the road checks, past the soldiers lounging at street corners, past the snapping dogs. We pedalled down the centre of the road, afraid that the sentries might shoot us in the darkness. Chantal's first three clients were Kate Webb, a journalist, Kent Potter, a courageous young British photographer, and myself. Our pictures were pinned to the wall; we were part of her family. Chantal was a beautiful woman, soft, smooth and round like a plum. We adored her.

Her house was partitioned into four rooms. Naked except for a sarong, we lay on the coconut-matting covering the bare wooden boards and smoked. Sometimes we had female company. Sometimes we had a traditional Cambodian massage. Sometimes we just talked among ourselves, reminiscing and reflecting on the adventures of the day. Often, one of us would launch into an impassioned soliloquy about the war.

One recurring theme was who was the greatest war photographer – the late Robert Capa, Larry Burrows or Don McCullin?

There was a lot of common ground as to why we were in Cambodia. With opium, our inner thoughts took wings. And it turned out that for most of us the enemy was not the deadly carnage in the Cambodian fields but the tedium of life itself; especially the perceived dreariness and conformity we had left behind in the West, to whose taboos and musty restrictions we dreaded having one day to return. During the day we might have experienced terrifying incidents and made life-and-death decisions as to where to go, and how long it was wise to stay on a battle-field. But the war also provided us with a certain freedom, which is why we liked being here. We felt we had broken loose and were accomplices in an escape from the straitjacket of ease and staid habits.

Lying down and smoking, eyes closed, we were scarcely aware of the outside, even when, through the open window, an occasional flash and boom of artillery reminded us of the battles raging in the countryside. Later on, when the American B52 carpet-bombing came closer to Phnom Penh, we would feel a sullen rolling vibration as though we were on the periphery of a great earthquake. The whole house quivered. Yet, thanks to the soothing balm of the opium, I recall a strange, almost childlike, satisfaction, a feeling of absolute content in the mysterious certainty that we were utterly secure where we lay. Then at some stage, at two or so in the morning, our thoughts drifted away and we sank into an ocean of forgetfulness. Time did not exist in the limbo of the *fumerie*.

Graham Greene, in *Ways of Escape*, said of the four winters he spent in Indo-China, it was opium which 'left the happiest memory', and I understand what he means. I took opium many times in Cambodia. It was sweet and left a lingering acrid fragrance on the palate. The ritual was seductive. I remember very well the old man who made us our pipes. He was spare and the skin on his face was wrinkled like *crêpe*.

With a metal spike, he turned a small sizzling ball of sticky opium paste the size of his fingertip over and over in the flame of a little oil-lamp until it was cooked; then he inserted it into the ivory pipe and handed the pipe to me. Little bluish clouds puffed as I drew on it. There were no great visions; just disembodied contentment. It brought tranquillity to the mind and spirit as we lay cocooned in this sanctuary Chantal had created for us in the intimacy of her home.

All manner of people visited her *fumerie* – French planters and their Cambodian mistresses, Frenchwomen and their lovers, diplomats, journalists, spies. None stranger, perhaps, than Igor, the resident Tass correspondent. Igor was an important KGB officer in Phnom Penh, a product of the new generation of sophisticated young Soviet spies who graduated from the Moscow spy school. A natty dresser with well-cut suits and wide flowery Italian ties, he spoke Cambodian and French. He cultivated the western press and was a good friend of Jean-Pierre Martini. But no one had ever seen him commit an indiscretion. He was too much of a professional. It became something of a challenge to get Igor drunk or, better still, into the opium parlour. Even when his skin was full of a fearsome concoction of vodka mixed with marijuana, a creation of some American journalists, he remained as solid as a rock. I have seldom found a drink more corrosive. The Americans loved it. And unlike them, Igor could take it.

On New Year's Eve 1970, Jean-Pierre and Igor organised a joint party. Jean-Pierre offered the champagne, I offered a tin of caviar saved from a stopover at Tehran airport, and Igor provided the food and vodka. Indicative of his rank and the respect in which he was held by the embassy was that he was given the Soviet ambassador's personal chef for the evening. There followed a memorable Georgian meal of meat skewered on swords, roasted and flambéed, washed down with much vodka and champagne. Afterwards, Igor drove me back to the studio at Le

Royal. I proposed a visit to Chantal's. To my astonishment and delight, he accepted. Now, I thought, perhaps I can tickle some of those KGB secrets out of him. It was not to be. We each smoked a pipe and passed out on the mat. In the morning when I awoke, Igor had vanished.

Eighteen

A Supper in Capri

These passages are linked by the first, written as a diary piece by Sybille Bedford. It records her second meeting with Martha Gellhorn, the American writer, intrepid war correspondent and, perforce also intrepid, sometime wife of Ernest Hemingway, and their joint impromptu dinner with Norman Douglas in 1948 in Capri, where he lived and held court, if he felt so inclined, in his local *trattoria*. Sybille, even at thirty-seven, was a relative ingénue; it was still five years before the publication of *A Visit to Don Otavio*. She was in awe of Gellhorn, as were many, and both women were in turn in awe of the irascible eighty-year-old Douglas.

'He did not come out well'

SYBILLE BEDFORD

Pleasures and Landscapes (1990)

Sybille Bedford was born Sybille Aleid Elsa von Schoenebeck in Charlotten-burg, Berlin in 1911. She lived with her father in Baden and her mother in Italy in her early years and then with her mother and her Italian artist stepfather in the South of France, where she became friends with German writers such as Thomas Mann and Bertold Brecht. A lesbian, she entered an arranged marriage of convenience with British army officer Walter Bedford, ex-boyfriend of W. H. Auden, and continued to use his name as a writer.

'Let's get into that bar and have some martinis,' Martha said. We did. Presently she and I went to have dinner. (A boy porter in Piazza had taken my bag straight to the pensione.) We went to the Savoia, the small trattoria a few steps from Piazza where Norman Douglas, walking down from the Villa Truto, ate at night. One went there – the food was seldom very good, and the wine, for anyone less hardened than Norman, just not undrinkable – in the hope of his company; his privacy, though, was inviolate. The convention was to wave to him as one came in; he would call out a greeting or a warning – 'Don't touch their squid tonight, my dear,' or 'The veal's tolerable.' You might approach his table and say a few words in return. Sometimes he ate alone, usually he assembled two or three or more companions; yet, great friend or distant, one would never sit down with him unless expressly asked to do so.

That evening he had a look at Martha and liked what he saw. He called to me to bring her over. The dinner went well, it seemed to me, because of Martha and Norman's misapprehension of each other's natures. He called her 'my poppet', declined to be aware that she was a formidable – and formidably committed – woman; what he chose to take in were her looks and charm. She might have been inclined to remain censorious and unamused (she had not read *Siren Land*, she had not read *South Wind*; she *had* heard of the pederasty, of which she disapproved with all the strength of her fundamentalist American Puritanism); what she took in was an exquisitely mannered old gentleman and his charm. The talk, as I remember, was chiefly about fish.

Anything about the late war, Nazis, collaborators and their tortuous allegiances, would have glanced off Norman's Rabelaisian urbanity. It would not have been appropriate, and it was not attempted.

The Trattoria Savoia closed down (not early). After cheerful good-nights in Piazza – 'Bless you, my poppets' – Norman stumped off for his steep walk home with pocket torch and stick. Martha and I went to our pensione, where a key had been left for us to find. The rooms, even under the weak bulb light, showed up clean and white, but they were stuffy, the shutters being closed. Owing to the peculiar topography of Capri back streets, the windows were near ceiling high: to get to them and undo those shutters one had to climb onto a pair of wooden stools. This we did and reached the small squares of open window – and there were Mauresque rooftops, stars, night air.

'Isn't this delectable?' Martha said. It was. Jasmine, citrus, oleander, warm stone, a hint of sea . . . We drew it in, leaning into the night, our elbows on the windowsill, our toes on the wobbly stools.

'We must stay up here,' Martha said. 'We don't have to go to bed yet in those stuffy rooms. Let's stay up here by the window. Let's watch the dawn come up. I want to talk.' We did talk. Martha talked. I can still feel us as we stood balanced on those stools, heads out in the air, like two characters in a surrealist stage production. Martha talked about Ernest, about Spain, about the angle of the Nationalists' fire on the Hotel Astoria in Madrid, the safer exposure of some rooms at the Dorchester in the London Blitz. Ernest, she said, had taught her about ballistics. She talked of her own ride (unauthorised) on the naked floor of an Air Force bomber, of the ascent towards Cassino, of living with Ernest, being married to Ernest. He did not come out well.

<hr />

'How they fade away, like the ghosts they are'

NORMAN DOUGLAS

Siren Land (1911)

Norman Douglas (1858–1952) divides opinions. Many would agree with Patrick Leigh Fermor's biographer, Artemis Cooper: 'Douglas was PLF's favourite writer. I find him unreadable.' But the opening chapter of Siren Land, *quoted here, which first appeared in* The English Review, *was said by editor Ford Madox Ford to have been 'the most beautiful thing we ever printed'. Italy, and particularly the south of Italy, was Norman Douglas's home territory; he commanded it by force of scholarship.*

John Sutherland in Lives of the Novelists *(2011) summarised Douglas thus: 'Douglas's Mediterranean travel writing then chimed with the public taste. There was a time when, in literary conversations, Norman Douglas was regarded as one of the smartest things going. Part of that smartness was his keeping, for the whole of his long depraved life, one jump ahead of the law.'*

It seems to me that the Sirens, like other old Hellenic ideals, are coming to honour again.

During their westward progress they tarried long about the headland of Athenaeum, which is the southern horn of the Bay of Naples now called Punta Campanella, and about its islands. A snowy temple, one of the wonders of the western world, rose in their honour near this wave-beaten promontory – for promontories were sacred in oldest days from their dangers to navigation; colonnades and statues are swept away, but its memory lies embedded in the name of the village of Massa Lubrense (delubrum). A wondrous mode of survival, when one comes to think of it: a temple enshrined in the letters of a word whose very meaning is forgotten, handed down from father to son through tumultuous ages of Romans and Goths and Saracens, Normans, French, and Spaniards, and persisting, ever cryptic to the vulgar, after the more perishable records of stone and marble are clean vanished from the earth.

A good idea of the country can be obtained from the well-known Deserto convent above Sorrento or, nearer the point of the promontory, from the summit of Mount San Costanzo which, if I mistake not, ought to be an island like Capri near at hand, but will probably cling to the mainland for another few thousand years. The eye looks down upon the two gulfs of Naples and Salerno, divided by a hilly ridge; the precipitous mass of Sant' Angelo, stretching right across the peninsula in an easterly direction, shuts off the view from the world beyond. This is Siren Land. To the south lie the islets of the Sirens, nowadays known as the Galli; westwards, Capri, appropriately associated with them from its craggy and yet alluring aspect; Sorrento, whose name has been derived from them – I wonder some adventurous scholar has not identified it with the . Homeric Surie – lies on the northern slope. A favoured land, flowing with milk and honey; particularly the former: Saint-Non mentions as proof of its fertility the fact that you can engage wet-nurses there from the ages of fourteen to fifty-five.

I am not going to describe its natural features; the thing has been done by five hundred travellers already. Imagine to yourself a tongue of limestone about three miles across and six long, jutting into the sea; a few islands hanging upon its skirts; villages and farms whose inhab-itants reflect the various cultures that have been imposed upon them during the last two thousand years of political changes. A microscopic territory; but overgrown with hoary traditions of which that of the sea-maidens is only one. We need merely think of those quaintly carved vessels which in olden days sailed in between Capri and Point

Campanella, bearing westwards certain gods and letters and aspirations – much of what is best, in fact, in our own modern civilisation. And more recent memories, grim and glorious, cluster thickly about its rocks and inlets . . .

It was no doubt during one of those spells of deathlike summer stagnation, known hereabouts as *scirocco chiaro* or *tempo di bafogna*, that Odysseus encountered the Sirens –

> While yet I speak the winged galley flies
> And lo ! The Siren shores like mists arise.
> Sunk were at once the winds; the air above,
> And waves below, at once forgot to move.
> Some daemon calmed the air, and smoothed the deep,
> Hushed the loud winds, and charmed the waves to sleep –

for scirocco is the withering blast whose hot and clammy touch hastens death and putrefaction.

This passage may have suggested to Cerquand the idea that the Sirens 'sont le calme sous le vent des hautes falaises et des iles', an interpretation which he subsequently discarded. Loosely speaking, this would imply that something had been created out of nothing; even as, on the same principle, Pan has been called the personification of the midday hush that can be felt. The Swiss painter Boecklin, whose Gothic exuberance often ran on lines antithetical to what we call Hellenic serenity, has yet divined the psychology of the matter in Das Schweigen im Walde – the shudder that attunes the mind to receive chimerical impressions, the silence that creates; though I cannot but think that the effect of this particular picture would have been improved by the omission of Madame Boecklin. So may those pioneers of navigation have felt when, becalmed in the noonday heat amid pale-shimmering cliffs, they grew conscious of the unseen presence. Sirens dwell here! For the genii of earth and air were ready enough to commune with untutored men of early ages, to whom everything unknown was marvellous. Such fruitful shadows cast by inanimate nature upon the human phantasy are not rare; the second-ary stage is reached when the artist endeavours to fix in stone these wavering shapes, or the bard in verse; the third is that of the philosopher or grammarian who explains them as the splashing of waves and what not.

What not, indeed? The Sirens, says one, are the charms of the Gulf of Naples. No, says another; they were chaste priestesses. They were neither chaste nor priestesses, but exactly the reverse. They were sunbeams. They were perilous cliffs. They were a race of peaceful shepherds. They were symbols of persuasion. They were cannibals. They were planetary spirits. They were prophets. They were a species of Oriental owl. They were the harmonious faculties of the soul. They were penguins.

Penguins! That is the final pronouncement of commentatorial erudi-tion.

Yet I must add my own mite of conjecture regarding the so-called 'eyed Sirens'. These, I hold, may well represent a pristine version of the Beasts in the Apocalypse. And Eustathius has already explained how they came by their feather-dresses. They used to be young girls like any other nymphs or naiads, but Venus was so annoyed at their persistent chastity that she changed them into birds. Just like Venus – the Venus of the grammarians.

So may they have felt, those ancient mariners, spell-bound in drowsy scirocco-chains; but I question whether this was the true genesis of the Sirens. The bird-termination . . . It recurs in the harpies, of Egyptian origin. Those Egyptians, too, had that notable conceit of the dead body being visited by its soul in the shape of a human-headed hawk (Die Seelenvögel), and it was also – says Doughty – 'an ancient opinion of the idolatrous Arabs, that the departing spirit flitted from man's brain-pan as a wandering fowl, complaining thenceforward in deadly thirst her unavenged wrong'. Leucothea, a Phoenician goddess, could likewise assume the bird-form, and – who knows? – some crazy enthusiast may yet succeed in establishing a cousinship between the Sirens and those enigmatical swan-maidens who winged their way from snowy Himalaya to grace the bridal couch of northern hero-kings.

For the rest, such days of heavy-lidded atmospheric brooding are rare in Siren land.

They are clear-eyed and caressing as a rule, these summer breezes; caressing and cleansing; they set all the shining leaves a-tremble and scatter town-memories and the fumes of musty learning. How the bizarre throng of water-witches and familiars grow uneasy in that brave light, and wan – how they fade away, like the ghosts they are!

———

'I was too alarmed to speak'

MARTHA GELLHORN

Travels with Myself and Another (1978)

Subtitled Five Journeys From Hell, Travels with Myself and Another *is a collection of what in Gellhorn's (1908–98) view is 'the only aspect of our travels that is guaranteed to hold an audience, a disaster'. Much of the African part of her writing is informed by the white supremacist viewpoint of many of her generation.*

———

This morning, Ali and Ibrahim turned up an hour late; Ali's fault; Ibrahim, left to himself, is a most reliable boy. We were too late to get to a mirador above a drinking pond, before dawn, to watch the elephants come for their morning splash. I was furious and Ibrahim was miserable; he had not slept all night, due to the bedbugs in Ali's hut. He looked dirty, unlike him, and very unhappy. We drove futilely, as the sun rose higher, and saw nothing; I was conscious of time lost and costly kilometres. We arrived at a dead end of track where another, older guide was setting off with three French people, a peroxided lady in peacock blue trousers and little white ballet slippers, two men just as oddly clad. Ali and their guide talked excitedly; Ali explained there were elephants in the bush, and urged me to follow. Filled with doubt, I tailed along behind.

The Frenchmen made jokes in their usual voices. I remembered two rules about proper bush behaviour: (1) Wear no bright colours. (2) Do not speak. Elephants have bad eyesight and are alleged to see nothing more than twenty feet away; but have fine hearing and an acute sense of smell. The older guide and Ali were both busy being very Red Indian, noting twigs, droppings, sifting dust to see how the wind blew. I thought them theatrical for our benefit. We walked single file deeper and deeper into the grass which was higher than my head. I doubted that this undertaking was well advised.

We heard a tree crash, some distance ahead, and Ali cavorted with excitement. On we went until we saw, at a reasonable distance, an enormous bull elephant silently eating the tasty top of a thorn tree. I focused my binoculars, had a good look and felt no urge whatever to proceed. The French, innocent and unafraid, city people to their ballet slippers and the toes of their pointed shoes, pushed on. I told Ali we would go back.

He led me on another track; I had lost all sense of direction as soon as we got into the bush; trees look alike, you see a few feet ahead of you on the narrow beaten path. I heard in the grass to my left a lion; have never heard one before, but knew at once what this snarling, coughing sound was. I was badly shocked and whispered to Ali, *'Un lion.'* *'Oui'*, he said. *'Où .'* 'Where?', when referring to a lion, is not the sort of question you expect from a game park guide; it did the exact opposite of inspire confidence. But it was not the lion that had frozen Ali and made his eyes roll: in front of us, some twenty yards away, silent as stone, stood elephants – we had come on a little clearing. There were two females and a big bull, motionless. Fortunately I did not see the two baby elephants behind the females, or my panic would have been greater.

I focused my binoculars with clumsy hands, terrified, and there sprang into view, far too close, an enormous still head, with small suspicious eyes under old drooping lids, looking into mine. The last thing in life I had ever wanted was to be face to face with elephants, on foot, in the bush, accompanied by an imbecile. Ali was desperately lighting matches and sifting dust; too late, I thought, if we are down-wind they'd have charged us by now. The elephant fears no animal except man, with cause; and is incensed by the human smell. At this point there was a crunch to our right and behold, much nearer, a much bigger bull elephant was gently pulling off bits from a tree top with his trunk.

Ali, his eyes rolling, whispered, *'Beaucoup élephant.'* I was too alarmed to speak, but pushed him, to indicate that we should get a move on. He went ahead, walking fast and silently. I followed, trying not to make a sound, and when he stopped, I raised my eyes from the path and saw that he had brought us, in a half circle, even closer to the elephants. The two baby elephants were now all too visible. I was rooted to the spot with fear, an expression I have often read but never experienced. I was also beside myself with anger, furious with the game warden, furious with Ali; imagine being in this Charlie Chaplin situation of the greatest peril, because the whole lot of them were bloody fools. The elephants, again soundlessly, lifted their ears, which stood out like tremendous swaying leaves, and silently turned to face us.

Ali began to take me, respectfully, by the bottom, to urge me away, his eyes were wide, staring, his mouth open in shock. I slapped him smartly on the shoulder and hissed, *'Cours! Je te suis!'* He ran, leaping on his huge flat feet, and I ran after him; I would not have believed that I could run so fast and so silently. I decided not to think about the lion in the grass; better just not to think of it. After some distance, Ali slowed down; we were still however in an odious fix, able to see nothing over the grass. *'Bon maintenant,'* Ali announced a bit breathlessly. It did not look *'bon'* to me.

We went on walking; the heat was the least of my concerns. Finally Ali came to a broad dust track, which he recognised. He stamped this with his bare foot, laughed, and said idiotically, *'D'accord.'* I have never so wanted to hit anyone, but I never have hit anyone and it's too late to start. Ali now turned and said smugly, *'Ali bon type. Blanc veut voir éléphant. Ali trouve éléphant toujours. Toujours.'* It seemed futile to point out that the elephants had found us, if anything; and that he was a menace to life and it would be a frosty day in Waza before I ventured into the bush with him again.

'A dear little dirty American from England'

SYBILLE BEDFORD

A Visit to Don Otavio: A Traveller's Tale from Mexico (1960, first published as *The Sudden View: A Mexican Journey,* 1953)

After the tribulations of the Second World War, Sybille Bedford decided that she 'had a great longing to move, to hear another language, eat new food, to be in a country with a long nasty history in the past and as little present history as possible.' She chose Mexico and revolved her tale around her Mexican host. 'Don Otavio . . . de . . . y . . . y has been ruined these thirty years. He has seventeen servants to look after him.'

We owe it all to Anthony. He had not been able to enjoy the driving of his automobile for long. Thirty miles out of Guadalajara, at Chapala, the lake began and the road ended. He made an attempt to continue on the rutted trail replacing it, but had to give up. A number of Indians, rigid in their blankets, looked on without comment. We studied the address on Anthony's bit of paper.

'I can hardly pronounce it,' said E.

'Just ask for Don Otavio's place,' said Anthony.

They said, 'A boat will come.'

'Indeed. A boat. *When?*'

'In the little future.'

A child was sent to the shore on lookout, Anthony gazed at his engine, I at my wristwatch, E flicked the pages of her detective story. The Indians sat well content.

But the boat did not come.

Then a mule cart passed. The Indians stopped it, made the old man who was driving turn round, dump his load, and pile on our bags instead. Anthony and I were helped on to a trunk, a space was cleared for E on the driver's plank. Somebody stuck flowers into the mule's hat. E was still sitting in the Cadillac firmly, clutching her book. 'Ask them how far it is,' she said.

'*Es un poquito retirado.*'

'They say it's a little retired.'

Then suddenly we were off. The Indians poked the driver and the beast, and shouted, '*¡Tlayacán, Tlayacán! ¡que les vaya bien!*' E bowed from her plank and said politely, 'boo-ainous deeas, moochas gratsias, *viva Mexico.*' The mule feigned a second's trot and everything began to shake, sway and rattle in the most concentrated manner.

The trail consisted of two not always parallel ruts of varying depth and gauge, caked hard, strewn with boulders, cut by holes and traversed by ditches. The cart had solid wooden wheels and no springs.

First we passed some stucco villas decaying behind tall enclosures. Sixty years ago, during the heydays of the dictatorship, Chapala had been a modish resort. The driver pointed, '*la casa de la hija de Don Porfirio Diaz.*'

'Look,' we said, 'that villa belongs to Diaz' daughter.'

'I am not going to be diverted by historical interest,' said E. The plank she was trying to remain on was narrow as well as wobbly.

'Doña Carmen comes here in the winter,' said the driver, 'but the *ferrocarril* her father built for her is broken.'

'A railway?' said E. 'A railway, where?'

'From Guadalajara.'

'Where is it now?'

'Broken. Now we have the road.'

'What road?'

'The road from Guadalajara.'

'But it doesn't go on.'

'Yes, to Guadalajara.'

'What *is* he talking about?'

'The Señora wants to know whether there was a road or railway from Chapala.'

'Yes, Don Porfirio's railway. Now the road.'

'We meant round the lake.'

'Round the lake one goes by boat.'

'The hell one does,' said Anthony.

'How did Don Porfirio and Doña Carmen go?' said I.

'Don Porfirio and Doña Carmen and the Excellencies did not go farther than Chapala.'

'Very sensible of them,' said E.

Soon we were in open country. On our left lay the lake, almost colourless under the still vertical sun; on our right, behind a fringe of fields, a row of humpy hills covered with lush green shrub. Nasty clusters of black carrion birds hung watchful in the sky. The trail, conservative in the rhythm of its vagaries, continued small hole, big hole, boulder, ditch; small hole, big hole, boulder, chasm. In turns we walked, we rode, we pushed, propped luggage, steadied shafts, picked up E's book and helped the mule. We sat by the chasms in discouragement. After some time, pigs appeared and baby donkeys, then a banana grove, and presently we reached a sub-tropical village. Women with children at their breasts peered at us from leaf huts.

'Anthony, is *this* your friend's place?' said E.

'What is this village called?' said I.

'The place of *el gringocito d'Inglaterra*,' said the old man.

'What's that?'

'A dear little dirty American from England,' said I.

302

'From the map it must be San Antonio Something,' said Anthony.

'Map!' said E. 'Don't tell me.'

'What about that American?' said Anthony, '¿Dónde? ¿Dónde?'

'Not American,' said I. 'Work him out in terms of *un cher petit boche d'Autriche.*'

'Oh,' said E, 'a nice young Englishman.'

'Let's call on him,' said Anthony.

'What a dreadful idea,' said I.

'My dear Anthony,' said E, 'you have much to learn. If this hypothetical personage chooses, for no doubt some very good reason of his own, to live in such a place as this, he does not do so in order to be called upon by the likes of us.'

'He may be lonesome,' said Anthony.

'Englishmen in sub-tropical villages never are.' After another hour, we came to another much larger village with proper mud houses and a market place. For three hundred yards, potholes were agreeably replaced by cobble-stones.

'Now what about this place?'

'Ajijic,' said the driver.

'I dare say,' said E.

Then the trail resumed its character with a will. The countryside grew wilder, westering rays struck the lake and the water glistened in milky rainbow colours. Birds appeared. On we dragged and shook and rumbled with no end in view. Then a train of mules came into sight, broke into a gallop, raced towards us in a cloud of dust, reined in and effected a trembling stand-still. A man leapt from the saddle. He bowed to E and handed her a large mauve envelope.

On crested paper, above a triple-barrelled signature, we read:

Villa El Dorado,
San Pedro Tlayacán

Your Madams, Distinguished Esquire – Your entire servant, being apprised to his profoundest confusion of Your unbecoming way to his undignified house, the disgraced rascals through obdurate tardiveness having returned the insufficient boat without Your Unparalleled Favours to his eternal shame, is sending three unworthy mules, scant shelter and a humble sustenance for Your Facile progress and implores You to dispense him for the abomination of the travel! Q.B.S.P.
Otavio de . . . y . . . y . . .

'Your friend seems very civil, Anthony,' said E.

The mules, fine well-groomed beasts, were hitched troika-fashion on to our equipage; a third was to be Anthony's mount. The shelter was two parasols, and the sustenance a large Edwardian tea-basket in full polish. This was deposited on the ground.

NINETEEN

The Thirties and Their Heritage

Travel writers in the 1930s and the late 1940s were rewarded with contemporary celebrity. There was a public thirst for escapism in difficult times. For example, the unknown Irish writer Robert Gibbings sold more than 130,000 copies of his *Sweet Thames Run Softly* in 1939. The genre attracted many of the most talented writers of the time. Only a few years covered the publication of the travel works of Robert Byron, Graham Greene, Evelyn Waugh, Norman Douglas, Fitzroy Maclean and Peter Fleming. Byron, Fleming and Douglas were travel writers by choice; the novelists Waugh and Greene were attracted to it by its popularity. Maclean, meanwhile, was a diplomat in the widest sense.

These were Englishmen but, with the exceptions of the self-confident Fleming and Maclean, most comfortable as Englishmen abroad, where they could don the aura of the privileged, educated Briton. Byron and Waugh were both insecure in a class-divided Britain. Douglas and Byron were closet homosexuals. Of the six, Fleming, older brother of the more famous Ian, was the one who established the image of the urbane adventurer-traveller. In these turbulent ideological times it was only a short step, indeed one taken by Greene, from explorer and writer to MI6.

'Bartering for camels'

PETER FLEMING

News from Tartary (1936)

Fleming's (1907–71) first travel book, A Brazilian Adventure, *recorded a journey up the Amazon to search for the lost Colonel Fawcett. He avoided any mention of his companions for most of the book; then he wrote* One's Company *and established himself as a solo traveller. So he was somewhat diffident about having agreed to join Swiss traveller and writer Ella Maillart (known as Kini) for what became a journey in the footsteps of Francis Younghusband across the whole of China to India. The journey was 3,500 miles. They took the route west from Peking, keeping north of Tibet and turning south to avoid the impassable Taklamakan Desert, and then into Xinjiang via the southern oases of Cherchen, Keriya, and Khotan before reaching Kashgar and then tackling the challenge of the Karakorum. Here they are negotiating for camels in preparation for the circuit of the Taklamakan.*

We had a splendid evening. It was a great relief – especially for Kini – to be talking Russian again, to be no longer dependent on my sparse and uncertain Chinese; and it was a great relief to be able, for almost the first time since we had left Peking, to speak openly of our plans. We were installed luxuriously in the second yurt, which was normally used as a store-room. We cooked a duck that we had with us and got out one of our precious bottles of brandy and had a gargantuan meal with Borodishin and Wang Sun-lin, his Chinese partner in trade. Wang both spoke and wrote Russian, and in the rumours of his existence which we had picked up on the road he had always been referred to in words connoting great scholarship and learning; it was strange to meet the tubby, insignificant reality behind our subconscious image of a tall, frail sage.

The atmosphere was a good deal mellower than it had any right to be. The news we had counted on obtaining at Teijinar was not obtainable. Ever since the outbreak of the civil war in 1933 communications between Sinkiang and the Tsaidam had been cut; no merchants had come through. After the first bloody rumours silence had fallen, and none could tell what was happening beyond the mountains. We were as far from being able to assess our chances of getting further west as we had been in Peking, nearly three months ago. It was maddening.

No news was unlikely to be good news, but neither of us was minded to turn back. We discussed the situation over maps with Borodishin, who had volunteered, as soon as he knew our plans, to do all in his power to help us. Borodishin said that the direct, the obvious route to Sinkiang lay through Ghass Kul, whence a comparatively easy road led you up over the Chimen Tagh and down to the oasis of Charklik. But the Tungans, or whoever else was in control of the southern oases, almost certainly maintained a frontier-post on this route, and frontier-posts were institutions which we, being heavily under-passported, were anxious to avoid. There was, however, said Borodishin, another road, much more difficult – indeed at this barren season barely negotiable – but preferable to the first because it was hardly ever used and therefore probably not watched. To follow it, we must leave the Tsaidam forthwith (an idea which greatly appealed to us) and strike southwest into the mountains, then bear west up the gorges of the Boron Kol, on whose lower waters Teijinar was situated; twelve marches, or thereabouts, would bring us to Issik Pakte, where there was a Turki encampment. Here news of the southern oases would surely be available, and if it was of a reassuring kind we could carry on for some twenty stages through the mountains and drop down on the oasis of Cherchen, well to the west of Charklik. Borodishin said that he would willingly act as our guide as far as Issik Pakte, but he could hardly come further, for he had no papers of any sort and White Russians in Sinkiang had a low survival-value. It was good to know, when we went to sleep that night, that though we should still be taking our fences blind we were at least going to get a run for our money. It was all we asked.

. . .

It took us very little time to discover that none of the Mongols would hire us camels for a journey from which camels were by no means certain to return; if we were to get animals at all, we should have to buy them. The Prince of Teijinar was away, but the day after we arrived an emissary came from his twenty-year-old son, requesting us to visit him; he asked for a day's notice, and we had heartening visions of a mutton feast, a little post-prandial haggling, and the speedy purchase of four fine camels. We said that we would come the next day.

Washed and brushed and dressed in clothes which might by a long stretch of a tramp's imagination have been called presentable, we set out in the morning, accompanied by Wang Sun-lin on a camel. It was a hot day and we had a two hours' ride back to the yurts of Teijinar. We had purposely made a light breakfast lest, when the time came for feasting, we should be unable to distend ourselves with the zest which civility demanded. By the time we reached the Prince's tents our hunger was in its prime, had not begun to stale and numb itself and lose its edge as we found it used to at the end of a long march. We looked forward keenly to the audience.

It took place in a yurt which was bigger and more magnificent than most, and outside which we discarded our whips, as custom decrees you must. (You may not whistle in a yurt either). Along the walls were stacked painted chests which clearly belonged to some part of Turkistan, and there were carpets both from China and Khotan. The old Prince's son sat opposite the door, with elders and notables squatting in two convergent ranks on either hand. He was a handsome, surly young man with a pout, who sat lollingly and made no outward show of courtesy. We took humble places near the door and paid our compliments through Wang. Then I went up, feeling like a child with a mayoral bouquet, and presented our cards, laid reverently athwart a ceremonial scarf, and after them our presents, with another scarf. They were not, I freely admit, very good presents; they consisted of a knife, a pack of cards, and a box of cigarettes. The young prince's face showed that he had hoped for something better from such fabulous beings.

Tea was served, with rancid butter in it; but not very much tea, and the neat, alluring, golden piles of tsamba which stood about the felts in wooden bowls were left inviolate. We eyed them wistfully, and the long silences were more than once broken by poignant internal whinnyings from the distinguished strangers. Laboriously, through Wang, we answered the usual questions, made the usual polite remarks; but the atmosphere was cold and unpropitious, and when we had finished identifying ourselves conversation languished. I brought out a tube of quicksilver from a broken thermometer and played with the stuff idly, hoping to capture at least their curiosity; but the foolish gambit failed, and we told Wang to open negotiations for the camels.

He did; a flicker of intelligence and interest passed through the dour assembly. But we soon saw that things were not going well; the young prince's face was surlier than ever, and Wang looked rueful. The talk dragged on. The prince asked an impossible price and wanted payment in solid silver which (as no doubt he knew) we had not got. At last, in disgust, we closed the interview, exchanged frigid farewells, and rode hungrily home. Next day we learnt that the young prince had sent out messengers forbidding all his subjects to sell us camels.

The question of camels apart, neither Kini, who had lived among the

Kirghiz in the Tien Shan, nor I, who had travelled more cursorily in Mongolia, could find in our experience a parallel for such treatment of guests by a nomad. Perhaps our presents were too small. Perhaps we were too meanly dressed, too poorly attended. Perhaps he took a dislike to our faces. Whatever the cause of his resentment, the young prince did himself no good, and us no harm. He badly needed dollars, as Borodishin knew; his father had to pay annual tribute to Sining, and the Chinese did a good deal more than protect their own interests in assessing the cash value of a payment made in kind. Moreover, we got our camels. The news of the embargo had hardly reached us when we received a call from the most venerable of the young prince's entourage, whom we had conjecturally identified as the Prime Minister. The Prime Minister was a shrivelled but vigorous old man with a long, tapering silver beard and a humorous eye; he was also a camel-fancier in a big way, and after much circuitous talk over the fire in Borodishin's yurt we knew that the Prime Minister's loyalty to his master's son was no match for his commercial sense.

In the end, for an average price of about £4, we bought one good camel from him and three more from a Mongol-Chinese half-caste called Yanduk.

. . .

The next day, just before noon, we started. No Mongol would come with us. We loaded up, said goodbye to Wang Sun-lin, and rode away from the yurts, past the bluffs, and out into a shimmering desert of piedmont gravel beyond which, formidable and mysterious, a great wall of mountains challenged the sky.

It was May 15th. We had been exactly three months on the road to India.

'. . . and the devil danced for us'

GRAHAM GREENE

Journey Without Maps (1936)

Stamboul Train *had established Greene's (1904–91) reputation as a novelist;* The Heart of the Matter, Brighton Rock *and* The Confidential Agent *would come later. Greene decided to go to the interior of Liberia seeking the dark interior of the dark continent. The title of the book,* Journey Without Maps, *reveals a motivation to be seen as, and earn the cachet of, an explorer. He was also coy about the last-minute decision, surprising for a man six years married and with a one-month-old child, 'after too much champagne at a party' to invite his twenty-three-year-old cousin, Barbara, to accompany him. She does not get a leading role in the book; much of the mystique of his intrepidity would otherwise have fallen away.*

It was the blacksmith of Mosambolahun then who now swayed forward between the huts in a head-dress of feathers, a heavy blanket robe, and long raffia mane and raffia skirts. The big drum beat, the heels stamped and the gourds rattled, and the devil sank to the ground, his long faded yellow hair billowing in the dust. His two eyes were two painted rings and he had a flat black wooden snout a yard long fringed with fur; when it opened one saw great red wooden tusks. His black wooden nose stuck up at right angles between his eyes which were almost flat on his snout. His mouth opened and closed like a clapper and he spoke in a low monotonous sing-song. He was like a portmanteau word; an animal, a bird and a man had all run together to form his image. All the women, except the musicians, had gone to their huts and watched Landow from a distance. His interpreter squatted beside him carrying a brush with which, when the devil moved, he kept his skirts carefully smoothed down lest a foot or arm should show.

The devils need an interpreter because they do not speak a language the native can understand. Landow's mutterings were fluent and quite unintelligible. Anthropologists, so far as I can gather, have not made up their minds whether it is a real language the devil speaks or whether the interpreter simply invents a meaning. Mark's explanation has the virtue of simplicity, that the Bande devil speaks Pessi, that the Pessi devil speaks Buzie; the Buzie devil, on the other hand, he continued with a convincing lack of consistency, spoke Buzie, but in so low a tone that no one could follow him.

The devil was paying his respects to the chief and to the strangers, so the interpreter explained in Bande, and was ready to dance for them. There was an uneasy pause while I wondered with the embarrassment of a man in a strange restaurant whether I had enough in my pocket. But a dash of a shilling was sufficient and the devil danced. It was not so accomplished a dance as we saw later by a devil belonging to a woman's society in Buzie country; the lack of religious enthusiasm in the Bande tribe, if it allows them to lead an easier life, less under the fear of poisoning, diminishes their artistic talent. Vitality was about the only quality one could allow Landow; he lashed a small whip; he twirled like a top; he ran up and down between the huts with long sliding steps, his skirts raising the dust and giving his progress an appearance of immense speed. His interpreter did his best to keep up with him, brushing him when he was within reach. The spirit was definitely carnival; no one above the age of childhood was really scared of Landow; they had all passed through his school, and one suspected that the blacksmith of Mosambolahun, the slack grimy town, had not maintained very carefully his unmasked authority. He was a 'good fellow', one felt, and like so many good fellows he went on much too long: he would sit on the ground and mutter, then run up and down a bit and sit down again. He was a bore as he played on and on in the blistering afternoon sun, hoping for another dash, which I simply hadn't got with me. One woman ran up and flung down two irons and ran away again, and he cracked his whip and raced and turned and spun. The villagers stood in the background smiling discreetly; it was a carnival, but it wasn't a carnival in the vulgar sense of Nice and the Battle of Flowers; it wasn't secular and skittish; like the dancing in the Spanish cathedral at Easter, it had its religious value.

I remembered a Jack-in-the-Green I had seen when I was four years old, quite covered except for his face in leaves, wearing a kind of diving-suit of leaves and twirling round and round at a country crossroads, far from any village, with only a little knot of attendants and a few bicyclists to watch him. That as late as the ninth century in England had religious significance, the dance was part of the rites celebrating the death of winter and the return of spring, and here in Liberia again and again one caught hints of what it was we had developed from. It wasn't so alien to us, this masked dance (in England too there was a time when men dressed as animals and danced), any more than the cross and the pagan emblems on the grave were alien. One had the sensation of having come home, for here one was finding associations with a personal and a racial childhood, one was being scared by the same old witches. They brought a screaming child up to the devil and thrust him under the devil's muzzle, under the dusty raffia mane; he stiffened and screamed and tried to escape and the devil mouthed him. The older generation were playing the same old joke they had played for centuries, of frightening the child with what had frightened them. I went away but looking back I saw a young girl dancing before Landow, dancing with the sad erotic appeal of projecting buttocks and moving belly; she at least didn't know it was the blacksmith of Mosambolahun as she danced like Europa before the bull, and the old black wooden muzzle rested on the earth and the eyes of the blacksmith watched her through the flat painted rims.

'Under cover in Central Asia'

SIR FITZROY MACLEAN

Eastern Approaches (1949)

Fitzroy Maclean (1911–96) was posted as a young British diplomat to Moscow before the Second World War. He travelled widely, usually in the 'soft-underbelly' Central Asia countries of the newly formed Soviet Union, areas that were closed to foreigners. Maclean was to enter the army in 1939 as a private and be promoted during the war to brigadier, one of only two men who did so. He also found the time to become MP for Lancaster in a 1941 by-election.

Here he is in Baku on the Caspian Sea in what was then the Soviet Socialist Republic of Azerbaijan.

On one of the desolate red hills that overlook the town I found a memorial to the British troops killed in fighting against the Bolsheviks twenty years before, an episode in our military history which few English people any longer remember. But the Soviet authorities have never ceased to do everything they could to keep alive the memory of Allied intervention, and while I was in Baku elaborate preparations were being made for the celebration of the twentieth anniversary of the death of the

Twenty-six Commissars of Baku, said to have been shot after they had been taken prisoner by the British.

I have always heard that the twenty-seventh Commissar (who somehow escaped) was no less a personage than Anastasi Mikoyan, today a prominent member of the Politbureau. Meeting him at official parties, I could not help wondering, as he pressed on us delicious wines 'from my little place in the Caucasus', whether this elegant Asiatic statesman still bore us any ill-will. Looking at his fierce, handsome, inscrutable face above the well-cut, high-necked, silk shirt, smiling so amiably at a visiting British celebrity, I felt that he almost certainly did.

. . .

After two or three days I had seen all I wanted of Baku, and directed my attention to the next stage of my journey. My first move was a blunder. I walked into the local branch of Intourist and informed the seedy little Armenian clerk behind the counter that I wished to book a passage across the Caspian to Central Asia.

I could not have upset him more if I had told him that six Turks were outside waiting to skin him alive. At first he said nothing. Then, when he had recovered sufficiently from the shock, he started, with truly oriental reiteration, to enumerate the reasons which made it impossible for me to go where I wanted. Central Asia was a closed zone; it was dangerous; it was unhygienic; it was of no interest; there were no ships running across the Caspian; if there had been any ships there would have been no room on board; why did I not go back to Moscow where everything was so much more cultured?

I decided that I had better go away and think again. Taking a seat in a restaurant I ordered a late breakfast of vodka and fresh caviar from the Caspian and settled down to read the local newspaper.

The front page, I noticed, was given up to the Twenty-six Commissars, and featured a highly fanciful drawing of their execution by a mixed firing squad composed of Tsarist officers, Turkoman tribesmen and British other ranks, but on the back page an article caught my eye which I was soon reading with the most lively interest. It related the experiences of a scientific expedition of some kind in the neighbour-hood of a place called Lenkoran in the extreme south of Soviet Azerbaijan, on the Persian frontier. The expedition, who had travelled by ship from Baku, had found much to interest them in southern Azer-baijan. The climate was subtropical and the flora exotic and luxuriant, while the fauna, it appeared, actually included tigers. The inhabitants, the writer added, were a little backward, but coming on nicely.

Lenkoran might be (and probably was) unhygienic; it might even be dangerous; but no one could tell me that it was not full of interest or that it could not be reached by sea from Baku. Triumphantly waving my copy of the *Bakinski Rabochi* or *Baku Worker*, I burst once more into the Intourist Office. This might not be Central Asia, but it was on the way there and sounded as if it was well worth having a look at.

But the little Armenian knew where his duty lay. No, he said, there were no boats. There had been boats, perhaps, but at present there were none and in any case, when there were boats, they were always full. Nor could you go to Lenkoran by land; there was no railway and no road, nothing but a great howling wilderness. Besides, when you got there it was unhealthy and unsafe, and of no interest whatever.

'But what,' I said, 'about the tigers?'

'Tigers, perhaps,' he replied pityingly, 'but no culture.'

I was clearly barking up the wrong tree. I left the office and strolled aimlessly down to the harbour. There, a mixed crowd of Tartars and Russians were loading ships or standing about and talking. Others queued up for what seemed to be steamer tickets.

I attached myself to the nearest queue, which was mainly composed of Tartars, wild, swarthy, unkempt-looking fellows in shaggy fur hats and tight-fitting skull-caps, who jabbered to each other gutturally in their own language.

For an hour or two nothing happened. Then the window of the ticket office snapped open and we started to move slowly forward.

Eventually I reached the front. 'Where to?' said the pudding-faced woman behind the grating. 'Lenkoran,' I said, wondering what her reaction would be. 'Three roubles,' she said, giving me a ticket. 'What time does the boat sail?' I asked, hoping she would not notice my foreign accent. 'In half an hour,' she said.

There was no time to be lost. Making my way back to the hotel, I extracted my passport from a reluctant management by means of a subterfuge, shouldered my kitbag and, running back to the docks, pushed my way through the crowd and on board the S.S. Centrosoyus, a bare minute before the gangway was taken up.

TWENTY

The Lure of Afghanistan

Only Greece and Persia even approach Afghanistan as an inspiration for travel literature, but they are left far behind. The turmoil, the history and the apparently unshackled grandeur of Afghanistan have drawn travellers and then drawn them back. The country infuses much of *Scraps*. Some of the best-known Afghanistan travellers, Thesiger, Chatwin and Byron, have their place in other relevant chapters, such as Chatwin's 'Lament for Afghanistan' in chapter seven.

One feature alone, the minaret of Djam, was a lure sufficient to be the destination and subject of Freya Stark's last major travel book. Eric Newby's *Short Walk in the Hindu Kush* is a classic and not simply for the entertainment it still gives, but because its self-deprecating style was the antidote that was needed to counter the 1930s tradition of serious adventuring followed by serious writing.

Jason Elliot fell in love with the country whilst still a late teenager in a wartime mujahideen village at war with the Russian invaders, and then returns ten years later in the midst of another war. When we discussed whether he would go again now, his answer was 'Why do you need to ask, when you yourself have done so'. Rory Stewart took the road on foot from Herat, not far from Freya Stark's minaret, all the way across the country to Kabul.

'... eight centuries passing over it as over the Sleeping Beauty'

FREYA STARK

The Minaret of Djam (1970)

The Minaret of Djam should not be there. It is as if Chartres Cathedral, its almost exact late-twelfth century architectural contemporary, were to be in the Hoggar Mountains of the Sahara. At sixty-three metres, it is all but the tallest brick minaret in the world, but it stands alone in a gorge in an area of northwestern Afghanistan's Ghor Province that is difficult to access. It may have been the site of the lost medieval city of Turquoise Mountain, reputed to have been destroyed by the son of Genghis Khan in the 1220s. But if so, how did the minaret survive?

I have often wondered what catches us so sharply in the landscapes of Asia. They are hardly ever as beautiful as ours. There is no Afghan plain that I have seen as lovely as the Thames valley from Cliveden woods, no mountains rising as serenely perfect as Alps from their pastures; and yet prospects innumerable in all these Eastern lands, held for a few hours, or even moments, are never forgotten. It is a matter of size perhaps – what the ancient peoples felt obscurely when they carved their human figures so much smaller than their gods (wives, incidentally, only knee-deep to the Pharaohs). The atmosphere in the Asiatic landscape is not normal to us, its disproportion with the human figure is too vast, and the Hindu Kush soaring behind some tiny gathering makes us feel our own mortality as well as the immortal all about us. What we know, too, is added to what we see: the landscape that in Europe ends with North Sea or Mediterranean just over the brow of a hill, here stretches along the great silk road to China, with names of wayside halts that have

319

accumulated magic through the ages, Louland or Khotan, Samarkand, Bukhara whose minaret – from whose parapet the condemned were thrown to destruction – held a light for travellers drifting in from the Red Sands, or passing on their way through Gobi to reach the Gates of Jade.

Names merely, you will say, but such as the pearl-master works on, encrusting its shred of grit with light; and it is this recurrent sweep of distance and time, strokes of days unconsciously recorded, unconsciously noted, stray travellers' or poets' words thrown casually, which like the jeweller's hammer beat out the jewel's unnumbered facets into some lonely but complicated climax of perfection – not landscape only, but Time and Change, rise and decline of nations, all welded into the traveller's moment as he passes, enriched beyond his stride.

. . .

We were about to reach the climax of our journey. A day's travel and one mountain range only lay between us, from the level and rather dull bed of the Shahrak valley northwards, then almost due east over high downland ridges, and north again down a tributary gorge to where a bunch of precipices met. Here the Hari Rud swerved round the minaret in one of those alluringly dotted blue lines by which a map expresses the unsurveyed. The ridge we still had to cross showed a sort of saddle, steep on its northern slope, between the two highest points of the Safed Kuh, 3525 and 3416 metres respectively; and we could see its tossing and beautiful skyline before us as we turned from our valley.

The minaret stands alone and perfect, with no other building near it except an almost invisible scrap or two of castle ruined on a high scarp above. Its whole surface from top to bottom is covered with rectangles, lozenges, stars, knots and fancies of deep-cut tracery in the hard-baked earth which the Islamic art of the eleventh and twelfth centuries knew how to handle to such purpose: nothing has gone from it except the

wooden balcony which must once have supported the *muezzin* when he
called his call to prayer, and some of the bricks near the foundation
which need to be replaced. The door too, which must once have given
access to a double staircase of a hundred and eighty steps that inter-
weave themselves inside, is now no more than a hole in the wall.
Otherwise the whole slender structure stands as its builders saw it, eight
centuries passing over it as over the Sleeping Beauty, with little except
the rustle of the poplars and the voice of birds and water to disturb its
sleep. An airman from Herat, wandering off his course in 1957, first saw
its surprising shape at the meeting of four wild and stony gorges; and the
inscription of Sultan Ghiyath al-Dunya wa'l-Din Abu'l-Fath Muhammad b. Sam, fifth sultan of the Ghurid dynasty AD 1163–1203, is all of its
history that is known.

This was the age before Chingiz Khan and his Mongols swept down
with their destruction; and in its short span one civilisation after another
flowered from the Persian stem, rising and vanishing, rich and evanes-
cent, in the Asiatic trade.

'God, you must be a couple of pansies'

ERIC NEWBY

A Short Walk in the Hindu Kush (1958)

*Eric Newby (1919–2006) was working in ladies' fashion in 1956 when the
germ of what has become one of the classics of travel literature was born.
The first chapter records in entertaining detail his exasperation with his
daily life, reduced to needles and cotton and 'Hyde-Clarke, the designer;*

Milly, a very contemporary model girl with none of the normal protuber-
ances; the sour-looking fitter in whose workroom the dress was being made;
and Newby.' So on returning from lunch one day, he stopped at the Post
Office and sent to his friend Hugh Carless, then working at the British
Embassy in Rio de Janeiro, a telegram: 'Can you travel Nuristan June?' and
soon received the reply: 'Of course, Hugh.'

They arrive in Afghanistan via Turkey and Iran, get driven out to the Pan-
jshir Valley to the north west of Kabul and thence begin their trek into
Nuristan, north and east of Kabul, to try to climb the as yet unclimbed Mir
Samir, with their only experience being from a day at an Introduction to
Mountaineering course in Wales before they left.

At the end of their adventure the mountain remains unclimbed. Newby
and Carless start back a little scarred, much wiser but still the exploration
amateurs that they had been all along. Then they encountered Wilfred
Thesiger, formidably severe by reputation, who was known to consider
himself an explorer and everyone else by implication to be mere tourists.

We crossed the river by a bridge, went up through the village of Shahnaiz
and downhill towards the Lower Panjshir.

'Look,' said Hugh, 'it must be Thesiger.'

Coming towards us out of the great gorge where the river thundered
was a small caravan like our own. He named an English explorer, a
remarkable throwback to the Victorian era, a fluent speaker of Arabic, a
very brave man, who has twice crossed the Empty Quarter and, apart
from a few weeks every year, has passed his entire life among primitive
peoples.

We had been on the march for a month. We were all rather jaded; the
horses were galled because the drivers were careless of them, and their
ribs stood out because they had been in places only fit for mules and

forded innumerable torrents filled with slippery rocks as big as footballs; the drivers had run out of tobacco and were pining for their wives; there was no more sugar to put in the tea, no more jam, no more cigarettes and I was reading *The Hound of the Baskervilles* for the third time; all of us suffered from a persistent dysentery. The ecstatic sensations we had experienced at a higher altitude were beginning to wear off. It was not a particularly gay party.

Thesiger's caravan was abreast of us now, his horses lurching to a standstill on the execrable track. They were deep-loaded with great wooden presses, marked 'British Museum', and black tin trunks (like the ones my solicitors have, marked 'Not Russel-Jones' or 'All Bishop of Chichester').

The party consisted of two villainous-looking tribesmen dressed like royal mourners in long overcoats reaching to the ankles; a shivering Tajik cook, to whom some strange mutation had given bright red hair, unsuitably dressed for Central Asia in crippling pointed brown shoes and natty socks supported by suspenders, but no trousers; the interpreter, a gloomy-looking middle-class Afghan in a coma of fatigue, wearing dark glasses, a double-breasted lounge suit and an American hat with stitching all over it; and Thesiger himself, a great, long-striding crag of a man, with an outcrop for a nose and bushy eyebrows, forty-five years old and as hard as nails, in an old tweed jacket of the sort worn by Eton boys, a pair of thin grey cotton trousers, rope-soled Persian slippers and a woollen cap comforter.

'Turn round,' he said, 'you'll stay the night with us. We're going to kill some chickens.'

We tried to explain that we had to get to Kabul, that we wanted our mail, but our men, who professed to understand no English but were reluctant to pass through the gorges at night, had already turned the horses and were making for the collection of miserable hovels that was the nearest village.

Soon we were sitting on a carpet under some mulberry trees, surrounded by the entire population, with all Thesiger's belongings piled up behind us.

'Can't speak a word of the language,' he said cheerfully. 'Know a lot of the Koran by heart but not a word of Persian. Still, it's not really necessary. Here, you,' he shouted at the cook, who had only entered his service the day before and had never seen another Englishman. 'Make some green tea and a lot of chicken and rice – three chickens.'

'No good bothering the interpreter,' he went on, 'the poor fellow's got a sty, that's why we only did seventeen miles today. It's no good doing too much at first, especially as he's not feeling well.'

The chickens were produced. They were very old; in the half-light they looked like pterodactyls.

'Are they expensive?'

'The Power of Britain never grows less,' said the headman, lying superbly.

'That means they are very expensive,' said the interpreter, rousing himself.

Soon the cook was back, semaphoring desperately.

'Speak up, can't understand a thing. You want sugar? Why don't you say so?' He produced a large bunch of keys, like a housekeeper in some stately home. All that evening he was opening and shutting boxes so that I had tantalising glimpses of the contents of an explorer's luggage – a telescope, a string vest, the *Charterhouse of Parma*, *Du Côté de Chez Swann*, some fish-hooks and the 1/1,000,000 map of Afghanistan – not like mine, a sodden pulp, but neatly dissected, mounted between marbled boards.

'That cook's going to die,' said Thesiger; 'hasn't got a coat and look at his feet. We're nine thousand feet if we're an inch here. How high's the Chamar Pass?' We told him 16,000 feet. 'Get yourself a coat and boots, do you hear,' he shouted in the direction of the camp fire.

After two hours the chickens arrived; they were like elastic, only the rice and gravy were delicious. Famished, we wrestled with the bones in the darkness.

'England's going to pot,' said Thesiger, as Hugh and I lay smoking the interpreter's King Size cigarettes, the first for a fortnight. 'Look at this shirt, I've only had it three years, now it's splitting. Same with tailors; Gull and Crake made me a pair of whipcord trousers to go to the Atlas Mountains. Sixteen guineas – wore a hole in them in a fortnight. Bought half a dozen shotguns to give to my headmen, well-known make, twenty guineas apiece, absolute rubbish.'

He began to tell me about his Arabs.

'I give them powders for worms and that sort of thing.' I asked him about surgery. 'I take off fingers and there's a lot of surgery to be done; they're frightened of their own doctors because they're not clean.'

'Do you do it? Cutting off fingers?'

'Hundreds of them,' he said dreamily, for it was very late. 'Lord, yes. Why, the other day I took out an eye. I enjoyed that.'

'Let's turn in,' he said.

The ground was like iron with sharp rocks sticking up out of it. We started to blow up our air-beds. 'God, you must be a couple of pansies,' said Thesiger.

'Even God doesn't know the future of Afghanistan'

JASON ELLIOT

An Unexpected Light: Travels in Afghanistan (1999)

For me, the seeds of interest in the area were first sown by Matthew Arnold's Sohrab and Rustum; *it was no more than the exotic pull of the place names. It was the same for Jason Elliot (b. 1965) who was twelve when he read the same names. He asked his father how to find them and received the enigmatic reply: 'I know which way the oxen go.' He set to dreaming of 'high tangled ranges, where maybe a man lay in wait beneath the lapis dome of a Central Asian noon, and watching far below a shimmering trail . . . the oxen leading the way over wind-haunted passes'. Years later, when he had really followed his muse, Jason understood that he had misheard his father. There are no oxen in Central Asia; his father had really said: 'I know which way the Oxus flows.' But he was already snared. He said, 'Once snared, as you so well know, one never fully leaves; a portion of one's heart is forever woven into the fabric of that place.'*

Elliot was nineteen when he arrived in Peshawar and arranged to be smuggled into Afghanistan to join a mujahideen village engaged in fighting the Russian occupiers. The first part of An Unexpected Light *tells this story, and of how he was drawn into a love affair with the country. Ten years later he returned to a still fractured Afghanistan; Taliban authority was temporarily the dominant force.*

It was the strangest thing, but as soon as I stepped out of that little plane onto Afghan soil, I felt as though an inner clock of mine, which had stopped since I had last been there, began to tick again.

. . .

There is nothing like being far from home in a country at war to reveal the fragility of your original plans, and with a deep sense of disappointment I knew my nerve was faltering. I had earlier hatched a private longing to go beyond the usual risks, to force myself over a kind of threshold of calculation, to jump into a situation where to assess the risks ahead was impossible. I wanted to be free, if only for a day, of the tyranny of knowing what to expect in advance; to ride, in effect, a high wave of uncertainty until I could no longer feel its motion. I wanted to prove that it was possible to travel in those very places that others shunned, and the central route was the perfect place to put all this to the test. I would be beyond everything; in an untried space, without friends or contacts, no foreknowledge, a place at war, freezing, inhabited by teenage cannibals. In Kabul it had seemed a reasonable enough idea. There was just one problem: I was now terrified of my own plan.

The bus came to a lurching halt. We were in a wild-looking village – I guessed it must be Ghorband, halfway to Bamiyan – and the passengers began hauling their loads onto their shoulders. It was the last stop and as I stepped into the muddy street, alone again, I felt suddenly abandoned. The passengers melted into the flow of passers-by.

'Where are you staying, brother?'

I turned; it was the young man who had been sitting behind me on the bus. Briefly I wondered at the question's intent, and looked back into a pair of luminously dark eyes set in mouse-like features.

'Is there a *mehman khana* in the village?' I asked, weakly.

'A *mehman khana!* Here?' He gave a cynical chuckle. 'Come on. You can stay with me.' He tossed the end of his *pattu* over the shoulder of his black clothes and began walking in the opposite direction. This was my invitation.

In the narrow main street two crippled Russian tanks, stripped to their hulks, sat at the muddy verge in front of ragged stalls. I hobbled behind my new host, slipping on icy patches under the weight of my rucksack as he trotted nimbly ahead. We followed the snaking road at the base of steep cliffs for a mile or so until another village appeared. Here a man coming the other way greeted us and, eyeing me, lowered his voice and asked:

'So who's your friend, Sayeed?'

'Him? He's my cousin from . . . Kabul.'

'Sayeed,' says the man, 'you haven't got a cousin in Kabul.'

'I have now,' muttered Sayeed, and led me forward into the labyrinth of mud-walled alleys before I could attract too much more attention. We climbed a ladder into a long room above a stable, and drank tea with mulberries and walnuts. The village was called Baham. It was freezing and overcast. Sayeed disappeared for half an hour and returned looking disappointed, apologising for not having found a chicken for our dinner.

'The Shibar pass will be closed,' he said gloomily.

At dusk we moved to a different house within a walled yard where he lit a stove in a tiny room. I stood on the doorstep and watched plumes of smoke rising from tiny houses set among leafless trees on the far side of the valley and heard the howls of wolves echoing from beyond them. It was Christmas Day.

Word spread quickly of a foreign visitor and we were soon joined by half a dozen other men whose curiosity overtook their natural good manners like water from a leaking dam. They huddled opposite, exchanging the unanswerable questions they dared not yet ask, while I braced myself inwardly for the inevitable eruption of enquiry. In good spirits I enjoyed these interrogation sessions, which were a small price to pay for the hospitality. Yet now I felt inexplicably weary, weary at my own ingratitude, but most of all weary at having to disguise my weariness.

The room was bare but for the carpets on the floor and a single peacock feather pinned to one wall beside a photograph of Sayeed as a young soldier. Gradually the grey light dimmed as if we were retreating steadily into a deep cave. Men came and went according to a logic of their own and only Sayeed's face, like a buoy flashing at the gates of a port, remained a constant in my vision. There was some doleful speculation over my chances for crossing the Shibar pass. We talked until our faces faded into shadow. Sayeed lit a paraffin lamp and we shared tea as the night tightened like a cold noose around us.

'So what about the future,' asked one of the men, inevitably. 'What do you think will happen to Afghanistan?'

'Even God doesn't know the future of Afghanistan,' I said, and they all laughed heartily at hearing this from a foreigner. But even in the shadows I could see the curls of their smiles turn downwards as they faded, as if they had tasted the bitterness of this perhaps ironic truth.

I added: 'From what I have seen, ordinary people all over the country are tired of war,' and the line of heads nodded in solemn assent.

'Ordinary people, yes,' said the village teacher. His manner was didactic, his tone resigned. 'But other countries aren't. Pakistan isn't tired of it. America isn't tired of it. Russia and Iran aren't tired of it. What do they suffer from this war?'

I had no reply.

'Nobody's tired of it except us!' he went on. 'So long as they have the money to give commanders who can pay others to fight, there's no way to stop the fighting.'

There was little reason to contest this; I had not met a single Afghan who hadn't expressed a longing for the war to end, nor encountered a single life unscarred by its cruel momentum. The misery was fueled from beyond, by players untouched themselves by the catastrophe.

'That's right,' said a voice in grave concord, 'this war is about money. In other countries people make money through business and trade, but here – war is the best business.'

Then out of the silence, a mournful, aged voice from the darkness made us turn. It came from an old man wrapped in his *pattu*, huddling in the shadows behind the stove.

'Afghanistan, Afghanistan.'

'"You," said the driver, "are a fucking nutter."'

RORY STEWART

The Places in Between (2004)

'In between' means between Herat, the first town in Afghanistan reached after entering from Meshed, in eastern Iran, and Kabul, the capital. Rory Stewart (b. 1973) walked the route in 2002 with dog Babur, visiting also the Minaret of Djam and the remains of the Bamiyan Buddhas soon after their destruction by the Taliban.

Any regrets I had about leaving Chaghcharan faded after half an hour on the road. My pack was still heavy, the hills tall and Babur reluctant, but I felt with the familiar motion of my muscles confidence and ease returning. The road ran gently up from the Hari Rud onto a flat plateau and then into rolling hills. Among the pug marks, footprints and hoof blows on the pale track, melting snow had left patches of dark, glutinous mud. To my right the same line of mountain peaks was curling, falling and rising again, in a silhouette, as regular as waves or ocean liners, heading east.

I pressed through a group of teenage donkey drivers in shabby turbans with dust-caked faces. They were fighting about who would ride the donkeys. When they saw me they poked Babur with their sticks, whistled, shouted questions, beat their donkeys so they careered into the side of my pack nearly toppling me over and told me I would never make it to Badgah by dark.

We soon left them behind. After another hour I sat down beside a mud wall and opened a green packet of army biscuits marked 'Biscuits Fruit S'. I didn't feel up to eating more than one so I offered the rest to Babur. He wouldn't touch them. Finally, in the late afternoon, we came down into a valley, with an old mud caravanserai at the base and two mud towers on the slopes above. The Hari Rud was mostly frozen and there was a line of bare silver poplars along the bank. A shepherd sat by the ice, playing a flute.

This was Badgah, 'the windy place', the home of Commandant Haji Maududi, who had once been with the Pakistani-supported warlord Gulbuddin Hikmatyar, and was now the owner of the only Stinger missiles in Ghor. I had a letter to him but he was away. We found his sixteen-year-old son in their mill. His hair and clothes were covered in a thick dusting of flour and he was very uncertain what to do with me, but after a long delay he led me to a guest room and then left me for the rest of the evening. He did not come to say goodbye the next day. I was grateful to be left alone.

The next morning it began to snow again. I turned off after ten minutes of walking to let Babur drink. Just above us the river was frozen. We watched four men from a neighbouring village stamp across the thirty-foot width of ice without pause. Then we turned away from the Hari

Rud, following a gorge through low hills. A gentle snow-hail started. Black hairs rose on Babur's golden coat and each one had a small ball of ice at its tip. But for some time the weather was still warm enough for me to walk without a coat. Then the hail strengthened and I pulled a coat out of my pack. We continued for about three hours through winding, brown, snow-stained hills, with the sun hidden in thick cloud. We had been luckier so far with the snow than the Emperor Babur:

> The farther we advanced, the deeper was the snow. At Chaghcharan the snow reached above the horses' knees. Two or three days after Chaghcharan the snow became excessively deep; it reached up above the stirrups. In many places, the horses' feet did not reach the ground and the snow continued to fall.
>
> One Sultan Pashai was our guide. I do not know whether it was from old age, or from his heart failing, or from the unusual depth of snow, but having once lost the road he never could find it again, so as to point out the way. We had taken this road on the recommendation of Qasim Beg [Babur's ancient chancellor].
>
> So, anxious to preserve their reputation, he and his sons dismounted, and after beating down the snow, discovered a road, by which we advanced. Next day, as there was much snow, and the road was not to be found with all our exertions, we were brought to a complete stand.

Babur the dog, in the heart of the blizzard, stopped to savour the bouquet of a wet grass hummock. The weather shifted and as we moved on, so did the sharp angles of the slopes, revealing new valleys on each side. My mind flitted from half-remembered poetry to memories of things I had done of which I was ashamed. I stumbled on the uneven path. I lifted my eyes to the sky behind the peaks and felt the silence. This is what I had imagined a wilderness to be.

At midday I reached the village of Gandab and from there left the road and took the narrow footpath up into the mountains. 'Stay high and right,' said the villagers. 'Don't be tempted by the path to your left.'

Halfway up the mountain the snow fell faster, obliterating the line of footprints that I had been following. Babur and I stumbled again and again into drifts, which were three or four feet deep, so we were both drenched. Visibility was down to fifty yards. Eventually we reached a ridge and a sudden clearing in the clouds revealed some peaks. But there was no sign of any path or village. Nine hundred feet above to my right was what appeared to be the shoulder of the mountain and a potential pass. I started up the hill through deep snow, sinking on every step and making slow progress. The powder slopes below seemed very long.

On this slope Babur lay down and wouldn't move. The weather was closing in again and it was snowing harder. I leaned over him. He was shivering and sucking air into his lungs and panting in an asthmatic wheeze. The fit continued for two minutes, while I held him and he trembled and fought for breath, and then it passed and he was able to stand again. I thought we should turn down the hill. But I could see no promising path.

We were both tired and cold and we would be pressed to reach Daulatyar by dusk. We were supposed to be travelling east so I set off on a traverse across a slope, dragging Babur behind me, hoping there were no crevasses. After half an hour of stumbling through more deep powder, we came over a lip. The fog lifted again and we could see on the next ridge a line of footprints heading downhill. We began to follow the prints and a little later, to my delight, saw an arrow of dark purple rock pointing into a village and tiny figures moving among the stands of poplars on the bank of the Hari Rud. We ran and slid down the snow-slopes into the broad valley of Shinia.

From the village, I kept moving east, walking across two half-frozen streams, jumping the cracks in the ice. Babur was reluctant and I struggled to drag him across the ice. We were now walking through hard sleet. Fog descended and the low hills on either side were hidden.

We came onto a vehicle track. Tyre-tracks had gouged the earth, leaving a glutinous dark-brown strip perhaps twenty feet wide. Because my boots stuck to the mud, I walked on the ice that had formed on the roadside ditches. This was better, except when the ice broke and soaked my feet in cold water. Babur was now coated in black mud. We had been walking for nine hours.

There were only another fifteen kilometres to Daulatyar and probably two hours of daylight left but I had forgotten how much deep mud and wet snow could slow my pace. I felt muffled in the snow-fog and imprisoned by the rain hood that I was wearing. I threw back the hood. I could hear and see again. The day was very silent and the plain seemed very large. The snow driving into my eyes at a forty-five-degree angle made me feel much freer, but my left foot seemed to be frozen to a cold, rigid iron plate.

Exhaustion and repetition created within the pain a space of calm exhilaration and control. And at this point, I saw two jeeps, weaving slowly towards us through the fog, over the rough track with their headlights on. They were the first vehicles I'd seen since Chaghcharan and the first people I'd seen for hours. When they reached me, an electric window went down. It was the Special Forces team from the airstrip.

'You,' said the driver, 'are a fucking nutter.' Then he smiled and drove on, leaving me in the snow. I had seen these men at work when I was in the army and in the Foreign Office and I couldn't imagine a better compliment. I walked on in a good mood.

TWENTY-ONE

Seeking Coloured Architecture

It was Robert Byron who announced that he wished to travel east to seek coloured architecture. But he was also following a path established by both Vita Sackville-West and Gertrude Bell before him. Few commentators have had the intellectual self-confidence of those of interwar Britain. They still saw it their duty to inform as well as comment, thus the occasionally pedagogic tone. None of them wrote with any apparent fear of contradiction.

'An endlessly beautiful parable'

GERTRUDE BELL

Persian Pictures (1894 and 1928)

Gertrude Bell (1868–1926) had the facility through family wealth and connections to travel freely, but she was also a talented linguist and student of Arab culture. She became more than an adventurer in Asia Minor and Arabia when the First World War drew her into becoming a political adviser, administrator and informant, particularly to Winston Churchill, alongside T. E. Lawrence. She took a leading role in the formation of Iraq.

Her death, aged fifty-seven, in July 1926, remains something of a mystery. The book was originally published as Safar Nameh, Persian Pictures: A Book of Travel *in 1894 and was republished in 1928, two years after Bell's death, as* Persian Pictures. *Much of it is adapted from the letters sent during her visit to her uncle Sir Frank Lascelles, who was British Ambassador to Tehran.*

The East is full of secrets – no one understands their value better than the oriental; and because she is full of secrets she is full of entrancing surprises. Many fine things there are upon the surface; brilliance of colour, splendour of light, solemn loneliness, clamorous activity; these are only the patterns upon the curtain which floats for ever before the recesses of Eastern life: its essential charm is of more subtle quality. As it listeth, it comes and goes; it flashes upon you through the open doorway of some blank, windowless house you pass in the street, from under the lifted veil of the beggar woman who lays her hand on your bridle, from the dark, contemptuous eyes of a child; then the East sweeps aside her curtains, flashes a facet of her jewels into your dazzled eyes, and disappears again with a mocking little laugh at your bewilderment; then for a moment it seems to you that you are looking her in the face, but while you are wondering whether she be angel or devil, she is gone.

She will not stay – she prefers the unexpected; she will keep her secrets and her tantalising charm with them, and when you think you have caught at last some of her illusive grace, she will send you back to shrouded figures and blank house-fronts.

You must be content to wait, and perhaps some day, when you find her walking in her gardens in the cool of the evening, she will take a whim to stop and speak to you and you will go away fascinated by her courteous words and her exquisite hospitality.

For it is in her gardens that she is most herself – they share her charm, they are as unexpected as she. Conceive on every side such a landscape as the dead world will exhibit when it whirls naked and deserted through the starry interspace – a grey and featureless plain, over which the dust-clouds rise and fall, build themselves into mighty columns, and sink back again among the stones at the bidding of hot and fitful winds; prickly low-growing plants for all vegetation, leafless, with a foliage of thorns; white patches of salt, on which the sunlight glitters; a fringe of barren mountains on the horizon . . . Yet in this desolation lurks the mocking beauty of the East. A little water and the desert breaks into flower, bowers of cool shade spring up in the midst of dust and glare, radiant stretches of soft colour gleam in that grey expanse. Your heart leaps as you pass through the gateway in the mud wall; so sharp is the contrast, that you may stand with one foot in an arid wilderness and the other in a shadowy, flowery paradise. Under the broad thick leaves of the plane-trees tiny streams murmur, fountains splash with a sweet fresh sound, white-rose bushes drop their fragrant petals into tanks, lying deep and still like patches of concentrated shadow. The indescribable charm of a Persian garden is keenly present to the Persians themselves – the 'strip of herbage strown, which just divides the desert from the sown,' an endlessly beautiful parable. Their poets sing the praise of gardens in exquisite verses, and call their books by their names. I fear the Muses have wandered more often in Saʿdi's Garden of Roses than in the somewhat pretentious pleasure-ground which our Elizabethan writer prepared for them.

'So stands Persepolis'

VITA SACKVILLE-WEST

Twelve Days in Persia (1927)

Vita Sackville-West (1892–1962) was a novelist, poet and garden designer, famed for the gardens of her Sissinghurst home. She came from an aristocratic and secure background and was married to the writer, politician and broadcaster Harold Nicholson for nearly fifty years. Meanwhile, she had many affairs, the more celebrated of which were with her talented and sometimes colourful friends, including her first love Rosamund Grosvenor, Violet Trefusis, and Virginia Woolf, for whose novel Orlando *she was the muse. Here Vita Sackville-West passes judgement with authority on the creative achievements of three different civilisations in a few paragraphs. Husband Harold Nicolson and other companions hardly merit a mention.*

The pastoral tribes have streamed by, simple survivals from a lost world; the steam-hammers have thudded round the site of what was once the Temple of Fire; now it is time to see what becomes of empires as arrogant as the British and, on so oracular a note, to end.

Persepolis is particularly suitable for such a purpose – to stand midway between the Bakhtiari country and the outposts of England as typified by the Anglo-Persian Oil Company. It is suitable because, although it was once the capital of the Persian Empire, its ruins now lie among surroundings as primitive as the plain of Malamir. The gaunt columns remain, thrusting up at the sky, but of the site of the city of Istakhr there is nothing but the nibbled grass. Persepolis gains in splendour from its isolation. Not another building stands anywhere near it; not a hut, not a guard-house, not a shepherd's shelter; only the vast green plain, encircled by mountains and the open sky and the hawks that wheel and hover between the columns. As a ship launching out on an expanse of sea, the great terrace drives forward on to the plain, breasting it, the columns rising like naked spars into the clear blue of the sky. At first sight it may seem smaller than one had expected to find it, but that is due to the immensity of the plain and to the mass of the hill against which it is pushed up. The terrace, in fact, juts squarely out, backing against the hill as though for defence; but the effect is less of a seeking for defence than of an imperial launching of defiance, a looking-out across the plain, a raised domination above the level ground: the throne of kings overhanging the dwellings of the people. But the dwell-ings of the people which once spread over the plain have disappeared, and nothing of the royal capital remains but the ruins that were once the citadel of Xerxes and Darius; the dwellings of the people, no doubt, were made of wattle and sun-dried bricks, ephemeral material, whereas the kings glorified themselves in stone. A thousand years, I suppose, will level the disparity between them. The propylaea of Xerxes, the palace of Darius, will have enjoyed a few thousand more years of survival than sun-baked bazaars which sheltered the potter and the barber.

So stands Persepolis, looking out over the deserted plain. The space, the sky, the hawks, the raised-up eminence of the terrace, the quality of the Persian light, all give to the great terrace a sort of springing airiness, a sort of treble, to which the massive structure of bastion and archways plays a corrective bass. It is only when you draw near that you realise how massive that structure really is. It has all the weight of the Egyptian temples; square, monolithic. The terrace itself is supported on enormous blocks, its angles casting square shadows; a double stairway climbs it, a stairway that at its landing-place is superbly dominated by huge winged bulls. Now you are in the midst of the ruins: the columns soar, support-ing no roof; square doorways open, leading into no halls. (But see, within the jamb of one doorway is carved a king wrestling with a lion, and within another a king stepping forward under the shade of a parasol; these were the kings that ruled, but here, following the easy rise of steps, comes a procession of captive kings.) A little further, and you are in the Hall of the Hundred Columns, a wilderness of tumbled ruins, but ruins which in their broken detail testify to the richness of the order that once was here: fallen capitals; fragments of carving small enough to go into a pocket, but whorled with the curls of an Assyrian beard; wars and dynasties roll their forgotten drums, as the fragment is balanced for a moment in the palm of the hand. Over this roofless desolation hangs the sun, cutting black square shadows, striking a carving into sharper relief; and silence reigns, but for the dry-leaf scurry of a lizard over the stones. This hall was roofed with cedar, says Quintus Curtius; and now the discovered ashes of carbonised cedar corroborate the account of the historians: this hall of Darius flamed indeed beneath the vengeance of Alexander. Little did it avail Darius that he should have caused the Avesta to be written in letters of gold and silver on twelve thousand tanned ox-hides.

The hand of man has never desecrated these ruins, no excavator's pick has ever rung upon these stones; tumbled and desolate they lie today, as they lay after the might of Alexander had pushed them over. The heat of the Persian summers has passed over them and bleached them; they have flushed in the light of many sunrises and bared themselves to the silver of many moons; the wild flowers have sown themselves in the crevices and the lizards scurry over the pavements; but it is a dead world, as befits the sepulchre of an imperial race.

Ruined cities. Ranging away from Persepolis, I remember other wrecks of pride, splendour, and majesty: the ziggurat of Ur against the sunset, the undulating mounds that were Babylon, the gay broken colonnades of Palmyra. Golden, graceful, airy, debased, Palmyra rises like a flower from the desert in an oasis of palms and apricots. At the apex of a flattened and irregular triangle between Damascus and Baghdad, Palmyra lies on the old caravan route, and the strings of camels still slouch beneath the triumphal arches of Zenobia and Odenathus. But the Street of the Hundred Columns is now nothing but a transparent screen of pillars, framing the desert, and in the precincts of the Temple of Baal clusters an Arab village, the squalid houses incongruously put together with the stones of the once magnificent centre of a pagan faith. What is Palmyra now? Where is the glory of Solomon who built Tadmor in the wilderness? A few tourists motor out from Beirut, and the desert traffic of camel caravans passes through on its leisurely way. The Arab children squabble in the gutters. There is a French *poste de police*. There is a derelict building, originally designed as an hotel. But now that even the Trans-Desert Mail no longer takes Palmyra in its rush – as it did when the Druses terrorised the southern route – it seems likely that Palmyra will return to the isolation to which it is geographically destined, and that the flush of its prosperity under the Roman Empire will resemble the flush of flowers over the desert in spring – with this difference, that spring for Palmyra is not recurrent. It happened once, and will not happen again; a miracle the more exquisite for its singleness and fugacity.

You come upon Palmyra unexpectedly, if you approach it from the Damascus side, going through a gorge crowned by Turkish forts, and coming out on to a full view of the desert with these surprising ruins standing in the white, pale sand. Lovely in colour, as golden as honey, the vistas of columns and arches give Palmyra a lacy quality; it is a series of frames, and nothing so much enhances the beauty of landscape as to be framed in a fragment of architecture. But on looking closer this architecture presents a puzzle: it is Roman, surely? but there is something not quite Roman about it; there are mistakes that the Roman builders would not have made. Indeed, the Romans did not build it, no; Arabs built it, dazzled by what they had seen or heard of the Roman models. Most people criticise Palmyra on this account. Certainly it is neither as pure nor as majestic as Baalbec. It lacks the grand solidity of Roman building, and the Roman sense of proportion is notably absent. But I like Palmyra. It is very feminine; it is gay, whimsical, and a little meretricious. It seems to have drunk the desert sun, and to have granted free passage to all the desert winds with a wanton insouciance. Palmyra is a Bedouin girl laughing because she is dressed up as a Roman lady.

And there, lastly, under the snows of Lebanon lie the mighty ruins of Heliopolis. The Temple of Bacchus retains its shape, but of the Temple of Jupiter only six columns survive out of the original fifty-four. Baalbec had its worthy enemies: Genghiz, Timur, and Saladin; besides the earth-quakes which have crashed pediment and capital to the ground. There lie the blocks of masonry, here gapes a vault; here is a column, propping itself against the wall of the Temple. It is a wilderness of masonry; havoc such as might have been wrought in a sudden onslaught by the anger of the very god to whom the greatest temple was dedicated, that Jupiter who at Baalbec was called Baal, not the hirsute Jove of the Romans, but a beardless god, covered with scales, and holding in one hand a scourge, and in the other, lightning and ears of corn. Baalbec has gone the way of those cities of antiquity on whose ruin no later city has arisen. True, a little town has grown up beside it, so that it enjoys neither the superb isolation of Persepolis nor the native sprinkling of Palmyra, but the little town is insignificant, and it is really the wreck of Heliopolis which dom-inates the lovely valley between Lebanon and Anti-Lebanon.

There is another difference between Baalbec and those two other cities. The plain of Persepolis is green indeed with the short grass, and at Palmyra the fruit trees of the oasis foam with blossom in the spring, but there is no sign of cultivation anywhere. Round Baalbec the fertile land is carefully tilled; the permanence of agriculture, that detailed, laborious, and persistent craft, is nowhere more strongly emphasised than here, where it pursues its quiet way undisturbed by the presence of a crumbled civilisation. It seems not irrelevant to wonder whether in the course of centuries the Anglo-Persian oil-fields may not revert to the solitudes of the Bakhtiari hills, while London, Paris, and New York lie with the wild flowers blowing over their stones, and fields of corn bend to the breeze for the bread of the population in some distant capital whose name we do not yet know.

<hr />

'The hours fled, the decanter flowed, the telegraphist was carried out, I fell into a torpor . . .'

ROBERT BYRON

The Road to Oxiana (1937)

Robert Byron (1905–41) affected a casual diary style of writing; this disguised his very careful crafting and re-crafting of the book over the three years following his return from his travels. The Road to Oxiana *(Oxiana referring to the region along Afghanistan's northern border) is studiedly episodic and loose in its structure. Its easy-going diary format is a careful invention to engage the reader; the reader is intended to participate in the randomness of the journey.*

Byron was not connected in any way with the poet, though he would allow it to be assumed that he was. He made the journey that was The Road to Oxiana *with Christopher Sykes, who would write a biography of Byron after his death in 1941, when his ship was torpedoed in the North Atlantic.*

It starts in Venice and ends in Peshawar, the first town in what is now Pakistan on the east side of the Khyber Pass. The narrative is divided mainly between their travels in Persia and Afghanistan. In the first of these three passages, the two are in the Golestan Province in the northeast of Persia. In the second they have reached Afghanistan and are visiting the northern hub of the country, Mazar-i-Sharif, then the seat of provincial government and centre of commerce. In the last they have reached what were then the most celebrated monuments in the country, the Bhuddas of Bamiyan. These are statues of the Bhudda, thirty-five and fifty-five meters high, that were carved out of the mountainside in the sixth century CE.

Gumbad-i-Kabus (200 ft), 24 April

After following the Bandar Shah road a little way back, we turned to the right down a track between wattle fences. High reeds obscured the view. Suddenly, as a ship leaves an estuary, we came out on to the steppe: a dazzling open sea of green. I never saw that colour before. In other greens, of emerald, jade, or malachite, the harsh deep green of the Bengal jungle, the sad cool green of Ireland, the salad green of Mediterranean vineyards, the heavy full-blown green of English summer beeches, some element of blue or yellow predominates over the others. This was the pure essence of green, indissoluble, the colour of life itself. The sun was warm, the larks were singing up above. Behind us rose the misty Alpine blue of the wooded Elburz. In front, tyre glowing verdure stretched out to the rim of the earth.

Bearings, landmarks, disappeared, as they would from a skiff in mid-Atlantic. We seemed to be always below the surrounding level, caught in the trough of a green swell. Sitting down, we might see for twenty feet: standing up, for twenty miles and even then, twenty miles away, the curve of the earth was as green as the bank that touched the wheels, so that it was hard to tell which was which. Our only chart was by things whose scale we knew: groups of white-topped kibitkas, dotted like mushrooms on a lawn – though even in their case it needed an effort of reason to believe they were not mushrooms; and droves of cattle, mares with their foals, black and brown sheep, kine and camels – though the camels were deceptive in the opposite sense, seeming so tall that it needed another effort to believe they were not antediluvian monsters. As the huts and animals varied in size, we could plot their distances: half a mile, a mile, five miles. But it was not this that conveyed the size of the steppe so much as the multiplicity of these nomadic encampments, cropping up wherever the eye rested, yet invariably separate by a mile or two from their neighbours. There were hundreds of them, and the sight, therefore, seemed to embrace hundreds of miles.

As plans of cities are inset on maps of countries, another chart on a larger scale lay right beneath our wheels. Here the green resolved, not into ordinary grass, but into wild corn, barley, and oats, which accounted for that vivid fire, as of a life within the green. And among these myriad bearded alleys lived a population of flowers, buttercups and poppies, pale purple irises and dark purple campanulas, and countless others, exhibiting all the colours, forms, and wonders that a child finds in its first garden. Then a puff of air would come, bending the corn to a silver ripple, while the flowers leaned with it; or a cloud shadow, and all grow dark, as if for a moment's sleep; though a few feet off there would be no ripple and no darkness; so that this whole inner world of the steppe was mapped on a system of infinite minute recessions, having just those gradations of distance that the outer lacked.

Our spirits had risen when we left the plateau. Now they effervesced. We shouted for joy, stopping the car lest the minutes that were robbing us of

345

the unrepeatable first vision should go faster. Even the larks in this paradise had lost their ordinary aloofness. One almost hit my hat in its inquisitiveness.

. . .

Mazar-i-Sheriff, 1 June

Yesterday morning Christopher called at the Mudir-i-Kharija's office to ask permission to visit the Russian Consulate. His excuse was that we needed some visas, of which there is in fact no hope, though it is tantalising to think that Bokhara is only fifteen hours from Termez by train. However, he had no chance of using this excuse, since even the Mudir-i-Kharija's deputy is asleep to us now. He therefore went by himself, breasted his way through a post of Afghan soldiers who presented their bayonets at him, and at length reached M. Bouriachenko, a small intellectual man who was sitting under a tree reading.

'You want visas for Samarcand?' said M. Bouriachenko. 'Of course you do. I will telegraph to Moscow at once to say that two Oxford professors of Islamic culture' – (God forgive us, we both left Oxford without degrees) – 'have arrived here and are waiting for permission to cross the Amu Darya. No, there is nothing to see at Termez. The place you ought to go to is Anau. Professor Simionov has just written a book on the Timurid monuments there. I wish I could give you the visas at once, but I'm afraid it will take a week or so to get a reply. Anyhow you are *here* for a bit, that's the main thing. We must have a party. Will you come?'

'When?' asked Christopher, forgetting to say thank you in his surprise.

'When? I don't know when. What does it matter? This evening? Would that suit you?'

'Perfectly. What time?'

'What time? Seven, is that all right? Or six? Or five to four? We can start now if you like.'

It was half-past eleven, and a blazing hot morning. Christopher said perhaps the evening would be nicer.

At half-past six we tiptoed out of the hotel so that the Muntazim should not hear us, reached the gate of the Consulate, where the guard brandished their weapons as before, and found ourselves in a series of courtyards shaded by trees; in the front yard stood a number of lorries and cars, including a red Vauxhall. M. Bouriachenko received us in a cool room free from icons of Lenin and Marx, and lit by a private electric light plant. I said, I supposed by his name that he must come from Ukraine. 'Yes, from Kiev, and my wife from Riazin.' She walked in, a young woman plainly dressed in dark purple, whose good-natured face was framed in hair drawn flat from a parting in the middle. Others followed her: an enormous wallowing man, slightly scented, from whose pitted face came the voice of a dove; his wife, a blonde with red lips whose golden hair was brushed straight back from her forehead; Master Bouriachenko, aged five and the spit of Chaliapin; a boy and girl belonging to the second couple; the doctor, a tubby little fellow with a black moustache and butcher's lick; another lady discreetly painted, whose fair hair was ruffled into a crest; the fat fair man I saw in the telegraph office, who said he had been a radio officer at Canterbury during the War; two natty young fellows just arrived from Kabul, who had taken a fortnight over the journey owing to the rains: and last of all a girl of fourteen, daughter of the painted lady, whose movements were beautiful to watch and who is destined to become a ballet dancer.

Judged by Russian standards, which differ from ours, the food was not really profuse; indeed how could it be? though they had bought, at considerable expense we discovered afterwards, the last sardines in the town. But it had that air of profusion which Russians always create about them, and as new guests kept wandering in, and new tables were brought, and new chairs, and the children hopped up on people's laps, the dishes kept pace and were still as full as ever of the sardines from India, paprika from Russia, fresh meat with onion salad, and bread. A decanter of yellow vodka, in which fruit was swimming, was endlessly replenished. The Russians, who gulped it off in cups, complained furiously of our slow sipping. But that was only at first.

The two young men from Kabul had been bringing a number of new English records that had been ordered from Peshawar; but they had all been spoilt in the wreck of their lorry by the storm at Haibak, and the loss was a tragic disappointment to this isolated community; though to hear them apologise for it, one might have thought the records had been ordered for us instead of them. As it was, tangos and jazz alternated with *Shehérezade, Boris Godunov,* and *Eugene Onyegin*. We danced, we sang, we sat down to eat, we danced again. Conversation was in Persian, and what made it odder, when talking to one's own kind, was the inevitable accompaniment of Persian gesture, the bowing of the head and fluttering of the eyelids, the hand on the heart, and the general assumption of self-deprecation. M. Bouriachenko and the man with the dove's voice addressed us as 'Sahib'. Perhaps they thought this sounded more equalitarian than the Persian Excellencies and Highnesses we used to them.

The hours fled, the decanter flowed, the telegraphist was carried out, I fell into a torpor, the Russians began to unload their emotions, and when I woke up I found Christopher gasping for breath under the souls of the whole community. It was two o'clock and time to go home. The hotel was only a few hundred yards away. But M. Bouriachenko, calling for the 'Consulski Vauxhall', insisted on driving us to it. This was an act of real friendship. For whether our walk was unsteady or not, it would have been unwise to run a risk of the Afghans observing it, a fact we appreciated when a sentry thrust his rifle into the window of the car.

This morning was painful beyond the usual run of next-mornings. We called at the Consulate after tea, bearing not flowers, but some boxes of cigars, and found them all sitting out in a sort of games court equipped with swings and parallel bars and a high net over which any number of people divided into two sides, can fist a soft football. A game was started for us, the party being increased now by three or four other men, proletarian savages, who are employed as chauffeurs and mechanics. The telegraphist looked older.

M. Bouriachenko told us that the only other Russians in this part of the country were four locust-fighters living in and about Khanabad. The locusts are a new plague here. They arrived from Morocco a few years ago, breed on the north slopes of the Hindu Kush, and thence descend on Russian Turkestan, where they menace the cotton crops.

Since there is a road from here to Khanabad, and another from there to Kabul which avoids the Haibak gorge, we have decided not to ride after all. This detour will take us 150 miles further east, to the edge of Badakshan, and the excuse for making it afforded by the blockage at Haibak is too good to miss. Christopher regrets the horse journey, but I think the detour will be more interesting.

The pleasure he takes in reducing the famed Bhuddas of Bamian to cultural rubble is part of what Jonathan Raban refers to as Byron's 'calculated affront' to the conventional bias of taste towards the classical.

Shibar (c. 9000 ft, 24 miles from Bamian), 9 June

I should not like to stay long at Bamian. Its art is unfresh. When Huan Tsang came here, the Buddhas were gilded to resemble bronze, and 5000

monks swarmed in the labyrinths beside them. That was in 632; Moham-
mad died the same year, and the Arabs reached Bamian before the end
of the century. But it was not until 150 years later that the monks were
finally extirpated. One can imagine how the Arabs felt about them and
their idols in this blood-red valley. Nadir Shah must have felt the same
1,000 years later when he broke the legs of the larger Buddha.

That Buddha is 174 feet high, and the smaller 115; they stand a quarter
of a mile apart. The larger bears traces of a plaster veneer, which was
painted red, presumably as a groundwork for the gilt. Neither has any
artistic value. But one could bear that; it is their negation of sense, the
lack of any pride in their monstrous flaccid bulk, that sickens. Even their
material is unbeautiful, for the cliff is made, not of stone, but of com-
pressed gravel. A lot of monastic navvies were given picks and told to
copy some frightful semi-Hellenistic image from India or China. The
result has not even the dignity of labour.

The canopies of the niches which contain the two figures are plastered
and painted. In the smaller hangs a triumph scene, red, yellow, and blue,
in which Hackin, Herzfeld, and others have distinguished a Sasanian
influence; but the clue to this idea comes from Masson, who saw a
Pahlevi inscription here a hundred years ago. The paintings round the
larger head are better preserved, and can be examined at close quarters
by standing on the head itself. On either side of the niche, below the
curve of the vault, hang five medallions about ten feet in diameter which
contain Boddhisatvas. These figures are surrounded by horseshoe auras
of white, yellow, and blue and their hair is tinged with red. Between each
medallion grows a triple-branched lotus; at least we supposed it to be
that, though in other surroundings it might be taken for an ecclesiastical
bracket upholding three glass globes. The next zone above is occupied
by a pavement in squares out of perspective, and the zone above that by
a wainscot of Pompeian curtains finished with a border of peacocks'

feathers. On top of this come two more rows of Boddhisatvas, seated against auras and thrones alternately, the thrones being decked with jewelled carpets. Between these stand large cups on stems, resembling Saxon fonts and sprouting cherubs. The topmost zone overhead is missing. The colours are the ordinary fresco colours, slate-grey, gamboge, a rusty chocolate-red, a dull grape-tint, and a bright harebell blue.

The subjects suggest that Persian, Indian, Chinese, and Hellenistic ideas all met at Bamian in the fifth and sixth centuries. It is interesting to have a record of this meeting. But the fruit of it is not pleasant. The only exception is the lower row of Boddhisatvas, which Hackin says are older than the rest. They achieve that air of repose, graceful, but empty, which is the best one can expect of Buddhist iconography.

TWENTY-TWO

———

Herodotus

Herodotus, *The Histories*

Herodotus has a chapter to himself as he may be considered the founder of travel writing as we know it now. His *Histories*, written in the Ionian dialect of Classical Greek, date from 440 BCE. They cover the history, customs, geography and politics of most of the then known world.

Every generation seems to think that the era of travel writing is over. Its death has been announced many times. No doubt when Herodotus returned from his travels, his contemporaries opined that after his efforts, there would be no need for further travel writing; it had all been written.

The fifth century BCE was the zenith of the influence of Greek civilization, so he was a contemporary of Pericles, Socrates, and Euripides. Although a Greek, he was born in Halicarnassus, in the then Persian Empire, which is modern-day Bodrum in Turkey.

Justin Marozzi writes in *The Man Who Invented History: Travels with Herodotus*: 'Herodotus is the world's first historian, but he is also its first foreign correspondent, investigative journalist, anthropologist and travel writer. He is an aspiring geographer, a budding moralist, a skilful dramatist, a high-spirited explorer and an inveterate storyteller. He is part learned scholar, part tabloid hack, but always broad-minded, humorous and generous-hearted, which is why he's so much fun. He examines the world around him with the benevolence of a Micawber, with an unerring eye for thrilling material to inform and amuse, to horrify and entertain.'

⁕

Herodotus 3.38 *The Histories*

In view of all this, I have no doubt whatever that Cambyses was completely out of his mind; it is the only possible explanation of his assault upon, and mockery of, everything which ancient law and custom have made sacred in Egypt. For if anyone, no matter who, were given the opportunity of choosing from amongst all the nations in the world the beliefs which he thought best, he would inevitably, after careful consideration of their relative merits, choose those of his own country. Everyone without exception believes his own native customs, and the religion he was brought up in, to be the best; and that being so, it is unlikely that anyone but a madman would mock at such things. There is abundant evidence that this is the universal feeling about the ancient customs of one's country. One might recall, in particular, an account told of Darius. When he was king of Persia, he summoned the Greeks who happened to be present at his court, and asked them what they would take to eat the dead bodies of their fathers. They replied that they would not do it for any money in the world. Later, in the presence of the Greeks, and through an interpreter, so that they could understand what was said, he asked some Indians, of the tribe called Callatiae, who do in fact eat their parents' dead bodies, what they would take to burn them. They uttered a cry of horror and forbade him to mention such a dreadful thing. One can see by this what custom can do, and Pindar, in my opinion, was right when he called it 'king of all'.

TWENTY-THREE

Who Made Scraps?

The best parts of *Scraps* are the passages I have permission to quote. The next best are the comments of my many friends and correspondents, who have chosen to share with me the books, indeed the very sentences, that inspired them to travel.

Some of us were drawn to travel by children's fiction. Tony Wheeler chose Arthur Ransome's *Swallows and Amazons*; Nick Danziger countered with *Tintin in America*; for me it was the almost forgotten *Mary Plain's Big Adventure* by Gwynedd Rae. Just staring at maps and turning names into images was also dreamland for Judith Schalansky and Dervla Murphy. Dervla sent me twenty or more pages of typewritten (looks like the old mechanical sort) and handwritten notes on her travel writing heroes, or friends, as she prefers to call them, even though she has met them only in print. It was accompanied by an invitation to discuss them over a glass of Guinness in her village. Every one of her choices shares her own need to open doors, with no idea what may lie behind. Her list includes several of the celebrated women travellers of the nineteenth and twentieth centuries: Mary Kingsley, Isabella Bird, plus an anonymous writer published in the 1780s by John Murray.

Alexandra David-Néel is one of these heroes. Dervla, who knew when she was just five years old that she wanted to go places, feels a kinship with Alexandra who, when still a child, 'craved to go beyond the garden gate, to follow the road that passed it by, and to set out for the

Unknown'. Years later they communicated. 'When I was running a Tibetan children's refugee camp in Pokhara, Nepal, my first book was published and Mme David-Néel kindly wrote to me. It is a little tragedy that this precious document was eaten by one of the rats which shared my room in the bazaar.'

I wanted to canvas the ideas of an éminence grise of travel literature, Jan Morris. I contacted her in her Welsh fastness. She called me and expressed surprise at my request, claiming not to be a travel writer.

'I write about cities, Bill; that's not travel.'

'In which case did someone else write *Coronation Everest* and *The Sultan in Oman*?'

No answer.

But then she became one of my most entertaining advisers. She told me to include Alexander Kinglake's *Eothen* 'for the humour'; I have. We discussed others and she said that she had reserved for last the book that she most admired, Charles Doughty's 1888 *Travels in Arabia Deserta*, and that she wanted to show me her favourite passage. She liked it so much that she often repeated it and had also sung it to herself. She would like to sing it to me. So I sat and listened to one of my heroes singing her favourite passage of travel prose over the phone to me. She asked if I had any such passages that were important to me. I mentioned Matthew Arnold's epic poem *Sohrab and Rustum*, which had thrown me into a virtual romance with the Oxus many years ago. I read her the haunting final lines and sent the whole by email. A few days later she emailed me to say: 'Dear Bill. Thank you for entertaining me. I am now also singing *Sohrab and Rustum*.'

To understand a little of Doughty I consulted Andrew Taylor (*God's Fugitive; The Life of Charles Montagu Doughty*) and learned just why he, Jan and T. E. Lawrence treat the book with such reverence, despite it being very difficult to read.

Tony Wheeler founded Lonely Planet with his wife Maureen. They journeyed together from London to Australia in 1972 and wrote *Across Asia on the Cheap*, which was the launch of the publishing business. I was jealous of Lonely Planet when I bought a competitor, Cadogan Guides, in 1989; LP seemed to have got to all the most exciting places just before we did. Tony gave me several books and passages that I would have missed. These include the Ana Briongos passage, which he uses whenever anyone asks 'why travel?', and Raja Shehadeh's *Palestinian Walks*.

I relied on John Julius Norwich for the selection from Patrick Leigh Fermor's *Mani*, partly because they were close friends. Leigh Fermor's meandering imaginations around the coronations of the Palaeologi, enhanced by the contrast with their supposed twentieth-century descendants as simple Peleponnese fishermen, is the passage that John Julius chose to read to the Patrick Leigh Fermor Society at the Hellenic Centre in 2015. His view: 'Paddy, alongside Freya Stark, was the finest travel writer of the twentieth century and possibly of all time'.

Michelle Jana Chan chose Isak Dinesen and Elspeth Huxley. 'Elspeth Huxley and Isak Dinesen's two love songs to Kenya and East Africa have carried me from my South London childhood to dusty roads around the world, my triggers to longing for another land. I was eight or nine years old when I read *The Flame Trees of Thika*, about Huxley as a little girl in Kenya in the early twentieth century. I wanted to be her, of course. I still kiss the walls, as Huxley did, when I leave somewhere I love, so that I too will return'.

Wade Davis is the author of *Into the Silence*, one of the travel books published so far in the twenty-first century that will surely still be selling in the twenty-second century. He wrote to me about *Seven Pillars of Wisdom*: 'I have a first edition, bought by the grandfather I never knew, an army surgeon whose life was shattered in that war, a man who was killed with my grandmother a decade before I was born by a drunk driver on a coastal road carved into the cliffs of Vancouver Island. My own father's life was then ruined by Hitler's war. *Seven Pillars of Wisdom* is my favourite book of travel. Please use the first seven paragraphs of chapter one.'

Moutaineer Sir Chris Bonington (author of twenty mountain and travel books including *I Chose to Climb* and *The Next Horizon: From the Eiger to the South Face of Annapurna*) chose Herzog's *Annapurna* but added W. H. Murray's *Mountaineering in Scotland* as the book that sent him first adventuring: 'I was a youngster brought up in Hampstead. Although I had been evacuated to the Lake District, I had never been north of the Border. Tales of the Alps or the Himalaya seemed too distant and unattainable, but I could hitch hike up to Scotland to find a wonderful expansive wilderness which I could venture into and explore much in the way that Murray had done before the War'. Bonington's *Tibet's Secret Mountain* (with Dr Charles Clarke) almost guided me to Sepukangri in 2003.

Rory MacLean is creating a travel library of his own with *Berlin: Imagine a City; Stalin's Nose; Under the Dragon;* and *Another Life* and *Back in the USSR: Heroic Adventures in Transnistria* jointly with photojournalist and adventurer Nick Danziger (*Danzigers's Travels*). Rory chose Bouvier, Leigh Fermor and several more.

Colin Thubron chose Patrick Leigh Fermor's *Mani* ('its baroque brilliance has yet to be surpassed'), the opening chapters of the two Redmond O'Hanlon works, and wanted me to use the passage from Freya Stark's *Ionia* – 'A work of the poetic economy, which is Stark's hallmark.'

Artemis Cooper is biographer of Patrick Leigh Fermor and editor, with Colin Thubron, of *The Broken Road*, the last part of the Leigh Fermor trilogy. She has been a friend since we travelled across the

Sahara together in 1984, a seminal adventure for me, and maybe for her too. She gave me ideas and anecdotes about several of the authors. She also gave me the title of the book during lunch one day by quoting Jonathan Raban.

Antony Cazalet was on the same 1984 Sahara expedition and has been a friend ever since. He is an informed raconteur and can force obedience from any motor vehicle with no more than a severe look. He proposed passages by his friend Wilfred Thesiger ('He liked the slim Dinka boys, because he could see their willies swinging from side to side even when they walked away') and also Lady Hester Stanhope, after whom he named his Staffordshire Bull Terrier.

Robin Hanbury-Tenison has far more experience than I in creating books such as *Scraps*. We discussed his choices as we sat on the banks of Loch Ness together on Robin's eightieth birthday in May 2016. He was celebrating the event by running the London Marathon, climbing several mountains, and other activities usually reserved for younger men. The final challenge was walking and riding across Scotland and he had persuaded me and others to join him. I, for one, usually lagged behind but consoled myself that I am thirteen years younger, so have time to train up to his speed.

My daughter Siena supported with such enthusiasm from Boston and brought so many supporters to me at Unbound, including Chris, her husband. The Jan Morris *Venice* passage is dedicated to their daughters, Aya and Violet, who will discover that the first sight of Venice is far more important in anyone's life than little matters such as puberty or early romance.

Nigel Winser chose *The Ascent of Everest* and its summit moment. Nigel and his wife Shane, on behalf of the Royal Geographical Society and independently, have advised and encouraged many of the actual and would-be explorers and travel writers of the current generation, including me with *Scraps* and my own minor wanderings, mainly in Central Asia.

Tim Butcher (*Blood River: A Journey to Africa's Broken Heart* and *Chasing the Devil: A Journey through Sub-Saharan Africa in the Footsteps of Graham Greene*) decided to propose not a book but something maybe even more enduring. He describes walking north of Cape Town into the Cederberg mountains and finding caves by the River Brandy, excavated by its flow; here travellers from more than five thousand years ago have left stories of themselves and a simple right handprint on the ceiling. 'I reached up and placed my own right hand right next to it. And in that muscle memory reaction I felt the power of the best travel writing: to amuse, to entertain, to connect with other travelers, to make one think about those that went before, to make you wonder how you would have tamed the same landscape'.

Alexander Frater (*Chasing the Monsoon, Beyond the Blue Horizon; On the Track of Imperial Airways*) inadvertently but memorably gave me the name and the theme for chapter seven.

Rob Kinder and 153 others recommended *The Ascent of Rum Doodle* with the hope that its republication might inspire a new attempt on this little known mountain.

Georgiana Campbell was a lone advocate for Norman Douglas, but that led me to the happy congruity of chapter eighteen, 'A Supper in Capri'. Her father, the Marquess of Salisbury, shared with me his knowledge of the literature of the exploration of Central Asia by Europeans and Russians. Only Robert Middleton (*Tajikistan and the High Pamirs*) and John Keay (*When Men and Mountains Meet, The Gilgit Game, Eccentric Travellers,* and most recently *The Tartan Turban,* a biography of Alexander Gardner) have the same depth of knowledge of this, my own favourite region for adventure. Add Bijan Omrani, editor of the *Journal of the Royal Society of Asian Affairs* and author of *Afghanistan: A Com-*

panion and Guide with Matthew Leeming, and we would soon fill another *Scraps* devoted to Central Asia alone.

Sir Christopher Ondaatje extolled Hemingway and Richard Burton: *'True at First Light* and Fawn Brodie's *The Devil Drives: A Life of Richard Burton . . .'.* These books changed my life. I read them, then sold my Canadian finance business, moved to England and then for the next eight years followed Burton, first in India and then Africa'. Christopher subsequently became a benefactor to, and eventually president of, the Royal Geographical Society. That is travel writing as inspiration . . .

Hemingway was also chosen by Liesbeth Hop, whilst we climbed Kilimanjaro together in 2004. She was telling me how she had been beguiled by Hemingway's *The Green Hills of Africa* when she was attacked by a black-necked spitting cobra. I saw it and she did not. Ernest would have approved her bravado when she continued the discussion in the air ambulance to Nairobi.

Eland is the independent travel publisher that has done more than any, including the giants of publishing, to promote and preserve the best of the genre and to resurrect many forgotten titles. It was nurtured by first John Hatt and now by Barnaby Rogerson and Rose Baring. Many of their authors are quoted here including Sybille Bedford, Nicolas Bouvier, Martha Gellhorn, Norman Lewis and Dervla Murphy.

Sir Peter Job guided me through a tour of Chinese and Japanese travellers (among then the ninth-century Monk Ennin) and wrote for me an essay-length recommendation for Isabella Bird.

My twin sister, Sukie, years ago titillated an interest in Central Asia by giving me a copy of Galen Rowell's *Mountains of the Middle Kingdom* (possibly the travel book that I return to most often in my whole library).

My son Benjiamino's tales of Argentina reignited my enthusiasm for Chatwin's *In Patagonia* and with his wife, Marce, introduced me to her native Colombia. The South American passages are dedicated to their son, Arturo, who is already travelling (around his cot).

Adrian Lower directed me to Paul Heiney's *One Wild Song*. Paul Heiney in turn reminded me not to disregard Joshua Slocum, as did James Hanly, the latter whilst we looked over the sea from the Musgrave oasis on the southern tip of Syros. The Greek passages are for Syros, Christopher and the extended Musgrave family. That includes Robert Wilson Wright, who sent me many ideas including choices from Nicolas Bouvier, Jason Elliot, Robert Byron and the Gertrude Bell passage from *Persian Pictures*. Some of these were also promoted from the saddle during a 150 kilometre bicycle ride around Sheep's Head in Kerry; the occasional advance warning 'this bit may be lumpy' gained new meaning for me.

My daughter Kara, with Rich Austwick in support, spent two years surrounded by the library from which *Scraps* has been created, and lived alongside me the editorial process and the journey that was the pre-selling and funding via Unbound; she helped make it fun with her infectious enthusiasm. Everything related to Italy here is dedicated to her. Her views follow Robert Byron's when arriving in Italy for the first time: 'I might have been a dentist or a public man, but for that first sight of the larger world.'

Cindy Blake housed the other half of the library and, having more experience than I, encouraged me through the editorial process.

My friend and fellow traveller Christian Larsson chose Elias Canetti, Paul Bowles and those who wrote of Morocco whilst we sat in his brother, John's, Marrakech garden, surely the loveliest in the whole Maghreb. All the mountain passages are for them and their families together with our friends Inki Reksten and Arne Naess, who loved the mountains and died in them, and Bjorn Knudsen, who showed us how to survive.

Sara Wheeler (*Chile: Travels in a Thin Country, Terra Incognita: Travels in Antarctica*) sent a persuasively impassioned advocacy of Apsley Cherry-Garrard, whose biography she wrote. Jason Webster (*Or the Bull Kills You, Duende, Andalus, Sacred Sierra*) chose *The Colossus of Maroussi*. Simon Talbot Williams also chose the Henry Miller and others. Alexander Turner found the John Masters passage. Pico Iyer (*The Global Soul, The Lady and the Monk*) sent many suggestions, including the Peter Matthiessen passage. Duncan Smith shared with me access to his collection of the Penguin Pink editions, their original travel collection.

Michael Pauls and Dana Facaros, together the backbone of the Cadogan Guide series in its heyday, introduced the Kipling passage. Michael Pauls also proposed passages from Mark Twain, with whom he shares an iconoclastic bent.

Kapka Kassabova (*Street Without a Name, Border: A Journey to the Edge of Europe*), Bulgarian-born and now resident in Scotland, asked for O'Hanlon setting off for the Orinoco and chose the John Gimlette passage from *Tomb of the Inflatable Pig*.

Sarah Anderson (founder owner of the Notting Hill Travel Bookshop in London) gave me the run of her fine library. Laurence Millman (*Last Places, Lost in the Arctic, Hiking to Siberia*) chose Peter Fleming. Dick Russell selected several Norman Lewis passages.

My sister Lee Sturgeon Day (now a children's book writer) introduced me to many books, including Michael Crichton's *Travels*, a book that Denise Goulimis told me 'changed my life, and for the better'.

Tim Mackintosh-Smith (*Yemen, Travels in Dictionaryland*, the Ibn Battuta Trilogy including *Travels with a Tangerine*) mailed from San'a, Yemen to say: 'Sorry, Bill, will call when I can – we're in a war, missiles flying overhead'. He didn't call; that's a good excuse for going there to seek him out sometime.

Michael Kerr (the *Daily Telegraph* and *Deskbound Traveller)* introduced me to books which I would not otherwise have found. Isabella Tree (*Sliced Iguana, The Living Goddess*) and Sarah Lutyens promoted Sybille Bedford. Richard Robinson found the Paul Fussell comment that provides the title to chapter ten. Nicholas Best (*Tennis and the Masai, Happy Valley: The Story of the English in Kenya*) found the Joseph Thomson passage.

Justin Marozzi (*Baghdad: City of Peace, City of Blood, The Man Who Invented History*) gave me his review of Herodotus and many more ideas, as did John Gimlette (*At the Tomb of the Inflatable Pig: Travels in Paraguay, Wild Coast: Travels on South America's Untamed Edge*).

Anthony Sattin (*The Gates of Africa, Pharaoh's Child, Winter on the Nile*) gave me advice particularly on travellers in Egypt, about which few know more than he.

Adam Day and Wendy MacClinchy gave me ideas, hospitality in Beirut and the company of Kaia and Satya.

Rick Grand Jean in New York, Michael Cahan in Chicago, Peter Schwartz in Ontario, and Kevin Butler in Santa Fe all joined the editorial group, as did Rupert McCowan, director of the Royal Geographical Society in Hong Kong.

Ben Holden (*Bedtime Stories for Grown-Ups*) gave me his ideas by the pool in Cartagena, Colombia and advised on the pitfalls of the permissions process.

David Mills recommended *Deeper Than Indigo,* as did Gillie Green, and Rory Stewart's *The Places in Between.* Patrick Arning promoted Alexander Kinglake. Other valuable ideas came from: Timothy Ogene; James Robinson; Sophie Ibbotson; Alasdair MacLeod at the RGS; Richard Taylor; Alan Eisner; Jasper Winn; Lady Mary Stewart; Max Lovell-Hoare; Isabelle Duncan, whilst we wandered around the High Atlas; Alan Palmer (another Morocco expert in both literature and travel); John

Drake; Jeremy Quarrie; Rustom Irani; Sara McWatters; Nina Martyn; Mark Whelan; Archie Drake; Jamie Bebb; Mercedes Lopez-Tomlinson; Ted Monroe; Robert Penn; Heidi Kingstone (*Dispatches from a Kabul Cafe*); Antony Kitchin and Dillon Coleman, who also travelled Afghanistan's Wakhan Corridor with me in 2007; Jenny Balfour Paul; Jason Webster (*Guerra, Duende*); Sir Terence Clark; Sara Nunan; Henry Thompson; Lizzie Sellwood; Hugh Monk; Clemmie Macmillan Scott; Judith Thurman (biographer of Isak Dinesen); Nick Laing (founder of *Steppes East*); Ivor Lucas; Jonathan Stedall; Brigid Keenan (*Diplomatic Baggage, Packing Up*); Daniel Klein; Gavin Graham; Arabella Dorman; Christopher Burness.

Clare Maxwell Dickens has been the most valuable of all because she took on the convoluted adventure of obtaining the necessary permissions with dedication and enthusiasm, somehow not dulled even to the end. She was also my most prolific contributor of ideas and editorial support. Many passages are included because of her advocacy: John Masters, William Least Heat-Moon and Pico Iyer.

The passage from *One Wild Song* by Paul Heiney is dedicated to Clare and to the memory of her very talented son Titus.

The Unbound team have guided me with enthusiasm and savoir faire: Isobel Kieran, Phil Connor, Xander Cansell, who encouraged me to use thematic rather than chronological chapters, Caitlin Harvey, Jimmy Leach, Dan Kieran, John Mitchinson, the bearded guru, and Anna Simpson, my admirably encouraging editor.

There seems to have been much marrying and baby-making amongst the executives and editorial team, which must be a sign of good office relations. It is a vibrant office and I sense that a model for some part of the future of publishing is being created there.

Richard Collins, my literary editor, deleted all my best bits; that was because he must be a humourless pedant, despite his obvious talents and experience in travel literature. However, he is at least a member of the book reading public. So I tried to reconsider some of his comments as if I were an objective third party. I found an item that had been annotated 'maybe this does not quite do the trick'. I read it again a couple of times and then wrote in the margin: 'You are right, RC. This is sententious rubbish. I must be more careful.' I began to reassess his notes. Eventually I understood that without his cool hand and scissor work *Scraps* might have been little more than a messy indulgence for its creator's whims.

Miranda Ward then attacked what was left after Richard's work. She clearly has all the talents that I lack (that is most of the necessary ones) and more, in particular a fine eye for accuracy and consistency of presentation.

I am indebted to both of them for their care, their skill and for leaving a couple of paragraphs intact.

Everything that I have been given has been useful. Some have sent essays or annotated photocopies of favourite pages. Some have just remembered the passage or the idea but not even the name of the book; I have a few such of my own. Please continue to send them to me at scrapsofwool@gmail.com or bill@billcolegave.com. Together we could create a *Scraps II*.

Copyright Acknowledgements

COPYRIGHT ACKNOWLEDGEMENTS

Extract from *At the Tomb of the Inflatable Pig* by John Gimlette, 1997, published by Hutchinson and reproduced by permission of The Random House Group Limited.

Extract from *The Snow Leopard* by Peter Matthiessen, 1978, published by Chatto & Windus and reproduced by permission of The Random House Group Limited.

In addition to the above licensed extracts, the Publisher and editor gratefully acknowledge the following for kind permission to reproduce extracts gratis: Alexander Aitken, Back Bay Books, Cassell, Daunt Books, Eland Books, Medina Publishing, I.B. Tauris, Tauris Park, Trotamundas Press.

Index

Abu Dhabi, 173
Afghanistan, 93–4, 214–18, 319–34,
    344–51
    Baltit, 215–16
    Bamiyan, 349–51
    Chaghcharan (Chakcharan), 93,
    330, 332, 334
    Chalt fort, 215–16
    Gumbad-i-Kabus, 344–6
    Kabul, 21, 318, 322–3, 327–8, 330,
    347–9
    Mazar-i-Sharif, 346–9
    minaret of Djam, 319–21
    Shibar, 349–51
Africa, 124–7, 136–7, 231–4, 252,
    297–9
    Maghreb, 112–13
    North Africa, 33, 112–13, 280–3
    West Africa, 44–6
    see also Congo; Egypt; Kenya;
    Liberia
Alaska, 114–20
Amazon, river, 74–7
Anker, Conrad, 62–3
Antarctic, 241–50
Arabia, 164–77, 191–3
Arctic, 47–9, 114–20
Arkansas City, 154
Arnold, Matthew, 326, 355
Auden, W. H., 290
Azerbaijan, 314–17

Bates, Henry Walter, 74
'Battle of Flowers', 313
Bedford, Sybille, 289–90, 360, 363
    Pleasures and Landscapes, 289–91
    A Visit to Don Otavio, 300–4
Bell, Gertrude, 165, 335–6, 361
    Persian Pictures, 335–7
Betjeman, John, 73, 88–9
    Shell Guide to Cornwall, 88–91
Bird, Isabella, 37, 40, 44, 360
    A Lady's Life in the Rocky
    Mountains, 40–3
Blixen, Karen (Isak Dinesen), 251–3,
    356
    Out of Africa, 253–4
Böcklin, Arnold, 294
Bonington, Sir Chris, 357
Bouvier, Nicolas, 21–2, 357, 360–1
    The Way of the World, 21–3
Bowles, Paul, 21, 32, 111, 361
    Without Stopping, 32–3
Bowman, W. E., 55, 68
    The Ascent of Rum Doodle, 68–72
Brecht, Bertolt, 290
Briongos, Ana, 35, 356
    Black on Black, 35–6
Browning, Elizabeth Barrett, 199
Bryson, Bill, 149–50
    The Lost Continent, 149–152
Bulgaria, 121–3

Burroughs, William, 155
Burton, Richard, 164, 231, 360
Butcher, Tim, 359
Byron, Robert, 2, 93, 205, 305, 318,
    335, 343–4, 361
    The Road to Oxiana, 343–51

Calvino, Italo, 197–8
    Invisible Cities, 197–8
Cambyses, King of Persia, 353
Canetti, Elias, 111, 361
Capa, Robert, 286
Cape Horn, 38–9
Cape Sunium, 108
Cape Verde Islands, 13–14, 140
Cévennes, 182–7
Chaliapin, Feodor, 347
Charlemagne, Emperor, 83
Chartres Cathedral, 319
Chatwin, Bruce, 4, 16, 92–3, 318, 360
    In Patagonia, 16–19
    What Am I Doing Here?, 93–4
Chenier, André, 52
Cherry-Garrard, Apsley, 230, 241, 362
    The Worst Journey in the World,
    241-4
Chicago, 78–81
China, 268–72
    Cultural Revolution, 224–5
    see also Tartary
Chingiz Khan, *see* Genghis Khan
Chukchi Sea, 117, 119
Churchill, Winston, 335
Clausewitz, Carl von, 138
Coleridge, Samuel Taylor, 109
Congo, 15, 142–8
Conrad, Joseph, 4, 14
    Heart of Darkness, 14–15, 142
Constantine XI, Emperor, 96
Constantinople, 83, 96–7, 99, 268
Cooper, Artemis, 120, 123, 292,
    357–8

Copland, Aaron, 32
cormorant boats, 188–9
Cornwall, 88–91
Crockett, William J., 195
Curzon, Lord, 213–14
    *The Pamirs and the Source of the
    Oxus*, 214–18

Dalai Lama, 219–20
Damascus, 165–6, 341
'Dance of the Bee', 259
Darius, King of Persia, 339–40, 353
Danziger, Nick, 354
Darwin, Charles, 44
David-Néel, Alexandra, 213, 218–19,
    354–5
    My Journey to Lhasa, 218–22
Davis, Wade, 54, 61–2, 168, 356
    Into the Silence, 61–4
Dickens, Charles, 81
Dinesen, Isak, *see* Blixen, Karen
Diocletian, Emperor, 96
Doughty, Charles, 164–5, 355
    Travels in Arabia Deserta,
    164–8
Douglas, Norman, 289–92, 305
    Siren Land, 292–6
Dumas, Alexander, 207–8
Durrell, Lawrence, 25–6

Eberhardt, Isabelle, 92, 111–12,
    280
    Dans L'Ombre Chaude d'Islam,
    111–13, 280–3
Egypt, 258–60
Eiger, the, 60–1
Eland Books, 360
Eliot, George, 203
Elliot, Jason, 318, 326, 361
    An Unexpected Light, 326–30
Euripides, 352
Eustratius, Emperor, 97–9

Facaros, Dana, and Michael Pauls, 197, 210–11, 362
Cadogan Guide to Rome, 210–12
féticheuse, Congolese, 144–8
Flaubert, Gustave, 257, 259
Fleming, Peter, 205, 305–6, 362
News from Tartary, 306–10
France
see Cévennes; Paris
François I, King of France, 265
Frater, Alexander, 92, 213, 227, 359
Chasing the Monsoon, 227–9
Frederick Barbarossa, Emperor, 83
Fuller, Alexandra, 251, 260
Scribbling the Cat, 260–2
Fussel, Paul, 178, 363

Galapagos Islands, 11–12
Gellhorn, Martha, 252, 289–91, 296, 360
Travels with Myself and Another, 296–9
Genghis (Genghiz, Chingiz) Khan, 93, 321, 342
Germany, 266–8
German Democratic Republic, 12–13
Gimlette, John, 73, 86, 362–3
At the Tomb of the Inflatable Pig, 86–8
Ginsberg, Allen, 155
Goba people, 261–2
Goethe, Johann Wolfgang von, 197, 203, 267
Italian Journey, 203–5
Gorky, Maxim, 19
Grand Teton National Park, 151–2
Grant, General Ulysses S, 152
Greece, 25–8
Kardamyli, 94–9
Litotes, 139

Patras, 26–7
Greene, Graham, 44, 205, 273, 286, 305, 311
Journey Without Maps, 311–14
Grosvenor, Rosamund, 338

Hanbury-Tenison, Robin, 358
Hari Rud river, 330–2, 334
Harrer, Heinrich, 59–60
The White Spider, 59–61
Heat-Moon, William Least, 149, 159–60, 364
Blue Highways, 159–63
Heiney, Paul, 37–8, 361, 364
One Wild Song, 37–9
Heliogabalus, Emperor, 96
Heliopolis, ruins of, 342
Hemingway, Ernest, 251, 289, 291, 360
For Whom the Bell Tolls, 124, 252
True at First Light, 252
Heraclitus, 111
Herodotus, 352–3, 363
Herzog, Maurice, 54–5, 357
Annapurna, 55–9
Hobbes, Thomas, 211
Holmes, Richard, 178, 184
Footsteps, 184–7
Homer, 27, 95
Hong Kong Chinese, 270–1
Humboldt, Alexander von, 74
Hunt, Sir John, 54, 64, 198
The Ascent of Everest, 64–7
Hussein, Saddam, 103
Huxley, Elspeth, 251, 255, 356
The Flame Trees of Thika, 255–7
Huxley, Gervas, 255
Huxley, T. H., 44

Icknield Way, 275
India, 34–5, 179–81, 227–9, 235–40

Chamba, 34–5
Cherrapunji, 228–9
Mustagh Pass, 235–40
Indo-China, 284–8
Iran, *see* Persia
Iraq, 103–7
Italy
    Capri, 19, 290–6
    Naples, 206–10
    Punta Campanella, 292–4
    see also Rome; Venice
Ivan the Terrible, 97
Iyer, Pico, 178, 188, 362, 364
    The Lady and the Monk, 188–90

Japan, 188–90
Jefferson, Thomas, 152
John Paul I, Pope, 211
Johnson, Samuel, 207

Kapuściński, Ryszard, 3, 92, 124,
    128, 141
    The Shadow of the Sun, 124–7
    Travels with Herodotus, 141–4
Kassabova, Kapka, 362
Keay, John, 359
Kenya, 253–7
Kerouac, Jack, 21, 149, 155
    On the Road, 155–9
Kerr, Michael, 363
kif-smokers, 281–3
Kinglake, Alexander, 128–9, 355,
    363
    Eothen, 2, 128–35
Kingsley, Charles, 43
Kingsley, Mary, 37, 43–4
    Travels in West Africa, 43–6

Kipling, Rudyard, 73, 78
    American Notes, 78–81
Kublai Khan, 197–8

Lake Constance, 267
'Lake of the Lilies, The', 42
Lake Victoria, 135
Lawrence, T. E., 164–5, 168, 178,
    335, 355
    Seven Pillars of Wisdom, 168–71
Le Corbusier, 199
Leigh Fermor, Patrick, 92–4, 120–1,
    263, 292, 356–7
    The Broken Road, 120–3
    Mani, 94–9, 263
    A Time of Gifts, 264–8
Leopold, King of the Belgians, 143
Lewis, Norman, 197, 205–6, 360,
    362
    Naples '44, 205–10
Lewis, Isle of, 275–9
Liberia, 311–14
Livingstone, David, 231
Lopez, Barry, 92, 114
    Arctic Dreams, 114–20, 263
Luther, Martin, 266

McCullin, Don, 286
Macfarlane, Robert, 54, 263, 275
    The Old Ways, 275–9
Maclean, Sir Fitzroy, 305, 314
    Eastern Approaches, 314–17
Mackintosh-Smith, Tim, 362
Mallory, George, 54, 62–4
Maillart, Ella (Kini) 306, 309
Mann, Thomas, 290
Marcus Aurelius, Emperor, 96
Marozzi, Justin, 352, 363
Masters, John, 21, 33, 362, 364
    Bugles and a Tiger, 33–5
Matthiesen, Peter, 100, 362
    The Snow Leopard, 100–2
Maximilian, Emperor, 265
Maziad bin Hamdan, Sheikh, 105–6
Mexico, 155–9, 300–4
    Chapala, 300–1

Guadalajara, 300–2
Sabinas Hidalgo, 157–9
Sangre de Cristo mountains,
150
Michael VIII the Liberator,
Emperor, 96
Michelangelo, 212
Middleton, Robert, 359
Mikkelsen, Ejnar, 37, 46–7
Lost in the Arctic, 46–9
Mikoyan, Anastasi, 315
Miller, Henry, 21, 25, 362
The Colossus of Maroussi,
25–8
Mississippi river, 153–4
Morris, Jan, 165, 197–8, 355,
358
Venice, 198–203
Mosambolahun, blacksmith of,
311–14
Mount Annapurna, 56–9
Mount Everest, 54, 62–7, 100
Mount Gurla Mandhata, 223–4,
226
Mount Kailas, 213, 224–6
Mount Kenia, 136
Mount Kilimanjaro, 54, 360
Mount Kinchinjunga, 215
Mount McLoughlin, 196
Mount Mézenc, 182
Mount San Constanzo, 293
Mount Shasta, 196
Muhammad, Prophet, 350
Murphy, Dervla, 4–5, 44, 354,
360
Full Tilt, 5–10
Murray, W. H., 357
Muscat, 192
Mussolini, Benito, 211

Naipaul, V. S., 178–9
An Area of Darkness, 179–81

Naples, 206–10
Nelson, Admiral Lord, 207
Nepal, 100–2
Nero, Emperor, 211
Netherlands, the, 264–6
Newby, Eric, 318, 321–2
*A Short Walk in the Hindu
Kush*, 321–5
Nicolson, Harold, 338

O'Hanlon, Redmond, 73–4, 128,
144, 357, 362
Congo Journey, 144–8
In Trouble Again, 74–7
Oman, 191–2
Ondaatje, Sir Christopher, 360
One Thousand and One Nights,
108
Ottoman Empire, 129–35,
167–8
Oxus river, 3, 21, 213–14, 326,
355

Pakistan, 6–10
Hunza Valley, 54, 214–18
Palestine, 29–32
Palmyra, 340–2
Paraguay, 86–8
Paris, 81–2
Park, Mungo, 44, 230–1
*Travels in the Interior
Districts of Africa*, 230–4
Patagonia, 16–19
Paul, Jenny Balfour, 178, 190–1
Deeper Than Indigo, 190–3
Pauls, Michael, *see* Facaros,
Dana, and Michael Pauls
Persepolis, 338–40
Persia, 336–43, 353
Philby, Harry St John Bridger,
164
Phnom Penh, 284–8

Piper, John, 89
Polo, Marco, 197–8

Raban, Jonathan, 128, 137, 349,
 358
 Driving Home, 137–40
Ransome, Arthur, 354
Rider Haggard, H., 135
Rio Negro, 76–7
Rome, 203–5, 211–12
 see also Vatican City
Rum Doodle, 68–72
Ruskin, John, 199

Sackville-West, Vita, 335, 338
 Twelve Days in Persia,
 338–43
Sa'di, 337
St Boniface, 266
St Constantine the Great, 96
St Enodoc, 89
St Peter, 211
Saladin, 342
Salalah, 192
Sandwich Islands, 40
Sattin, Anthony, 363
Schalansky, Judith, 4, 11, 354
 Atlas of Remote Islands,
 11–14
Schubert, Franz, 267
Scott, Captain Robert Falcon,
 230, 241
Shackleton, Sir Ernest, 230, 244
 South, 244–50
Shannon Island, 46–7
Sharjah, 192
Shehadeh, Raja, 28–9, 356
 Palestinian Walks, 28–32
Siberia, 52–3
 Lake Baikal, 37, 52–3
Sirens, 294–6
Slocum, Joshua, 37, 50, 361

*Sailing Alone Around the
 World*, 50–1
Socrates, 352
Solomon, King, 341
Speke, John Hanning, 231
Spray voyage, 50–1
Stalin, Josef, 19
Stanley, Henry Morton, 231
Stark, Freya, 108, 318, 357
 Ionia, 108–11
 The Minaret of Djam,
 319–21
Stein, Gertrude, 32, 161
Steinbeck, John, 3, 21, 23
 Travels with Charley, 23–4
Stevenson, Robert Louis, 178,
 181–2, 184, 186–7, 276
 *Travels with a Donkey in the
 Cévennes*, 181–3
Stewart, Rory, 318, 330, 363
 The Places in Between, 330–4
Strayed, Cheryl, 178, 193
 Wild, 193–6
Swain, Jon, 280, 283–4
 River of Time, 283–8

Tartary, 306–10
Taylor, Andrew, 355
Tenzing Norgay, 54, 64–7
Tesson, Sylvain, 37, 52
 *The Consolations of the
 Forest*, 52–3
Theroux, Paul, 251, 257, 263
 Dark Star Safari, 257–60
 The Great Railway Bazaar,
 272–4
Thesiger, Wilfred, 3, 92, 102–3,
 164, 172–3, 318, 322–5, 358
 Arabian Sands, 172–7
 The Marsh Arabs, 102–7
Thomson, Joseph, 128, 135, 363
 Through Masai Land, 135–7

Thubron, Colin, 120, 213, 223,
    263, 268, 357
    Behind the Wall, 268–72
    To a Mountain in Tibet,
    223–6
Tibet, 100–2, 219–26
    Kum Bum lamasery, 219
    lake of Manasarovar, 225–6
    Lhasa, 219–22
    Shepeling monastery, 224
    Shey Gompa, 100–2
Tierra del Fuego, 12
Tinbergen, Niko, 146–7
Trefusis, Violet, 338
Trollope, Frances, 81
Turkey, 22–3, 108–11
    Erzurum, 22, 36
Priene, 109

Twain, Mark, 73, 81, 149, 152,
    210, 362
    The Innocents Abroad, 81–5
    Life on the Mississippi,
    152–4

United States of America, 23–4,
    150–2, 160–3
    Kentucky Bend, 153–4
    Mojave Desert, 194–6
    Rocky Mountains, 40–3

Seiad Valley, 194–5
Turtle Mountain, 162
    see also Chicago; Mississippi
    river
Ur, ziggurat of, 340

Vatican City, 211–12
Vaughan Williams, Ralph,
    276
Venice, 82–5, 198–203

Wallace, Alfred Russel, 74, 76
Waugh, Evelyn, 305
Wellington, Duke of, 242
Wheeler, Sara, 362
Wilson, Angus, 273
Winser, Nigel and Shane, 358
Woolf, Virginia, 338
Woolley, Sir Leonard, 107

Xerxes, King of Persia, 339

Yogistan, 68–9
Younghusband, Francis, 230,
    235, 306
    The Heart of a Continent,
    235–40

Zenobia, arch of, 341

Special Thanks

With special thanks to the following supporters who have kindly sponsored the inclusion of extracts from these writers:

Chris Feige

Frank Blake

Jamie Bebb

Mark Whelan

Barbara Yu Larsson

Alan Eisner

Adam Day

David Cooke

Adrian Lower

Peter Job

Jack Kerouac

Mark Twain

Ernest Shackleton

Bruce Chatwin

Alexandra David Néel

Peter Fleming

Robert Byron

Wilfred Thesiger

Paul Heiney

Isabella Bird

Supporters

Unbound is a new kind of publishing house. Our books are funded directly by readers. This was a very popular idea during the late eighteenth and early nineteenth centuries. Now we have revived it for the internet age. It allows authors to write the books they really want to write and readers to support the books they would most like to see published.

The names listed below are of readers who have pledged their support and made this book happen. If you'd like to join them, visit www.unbound.com.

Asad Ahmed

Tony Allen

Robert Allison

Sarah Anderson

Sophia Anscomb

Patrick Arning

Nigel Aslin

Camilla Astrup

Rich Austwick

Maggie Bailey

Jenny Balfour-Paul

Graham Bannister

Keith Barnes

Jamie Bebb

Cindy Blake

Frank Blake

Liz Blake

Anna Maj Boldt-Christmas

Martin Boldt-Christmas

Charlotte Bontoux

William Bonwitt

Matthew Bowers

Jane Braithwaite

Ana Maria Briongos

Hilary Brodsky

Haz Brown

Nick Browne

Kevin O. Butler

Michael Cahan

Georgiana Campbell

Toby Campbell

David Cantillon

Andrew Cartwright

Michelle Jana Chan

Terence Clark

Benjamin Colegrave

Kara Colegrave

Siena Colegrave

Dillon Coleman

David Cooke

Penelope Crichton

Hazel Critchley

Nick Danziger

Adam Day

Graham Defries

Clare Dickens

Hans Dols

Dawn Downes

Archie Drake

John Drake

Christian Drury

Isabelle Duncan

Alan Eisner

Jennie Ensor

Chris Feige

Pat Feige

John Fenwick

George and Pooh Gephart

Cathy Giangrande

John Gimlette

Simon Glasgow

Denise Goulimis

Gavin Graham

Richard Grand-Jean

Christopher Green

Deborah Grossman

Langdon Hamilton

Robin Hanbury-Tenison

James Hanly

Dave Harvey

Sue Haswell

Patrick Hayden

David Hebblethwaite

Mark Henderson

Tim Heughan

Jeremy Hill

Ben Holden

Mikael Horal

Michael Imber

Andrew James

Peter Job

Alison Johnson

Andy Johnson

Mark Johnson

Michael Jones

Magnus Karlson

Patrick Keogh

Dan Kieran

Rob Kinder

Philip King

Anthony Kitchin

Susan Knox

Bjorn Knudsen

Ginny & Dick Kurth

Nicholas Laing

Mark Landau

Barbara Yu Larsson

Carl Larsson

Christian Larsson

John Larsson

Kaj Larsson

Louise Lawson

Lottie Leefe

Peri Ann Levent-Sinclair

Michael Lingens

Mercedes Lopez-Tomlinson

Barry Lovern

Adrian Lower

Brian Lunn

Adam Maberly

Rory MacLean

Clementine Macmillan-Scott

Peter Maddock

Chris Mallows

Simon Mansfield

Michael Mates

Ewan McCowen

Margaret McFarland

Alice McLuskie

Kathryn McNicoll

John McVittie

Ben R. Miller

John Mitchinson

Hugh Monk

Jan Morris

Michelle Moses

Hugh Mullan

Dervla Murphy

Ross Arne Naess

Carlo Navato

Jeremy Norman

Alan Palmer

Oliver Parr

Sarah Parson

Ronald Paterson

Haven Pell

Nick Pellew

Fred Pilkington

Gregory Pilkington

Justin Pollard

Harry Ponsonby

David Potter

Carolyn Pottinger

Jeremy Quarrie

Margaret Reeves

Chloe Riddell

Richard Robinson	Charlotte ter Haar
Stian Rødland	Isabella Thomas
Lesley Ronaldson	Colin Thubron
Marion Rowsell	Isabella Tree
Harry Saint	Sam Trusty
Sarah Salter	Boysie Turner
Amanda Sander	Peter Vela
Christoph Sander	Michael Walker
Fred Satow	Sir Harold Walker
Brittany Schermerhorn	Mandy Warnford-Davis
Peter Schwartz	John Wates
Damian Severgnini	Deborah Watson
Hazel Slavin	Tony Wheeler
Duncan J. D. Smith	Mark Whelan
David Stewart	William Wilks
Mary Stewart	Cary Williams
Lee Sturgeon-Day	Anthony Wilson
Richard Szpiro	Nigel and Shane Winser
Simon Talbot-Williams	Robert Wilson Wright